STUDIES IN
THE COVENANT
OF GRACE

DAVID L. NEILANDS

Presbyterian and Reformed Publishing Co.
Phillipsburg, N. J. 08865

Printed in the United States of America
ISBN 0-87552-365-X

Scripture quotations are from:
The Holy Bible, New International Version, copyright © 1978, New York International Bible Society, used by permission;

The New American Standard Bible, © The Lockman Foundation, 1960, 1962, 1963, 1968, 1971, 1972, 1973, 1975;

J. B. Phillips: The New Testament in Modern English, Revised Edition (© J. B. Phillips, 1958, 1960, 1972);

and the King James Version.

CONTENTS

PREFACE

Why another volume on the subject of the covenant of grace? The answer to that question is precisely why this study was undertaken in the first place. The church is no longer covenant conscious. We have failed to grasp the importance of covenant theology, covenant thinking and covenant living. Even Reformed churches that once knew the glory of the covenant of grace have lost this vital life-giving fountain of scriptural teaching. It was the Reformers that discovered again the biblical teaching of the covenant of grace. But this is another part of the Reformation heritage that we have lost. Would that God would give us another Reformation in our own day that we might also discover again the scriptural teaching of the covenant.

The contents of this book are studies that were first given to the adult Sunday school class of the Covenant Orthodox Presbyterian Church of Berkeley, California. It took us nearly two years to cover this material. It is because the lessons were so well received (and at the urging of some) that I was encouraged to put them into a more permanent form. It is my hope that other Bible classes will also find the material useful and stimulating. With that purpose in mind there has been added a series of questions to help in class discussion.

Is this book any different from other books on this subject? The subject of the covenant of grace is usually presented under a series of topics covering various aspects of the covenant. This work represents a series of expository Bible studies. It begins with a study of the covenant made with Abraham in Genesis chapter 17. This does not mean that the covenant was first revealed in that passage. We could have started the study at Genesis 3:15 and watched it unfold until in Genesis 17 God formalizes the covenant relationship with Abraham and his seed.

A great deal of emphasis has been placed on God's promise to Abraham in Genesis 17:7 where He promises to establish "an everlasting covenant, to be a God unto thee and to thy seed after thee." That is the heart and soul of the covenant. We return to that passage again and again throughout these studies. It is amazing how many times those actual words or their equivalent are repeated throughout the rest of the Bible.

From the study of Genesis 17:1-14 we have extended the study to the rest of Scripture, including both Old and New Testaments. We see the covenant's final and glorious fulfillment in our study of Revelation chapter 21. The book includes a discussion on the subject of the sacrament of circumcision and its importance. That leads us into the subject of baptism as its New Testament counterpart. The book closes with a series of studies on infant baptism.

Why should a New Testament Christian have any concern about covenant promises which were made to Abraham nearly 4,000 years ago? It is our relationship to those covenant promises that determines our eternal destiny. We believe that the New Testament makes it quite clear that those Old Testament promises are also applicable to us. Underlying that truth is the related truth of the unity of the church. We have therefore sought to establish beyond any doubt the unity of the New Testament church with that of the Old Testament church.

In these expository Bible studies we have dealt with the pertinent passage in its larger context. We believe that this method represents the strength of this work for it represents a serious effort to understand the meaning and application of the whole passage rather than the one or two verses directly related to the subject of the covenant. We have simply tried to discover what the meaning of the passage under consideration is teaching us and something of its application for us today. By this approach we have sought to avoid the charge of forcing our interpretation upon a passage or of taking it out of context. The reader must not conclude that the passages under consideration are isolated passages. These are only representative of many other related passages of Scripture.

In his book *Children of Abraham* David Kingdon has presented a Reformed Baptist view of baptism, the covenant and children. We have quoted this book several times and criticized some of its conclusions. It is our hope that these studies will promote our understanding of Scripture and also promote the unity of the visible church of Christ.

I want to acknowledge my debt of gratitude for the work of Professor John Murray. Though he died in 1975, his works will be a blessing to the church for many generations to come. I cannot, nor would I want to, hide my deep respect for his Scotch piety and learning. His works have been of great assistance to me as I have wrestled with the meaning of certain biblical passages. Professor Murray believed the text of Scripture to be the very Word of God and therefore he approached it with humility and deep reverence.

I want to extend my sincere thanks to the Rev. Robert K. Churchill for his review of most of the manuscript, his constructive criticism and encouragement, also to the Rev. Richard M. Lewis, my pastor, for his kindness and assistance.

Finally, I want to express my appreciation for the work and encouragement of Sandra Emerson. Without her enthusiasm and insistence this book would never have been written. Her insistence was matched by her labor. It was she who typed the manuscript.

May Christ our Prophet, Priest and King be pleased to use this work for the advancement of truth, unity and piety in His kingdom.

David L. Neilands

1

THE LORD SPEAKS TO ABRAM

Genesis 17:1-3

Introduction

It does not seem possible to overestimate the importance of the 17th chapter of Genesis. It's truly a glorious passage in the history of divine revelation.

The passage is a marvelous revelation of God and His infinite grace. It reveals His great condescension in His dealings with men, even to the extent of binding Himself to the performance of certain promises.

As the meaning of the passage unfolds, we shall see that it has a vital meaning to *us* and also that its promises reach beyond time unto the eternal ages.

The Lord Appears to Abram

And when Abram was ninety years old and nine, the Lord appeared to Abram, and said unto him, I am the Almighty God; walk before me, and be thou perfect (Gen. 17:1).

a. The chapter opens by telling us that the Lord appeared to Abram when he was 99 years old. Chapter 16 had closed with the information that Abram was 86 when Ishmael was born. The Lord had already promised Abram in Genesis 15:5 that his seed shall be as numerous as the stars. In view of the ages of Abram and Sarai, it now appeared to Abram that God's promise was to be fulfilled through Hagar's son, Ishmael, who was now 13 years old.

b. *A New Name.* On this occasion the Lord introduces Himself to Abram with a name not previously used. A new name meant a further revelation of God. The new name was "El Shaddai." It is translated in the King James translation, "Almighty God" and in the NASB as "God Almighty."

The Lord himself thought it significant to point out to Moses that "El Shaddai" is the name by which He revealed Himself to Abraham, Isaac and Jacob. "I appeared to Abraham, Isaac and Jacob as El Shaddai, but by My name Jehovah, I did not make myself known to them" (Exod. 6:3).

1

If this is a new name and involves a new revelation, it must have special meaning and surely it must in some way be appropriate to the occasion. The name, "El Shaddai," appears to involve the following meanings:

1. The all-sufficient One.
2. The Overpowerer.
3. The Destroyer.
4. The all-powerful One.

So it can readily be seen why the name has been translated into English as "God Almighty." El Shaddai is the omnipotent God who is all-powerful and works wonderful deeds on behalf of His people. Through His supernatural power He overpowers nature in the service of His gracious designs.

We are accustomed to thinking of God's name "Jehovah" as being His covenant name, but this was not true until the time of Moses as recorded in Exodus 6:3. The covenant name for Abraham, Isaac and Jacob is "El Shaddai." It was that designation which God used as He unfolded to Abraham the promises and blessings which he would provide for His people. For Abraham, Isaac and Jacob, El Shaddai was the covenant God in whom they rested for their present strength and their hopes for the future. We, like them, must learn to rest in His sovereign power and His all-sufficiency. Our covenant God has power to fulfill His promises although the order of nature may appear against them.

c. "Walk before Me, and be thou perfect." God, The Almighty, calls upon Abraham to walk continually before Him. Abraham is to walk with the consciousness of the Almighty's presence. His life and conduct are to be lived in the knowledge that it is God Almighty who keeps him and fills his life with grace. Do we walk in the consciousness of the divine presence? Do we walk by faith knowing that we have been redeemed by divine grace?

And I will make my covenant between me and thee, and will multiply thee exceedingly (Gen. 17:2).

a. The biblical record shows that God had appeared to Abraham prior to this appearance in Genesis 17. He had made promises to him; some of which are now repeated. Chapters 12, 13, and 15 record some of those promises. It is even recorded in 15:18 that the Lord entered into a covenant relationship with Abraham. The idea, here in Genesis 17, seems to be the expression of settling, arranging or formalizing the covenant. Here the Lord takes steps in order to fulfill the covenant and seals it with a perpetual ordinance.

That the covenant relationship is predominant in this chapter is witnessed to by the repetition of the word covenant. It is repeated 13 times. Nine times it is referred to as "My covenant," three times as "everlasting covenant," and once as "the covenant."

A simple reading of the passage shows that the initiative is the Lord's. He declares what He will do. He announces the promises to be accomplished. He declares the sign of the covenant. It is all the Lord's doings. Five times in the first 9 verses of this chapter, the Lord says, "I will." The Lord sealed His promises by His covenant oath.

b. At this point the Lord announces to Abram that He is going to multiply him exceedingly. That same promise is dealt with in more detail in verses 4-6. It is also a repetition of a similar promise made in chapters 13 and 15. Certainly the repetition of the promise shows its importance. But why is it here in this introductory verse? I think there are two reasons. First, Abraham is to learn that the Lord does not forget His promises. Second, if the Lord could fulfill that promise to Abram who was now 99 years old, surely El Shaddai could fulfill His other promises for it would demonstrate that the Lord works wonders.

And Abram fell on his face: and God talked with him, saying (Gen. 17:3).

a. At the voice of God, Abram prostrated himself before the Lord. It was an expression of his deep humility in the presence of God. There seems also to be a feeling of trust and confidence in the Lord as he is overpowered by great joy at being in communion with God.

Calvin also sees in this prostration his appropriation and the reception of the promise. In this sense the prostration is an act of faith.

b. "Elohim talked with him." The meaning of "Elohim": The One to be dreaded or feared; it is plural in its form and therefore expresses God's majesty, magnitude, fulness and richness. It signifies the manifold perfections of God. Elohim is the Creator, upholder and moral governor of the universe. It occurs more than 2500 times in the Old Testament.

Here is a picture of Elohim, the Creator and sustainer of the universe in intimate fellowship with His covenant people.

Questions for Discussion

1. What's in a name, especially when it is God's name?
2. What is the meaning of "El Shaddai"?
3. Did this name have any special meaning to Abram?
4. Does God's name of El Shaddai have any special meaning to us today?
5. What was involved in God's call to Abram? Is the call of a Christian any different?
6. Who initiated the covenant relationship? Do we ordinarily speak of a covenant in this sense?
7. What are the differences between Genesis 12, 13 and 15 and the covenant relationship of Genesis 17?

8. What promise is given to Abraham in verse 2? Discuss the significance of this promise.

9. How did Abram respond when God spoke to him? What did his response mean? How does reverence fit into our thinking today?

10. What is the meaning of ''Elohim''?

11. How does God communicate His message and His will for us today?

2

A NEW NAME

Genesis 17:4-6

Introduction

1. In the first three verses of this chapter the Lord comes to Abram. The purpose of His coming is to formalize the covenant relationship with Abram.

2. In this situation the Lord discloses a new name for Himself. It is El Shaddai, God Almighty, the All-Sufficient and the All-Powerful One.

3. Within this covenantal relationship the Lord is going to make promises to Abram. His life is to be lived in the light of those promises.

Verse 4:

As for Me, behold, My Covenant is with you, And you shall be the father of many nations.

a. "As for Me." This appears to be the introductory statement of the formal covenant. We might paraphrase the thought "I make this covenant with you." The emphasis is on what the Lord will do. These are the words of a formal contract or treaty. In our legal contracts today we speak of "the party of the first part" and "the party of the second part." The Lord is "the party of the first part." The obligations of Abram, "the party of the second part," are taken up at verse 9 where God said to Abraham "Thou shalt keep my covenant."

b. Much has been written in recent years in the development of the idea that passages such as Genesis 17 follow the format of treaties entered into between kings that have defeated other kings in battle. The victor and the vanquished enter into treaty obligations. The victor makes certain promises but he also requires certain obligations. The Lord is making a declaration of His promises, but as he does so He also declares who are to be the subjects of the covenantal treaty.

c. A "father of many nations" immediately broadens out the covenant relationship. It is to include not only Abram but the "multitude of nations" who shall be related to Abram.

d. The promise of a numerous seed had been given to Abraham on previous occasions.

5

1. Genesis 12:2: It occurs when God calls Abram to leave Haran and to seek a country which the Lord would show him. In the context the Lord promises in verse 2 "I will make of thee a great nation, and I will bless thee, and make thy name great; and thou shalt be a blessing." This promise was made to Abram when he was 75 years old.

2. Genesis 13:15-16: The promise is repeated possibly three or four years later at the time Lot and Abram separate. "For all the land which thou seest, to thee will I give it, and to thy seed forever. And I will make thy seed as the dust of the earth: so that if a man can number the dust of the earth, then shall thy seed be numbered." Who can number the dust of the earth? Yet that is the promise given to a man nearing 80 and yet without children.

3. Genesis 15:5-6: Again the promise is repeated. The renewal is given possibly five or six years later than the last promise so that Abram is about 85 years old. The context shows that Abram was concerned about his future posterity inasmuch as he was yet childless. Were the children of Eliezer, his steward, to be counted as the seed of the promise? The Lord's answer was, "No." He shall bear his own seed. At this point we are told, "And He brought him forth abroad, and said, Look now toward heaven, and tell the stars, if thou be able to number them: and He said unto him, So shall thy seed be. And he believed in the Lord; and He counted it to him for righteousness."

We cannot stop now to explore the depth of meaning in this last text except to point out that though he was still childless at 85 yet he rested his faith in God's word and promise. He looked to the Lord to fulfill His promise, a promise that appeared to be impossible. Abraham's faith was counted to him for righteousness. Do *not* forget that text. It's important.

Verse 5:

Neither shall thy name any more be called Abram, but thy name shall be Abraham; for a father of many nations have I made thee.

a. Abram receives a new name. Abram, meaning high father or exalted father, has his name changed to Abraham, meaning father of a multitude. At the point of changing his name the Lord also adds the meaning and the reason for the change when He adds, "For *I will* make you the father of a multitude of nations. And *I will* make you exceedingly fruitful, and *I will* make nations of you, and kings shall come forth from you" (vss. 5-6).

b. It is the Lord, who had just revealed Himself under a new name, who now also gives Abram a new name. By changing his name the Lord was sealing His promise by a pledge. His new name Abraham was a daily reminder that the Lord had given him a promise that he would yet be the father of a multitude of nations. The new name was an expression of the reality yet to be fulfilled.

c. The promise "kings shall come forth from you" was gloriously fulfilled in

Jesus Christ. Matthew 1:1 records, "The book of the genealogy of Jesus Christ, the son of David, the son of Abraham."

Galatians 3:16

Now the promises were spoken to Abraham and to his seed. He does not say, "And to seeds," as of many; but *rather to one*, "And to thy seed," which is Christ.

a. Paul's reference is to the phrase "and to thy seed" which is found in Genesis 13:15 and 17:8. How can we reconcile Paul's reference to "seed" as meaning one when the promises in Genesis speak "of a multitude of nations"?

b. What Paul is saying is that inasmuch as these promises were given to Abraham and his seed, they were given unto *Christ* because *He is the Seed* referred to in the promises. Paul's exposition of this phrase "and to thy seed" is that in the Abrahamic promise the Messiah is concealed. The fulfillment of the promise in its highest meaning is to be found in Christ.

c. The passage has a similarity to the divine promise in Genesis 3:15. There the reference is to the "seed" of the woman. It is "her seed" that is to strike the fatal blow to Satan. The reference then is to none other than Christ.

d. Does Paul's argument invalidate the promise to Abraham that he would be the father of a multitude of nations? Not at all. The *primary* meaning of the seed is to be found in Christ, but Paul gives us the *secondary* meaning in verse 29 when he says that if we "belong to Christ, then you are Abraham's seed, and heirs according to the promise."

e. Paul has clearly set forth the unity of God's people as it rests in the promise to Abraham and finds its glorious fulfillment in Christ. Believers in Christ are children according to the promise made to Abraham just as much as Isaac and Jacob.

Questions for Discussion

1. Discuss the significance of the words "As for Me" in verse 4.
2. What was the promised extent of Abram's seed? Remember his age.
3. Trace the origin and history of the promise to Abram of a numerous seed.
4. What is the meaning of Abram? What is the meaning of Abram's new name?
5. Why did God give Abram a new name?
6. How would Abraham's faith be affected by his new name?
7. Discuss the relationship and problem presented in Galatians 3:16.
8. How does Genesis 3:15 fit into the promise given to Abraham?
9. Does it appear from this lesson that names are important to God? Do we give the same consideration to names as God?
10. Do we give any biblical consideration to the names we give our children?

3

THE EVERLASTING COVENANT:
A GOD UNTO THEE

Genesis 17:7

Introduction

1. As the Lord prepares to formalize the covenant of grace with Abraham, He reveals Himself under a new name, El Shaddai, God Almighty.

2. The Lord then proceeds to set forth the provisions of the covenant of grace.

3. The first promise is given in verses 4-6. That promise given to Abram at 99 years old was that he would be "the father of many nations." The promise of a numerous seed had been given to him on three previous occasions but as yet his wife, Sarai, had borne no children. With this first promise the Lord now changes his name from Abram to Abraham which means "the father of many nations."

Verse 7:

And I will establish my covenant between Me and thee and thy seed after thee in their generations for an everlasting covenant, to be a God unto thee and to thy seed after thee.

I. a. This verse sets forth the second provision in the covenant of grace.

b. Though in the first provision Abraham is given the promise that he should yet be the father of a multitude of nations, it remains for the second provision to confirm that the covenant extended to his seed after him.

The provisions of the covenant are to continue on to his children and to their heirs after them. It is the Lord who binds the seed of Abraham to Himself in the covenant relationship.

II. a. But what is the duration of the covenant? It is "an *everlasting* covenant." The Lord wants no mistake concerning the time element of the covenant. That same phrase is repeated three more times in this chapter. Speaking of the land of Canaan in verse 8 He promises "an everlasting possession." Referring to circumcision in verse 13 He says that it is the sign "for an everlasting covenant." Again in His promise to Sarah and the promised son Isaac in verse 19 He says, "and I will establish My covenant with him for an everlasting covenant, and with his seed after him."

The provisions of the covenant are *eternal*. Now "eternal" is not just a long time. It extends on into eternity. This provision that the covenant is to extend to all eternity has caused problems. Admittedly there are problems but we shall try to deal with them as they come up. As we look further into the text I believe that we shall be convinced that the provisions of the covenant are indeed everlasting.

III. "To be a God unto thee and to thy seed after thee."

a. What is it that the Lord is promising Abraham and his seed for ever? It is the tremendous promise that "I will be your God."

A fuller form of the promise is recorded in Leviticus 26:12: "And I will walk among you, and will be your God, and ye shall be My people." That statement is the very essence of the covenant of grace. In that one statement the *promises of the covenant are summarized*. In the words of Leviticus 26:12 the Lord is promising three things:

1. I will walk among you.
2. I will be your God.
3. Ye shall be My people.

These three items teach us that the covenantal relationship involves nothing less than *union* and *communion* with Jehovah, the God of Israel.

b. What is involved in the promise? What are some of the items involved in union and communion with Jehovah?

I Will Walk among You

a. Restoration

When Adam broke the covenant of works it resulted in expulsion from God's garden and separation from His presence. The covenant with Abraham restores that broken fellowship. The promise is that the Lord will walk among you. He will dwell in your midst. This promise involves the complete restoration of our normal relationship to God. All the ground of alienation and every barrier to fellowship is removed.

When the Lord restores He gives us the assurance of His love for us. Romans 5:8: "But God commendeth His love toward us, in that, while we were yet sinners, Christ died for us." In love He sent His only begotten Son to pay the price of our redemption.

b. Fellowship

1. "I will walk among you." That statement denotes the closest possible fellowship. He communicates Himself in His fulness to His people for they are the objects of His love. John could write, "and truly our fellowship is with the Father, and with His Son Jesus Christ" (I John 1:3).

2. The Psalms capture the need and the blessings found in fellowship with God. Psalm 73:25-26: "Whom have I in heaven but thee? and there is none upon earth that I desire beside thee. My flesh and my heart faileth: but God is the strength of my heart, and my portion for ever." Do we have that same consuming passionate desire for fellowship with the Lord?

3. "I will walk among you" reminds us of God's fellowship in the garden with Adam and Eve before their fall into sin. They had perfect fellowship with the Lord. Genesis 3:8 seems to record the *normal* fellowship when it says "And they heard the voice of the Lord God walking in the garden in the cool of the day." That fellowship broken by sin has been restored in Christ.

I Will Be Your God

   a. Divine Presence

1. Included in the promise "And I will be your God" is the promise of God's presence.

2. *Exodus 33:12-17* teaches us the importance of the divine presence as understood by Moses. In chapter 32 we have the sin of the people in worshiping the golden calf. The Lord's anger was kindled against the people. He brought misery upon them because of their sin. In 33:3 He threatens to withdraw from their midst lest He consume them. In His place He promises an angel in 32:34 and 33:2.

In verses 12-13 Moses is responding to the Lord's threatenings. Verse 12 may be paraphrased: "Lord thy commandment to me was 'Bring up this people.' But you haven't told me who it is that you're sending with me. Furthermore, you have said that I know you intimately and that I have found favor in your sight."

Verse 13: If I have indeed found favor in Thy sight then teach me Thy ways so that I may continue in Thy favor and count this nation as *Thy people*.

Moses is pleading for grace to be extended to the people because he had found grace in Jehovah's eyes for himself alone. Lord, If I am thine let the nation be thine also. Lord, remember they are "Thy people."

In verse 14 the Lord responds to this pleading with the promise that "My presence shall go with thee, and I will give thee rest."

The word translated "presence" is literally "face." Isaiah commenting on this and other similar events says in 63:9 "In all their affliction he was afflicted, and the *angel of His face* saved them, in His love and in His sparing He redeemed them; and He took them up and carried them all the days of old." What a glorious picture of the presence of God! In their afflictions there was affliction to Him. It displays the love and affection of a father. It is our heavenly Father who bears our burdens and carries our sorrows. Because the Lord is our God, He feels the sufferings of His people as His own sufferings.

According to Isaiah 63:9 it was "the angel of His face" who saved them

10

from all these afflictions and sufferings. Who then is this "angel of His face"? The angel of His face is the angel who is His face or in whom His face is made clear. In Him the Lord is Himself present. Paul's comment in II Corinthians 4:6 is quite illuminating: "For God who said, 'Light shall shine out of darkness,' is the One who has shone in our hearts to give the light of the knowledge of the glory of God in the *face of Jesus Christ.*" *The angel of His face* is none other than Jesus Christ the second person of the holy Trinity.

Is not that which the Lord promised in Exodus 33:14 "My face, My presence, shall go with thee"? Therefore, the angel promised in verse 2 becomes the face of Jehovah. Malachi refers to this One as the "messenger of the covenant" (3:1).

In verse 15 Moses finally seizes the promise, yet in such a way that he clearly shows his dependence upon the Lord's presence. "If you don't go with us, then don't carry us up to the promised land."

Notice carefully Moses' reasoning in verse 16. First he asks a question: "For how shall it be known that I and Thy people have found grace in Thy sight?" Secondly, he gives the answer: "Is it not by Thy going with us?" Thirdly, he draws a conclusion: "So shall we be separated, I and *Thy people,* from all the people that are upon the face of the earth." The presence of the Lord among His people flows from His grace. It is a covenantal promise. The possession of the land without the Lord's presence is of little or no value. The Lord's presence separates His people from all other peoples and nations. The Lord's presence and guidance of His people is a revelation to the other people of the world. The glory of the Lord is seen as He guides and cares for His people.

3. Who can plumb the depths and the height of the promise "I will be your God"?

a) God Himself chose a people to whom He would be their God. It is the Lord who chose to set His divine love upon a people. He gives Himself to those people. He is their infinite portion.

b) His perfections are revealed to us as the highest possible knowledge. His divine perfections are pledged to us for our redemption, our protection, our blessedness and our final glorification to be with Him eternally.

c) It is because of the promise "I will be your God" that He admits us to communion with Himself. It is the people among whom He walks that He invites to have fellowship with Him.

d) His grace and favor is life, and His loving kindness better than life. The highest possible exaltation is to be found in the presence of God and the enjoyment of His love and fellowship.

e) The promise includes all conceivable and all possible good.

And Ye Shall Be My People

a. The Lord is saying to His covenant people: "You are Mine." The people

11

among whom the Lord walks, and to whom the Lord is God belong to the Lord. As Leviticus 26:9 teaches us, it is to this people that the Lord is establishing and confirming His covenant.

b. Deuteronomy 14:1-2 is only one of the many passages that gives us something of the meaning of the promise "Ye shall be My people":

> Verse 1: "Ye are the sons of the Lord your God: ye shall not cut yourselves, nor make any baldness between your eyes for the dead."

> Verse 2: "For thou art an holy people unto the Lord thy God, and the Lord hath chosen thee to be a peculiar people unto Himself, above all the nations that are upon the earth."

1. Deuteronomy 14:1:

a) The verse contains a directive to Israel concerning their actions in mourning for the dead. Two things are forbidden:

(1) They are not to cut or wound themselves.

(2) They are not to shave their foreheads.

Why are these two things forbidden to those that mourn? Notice that the prohibitions are preceded by the statement: "Ye are the sons of the Lord your God." It is because they are the children of God that they are forbidden to cut themselves or shave themselves for the dead.

It seems that these were heathen practices. Both practices involve a disfigurement of the body and appear to represent the heathen customs which display the wild excesses of grief for the dead. They mourn thus because they have no hope.

But the people who belong to the Lord have a covenant relationship with Jehovah. We cannot mourn as those who have no hope. Paul reminds us that we do have a hope. Those that sleep in Jesus will God bring with Him at His coming (I Thess. 4:13-18). Jehovah is not the God of the dead but of the living.

b) "Ye are the sons of the Lord your God." That statement speaks to us of *union* and *communion* with our heavenly Father. To those in union with God death should have no power. For the children of God there is no place for the disfiguring of the body, for the dominion of death has been broken. Christ has died but He conquered the tomb by His resurrection.

Does death have power over "the sons of the Lord" so that it can separate them eternally from "the Lord your God"? Where the sonship of God is, there also is the divine inheritance which is the promise of eternal life.

c) Did you ever notice the double use of the concept conveyed by the word inheritance? I Peter 1:3-5: Our heavenly Father has begotten us to a living hope through Christ's resurrection "to an inheritance incorruptible and undefiled, and that fadeth not away, reserved in heaven for you." The *children of God* are to *receive* an eternal inheritance secured for them by Christ's death and resurrection.

Psalm 33:12: "Blessed is the nation whose God is the Lord. The people whom He hath chosen for His own inheritance." The children of God have been chosen to be His own inheritance. According to Psalm 74:2 it is the people whom He has redeemed that constitute His inheritance.

The Lord's people are *His eternal inheritance;* therefore the pagan rites of mourning have no place among God's people.

2. Deuteronomy 14:2:

a) This verse continues to state the reason why "the children of the Lord" must not be defiled by heathen practices. Because they are "the children of the Lord" He forbids them participation in heathen practices. But that raises a question: What does it mean to be a child of the Lord? Verse 2 gives us something of the *meaning* of that phrase. It describes them as:

    (1) A holy people
    (2) A peculiar people

(1) A Holy People

(a) Separation: To be holy signifies a separation to God. The text describes them as "an holy people unto the Lord thy God." The Lord had chosen them and separated them unto Himself.

(b) Sanctified: To be sanctified is to be devoted to God. Paul refers to the church of God at Corinth as "sanctified in Christ Jesus, called to be saints" (I Cor. 1:2). In this passage he is not referring to the progressive work of sanctification but a once for all act of God. The Lord had called these people unto Himself. They were saints—living saints. He had sanctified them. They were His holy people. He had devoted them unto Himself. I Corinthians 3:17 is very instructive. He says that "if any man defile the temple of God, him shall God destroy: for the temple of God is holy, which temple ye are." The children of God are God's holy temple.

(2) A Peculiar People

(a) "The Lord hath chosen thee to be a peculiar people unto Himself." It is by a sovereign act of God that the people are chosen to be His people (see Deut. 7:6-9).

(b) "A peculiar people" might be translated "a people of possession." Paul gives us the meaning in Ephesians 1:14 when referring to the Holy Spirit he writes, "who is given as a pledge of our inheritance, with a view to the redemption of *God's own possession* to the praise of His glory." To be a "peculiar people" is to be God's own purchased possession. God's chosen people are His redeemed people and therefore *belong to* the Lord.

We should now see *first* of all what it means *to be sons of God* and *secondly* why Israel was commanded not to participate in the heathen rites related to the dead. The children of God are God's holy people. His own possession *purchased* at the cost of giving His only begotten Son to die on Calvary. So it is that the children of God have been *separated from the world* and have no right to participate in that which is unholy. Children of God have been *consecrated* unto Jehovah; take heed then of the warning not to defile the Lord's temple which ye are. The whole of the life of God's people is to be shaped, regulated, guided and directed by their relationship to Him and to His Holy Word.

Questions for Discussion

1. What covenantal provisions are added in Genesis 17:7?
2. How long are the covenant provisions to last? Doesn't that answer give us problems?
3. What do we mean when we say that "to be a God unto thee and to thy seed after thee" is the essence of the covenant?
4. What is the relationship of Leviticus 26:12 to Genesis 17:7?
5. What are the three great promises of Leviticus 26:12? What is involved in those promises?
6. Are we walking and living in a normal world?
7. Discuss the importance of God's presence. What does it mean to be "separated"?
8. What instructions does Deuteronomy 14:1-2 contain? What are the reasons for these prohibitions? Is there any application to the Christian here?
9. What is our inheritance? Does God have any inheritance?
10. What is the meaning of the phrase "a peculiar people"? Who are "peculiar people"? Are we living and known as "peculiar people"?

4

THE COVENANT PROMISE
AND
NEW TESTAMENT CHRISTIANS

I Peter 2:9-10

Introduction

We have tried to show something of the meaning of the covenantal promise as found in Leviticus 26:12 with the following three parts:

1. I will walk among you.
2. I will be your God.
3. Ye shall be My people.

Each one of those parts speaks clearly of *union and communion* of Jehovah with His people, and His people with Jehovah.

Applies to New Testament Christians

But you may have been asking yourself the question: Does this promise belong to *me* as a New Testament Christian? I want to answer that question only briefly at this point by reference to only one New Testament passage.

> **But you are a chosen race, a royal priesthood, a holy nation, a people for God's own possession, that you may proclaim the excellencies of Him who has called you out of darkness into His marvelous light; for you once were not a people, but now you are the people of God; you had not received mercy, but now you have received mercy (I Peter 2:9, 10 NASB).**

To whom was the book of I Peter written? Some believe that it was written to Jewish Christians in Asia Minor; however, some including Augustine have disagreed with this conclusion. Certainly the letter was written to Christian churches then located in Asia Minor. Those churches undoubtedly included both Jewish and Gentile believers. According to verse 3 he is writing to "born again Christians." It is written to the New Testament church; believers in the Lord Jesus Christ.

I Peter 2:9-10 contains a series of eight Old Testament quotations, four in each verse. It is of interest and also of considerable value for us to know where those quotations come from.

15

Verse 9	Old Testament Reference
1. A Chosen Race	Isa. 43:20; Deut. 7:6; 14:2
2. A Royal Priesthood	Exod. 19:6
3. A Holy Nation	Exod. 19:6; Deut. 14:2
4. A People for God's Own Possession	Exod. 19:5; Deut. 14:2; 7:6; 10:15

Verse 10	
5. Not a People	Hos. 1:9-10; 2:23; Isa. 65:1
6. The People of God	Hos. 1:10
7. Not Received Mercy	Hos. 2:23
8. Received Mercy	Hos. 2:23

Verse 9 contains a list of four characteristics which describe the kingdom of Christ. In compiling that description Peter reached back to the writings of Moses, specifically Exodus 19 and Deuteronomy 14.

In Exodus 19 the children of Israel were camped at the foot of Mt. Sinai. They had just been redeemed by the Lord from Egypt. Now they were about to enter into covenant relationship with Jehovah as a nation of redeemed people. Jehovah is reaffirming the covenant of grace which He instituted with Abraham. Exodus 19:5-6 is the Lord's description of His covenant people Israel.

In Deuteronomy 14 Israel has completed its 40-year journey in the wilderness. They were now ready to move into the promised land. Moses reminds them of who they are and of their covenant relationship to Jehovah. Verse 2 is a description of Israel as the Lord's own possession.

It is extremely significant that Peter in I Peter 2:9 now gathers up those two descriptions and combines them into one glorious description of the New Testament kingdom of Christ.

(1) A Chosen Race. The reference is to the Lord's choosing. The church of all ages is a people chosen of the Lord by His grace. The Lord has set His love upon a chosen people, then He planned their redemption. He has sent His Spirit unto the far corners of the earth to seek His chosen people. Not one of those whom the Lord loved will be lost.

(2) A Royal Priesthood. The Lord's people constitute a royal priesthood because they belong to the one family of the children of God. How could it be that we who were born slaves of sin should now be exalted to regal splendor? It is answered for us in Revelation 1:5-6, "Unto Him that loved us, and washed us from our sins in His own blood, and *hath made us kings and priests* unto God and His Father; to Him be glory and dominion for ever and ever." He brought us into His family and made us His adopted children. Christ by His sacrifice on our behalf has raised us to the exalted position of kings. We are royalty! Children of the Heavenly King.

How could such sinners whose sinful crimes render us abominable before God be counted worthy to be priests unto God? It is only as we have been washed in

Jesus' blood that we have been *consecrated* to such holy service. Because we have been sanctified in Jesus' blood we may freely (vs. 5) draw near to God, bringing spiritual sacrifices, praying, blessing and worshiping. In worship we are performing our priestly functions.

Because we are kings and priests unto God we must no longer serve the world. With Christ we must rule over our sinful desires. In the kingdom of God every redeemed soul is a royal priest.

(3) A Holy Nation. Whether Peter was thinking of Exodus 19:6 or Deuteronomy 14:2 it is beyond any doubt that the original Old Testament reference referred to the nation of Israel. However, it is also beyond any doubt that the text of I Peter 2:9 refers to the New Testament church.

The meaning is the same whether we consider the Old Testament or the New Testament kingdom. The distinguishing characteristics are the same. *Separation* from the world. The church ceases to be the kingdom of God when it is in subjection to the kingdoms of this world. *Consecration* to God: Peter in chapter 1 verse 2 says that the church is an elect or chosen people, by the sanctifying work of the Spirit. We have been devoted to God. We are His, totally His. Because we are the Lord's we are to walk in obedience to Christ. As a holy nation we are so to glorify God that the nations of the world may see the distinction. It is the work of Satan to eliminate that distinction.

(4) A People for God's Own Possession. As we saw in our study of Deuteronomy 14:2 (see chap. 3) "peculiar people" is better translated "a people of possession." Peter's words are consistent in carrying over the Old Testament words and meaning. It is therefore clear that even as the Old Testament church was God's own possession even so is the New Testament church God's own possession. We have been made His by the "sprinkling of the blood of Jesus Christ" (I Pet. 1:2).

We have been made "God's own possession" so that we may proclaim the praises "of Him who has called you out of darkness into His marvelous light." We are God's to bring praise to His Name in everything. We can no longer serve self for we are not our own. We have been bought with a price (I Cor. 6:19-20).

Conclusion to Verse 9: We should learn from this verse that there is no antithesis between God's people in the Old Testament and God's people in the New Testament.

The unbelievable grandeur of the declaration contained in verse 9 is enhanced by the statement in verse 10.

Who are these people that verse 9 designates as (1) a chosen race, (2) a royal priesthood, (3) a holy nation, and (4) a people for God's own possession? Verse 10 answers that question in a rather remarkable way with a series of two contrasting statements. Again as in verse 9, Peter reaches back into the Old Testament to the prophecy of Hosea. Peter has not given a verbatim quotation found in Hosea but has given us the meaning of the passage.

The first contrasting statement is taken from the second part of *Hosea 1:10:* *"Once* you were not a people, *but now* you are the people of God."

(5) Once you were not a people. Strange as the language may appear to us the words of the original setting in Hosea refer to Israel. In Hosea 1:9 the Lord had declared that Israel was not His people and He would not be their God. Notice the language of Genesis 17:7 and especially Leviticus 26:12. Because of the spiritual adultery the Lord had disowned them. They were no longer His people and He would not be known as their God. Because of their sin they were cut off from the blessings of the covenant. The sins of the people brought a separation from God.

(6) But now you are the people of God. But in verse 10 we see again the matchless grace of God. The very language which he uses goes back to the covenant promises given to Abraham in Genesis 13:16, 15:5 and 17:5-6. The Lord remembers His everlasting covenant which He made with Abraham and his seed. So the people who had been cut off because of sin would be called back to be "the sons of the living God" because of the gracious provisions of His covenant.

The second contrasting statement is taken from *Hosea 2:23:* ". . . and I will have mercy upon her that had not obtained mercy; and I will say to them which were not my people, Thou art My people; and they shall say, Thou art my God."

(7) Once you had not received mercy. Again, the prophet is speaking to Israel. Because of her idolatry Israel is to be judged by the Lord. In pronouncing judgment in verse 4, He says: "And I will not have mercy upon her children; for they be the children of harlotry." Because they had forsaken the Lord to serve other gods the Lord withdrew His mercy and compassion. Idolatry brings separation from the Lord.

(8) But now you have received mercy. But again the Lord shows His eternal love and grace to His people. In verse 14 He begins to speak of His love for His people and how He will plead with His church. Then in verse 18 He speaks of the covenant that He will make for them. In verses 19-20 He speaks of His betrothal to His people forever, in righteousness, in justice, in loving kindness, in mercies, in faithfulness. Then you will know Jehovah.

The whole of this section, verses 1-22, is then gathered together in one climactic statement in verse 23. To those who had been cut off from His mercy, to them He will show mercy. Notice again the covenantal language of Genesis 17:7 and especially Leviticus 26:12. To those who had not been His people He will say: "Thou art My people." They will respond: "Thou art my God."

That's the language which Peter gathers together in I Peter 2:9-10. The precise language which the Lord had used in describing His Old Testament people, and

His relationship to that people is now used to describe the Lord's New Testament people. To both of them He says: "Thou art My people." They respond: "Thou art my God." This is so because they are both one chosen people to whom he has extended His gracious covenant blessings. They both enjoy the same union and communion. The redeemed of all ages constitute *one* holy church purchased by Jesus' blood and righteousness.

Is there yet any doubt in your minds that Peter in I Peter 2:9-10 is applying the language of Hosea 1:10 and 2:23 to the New Testament church and is therefore including the Gentiles? If there is then I would refer you to Paul's statement in Romans 9:24-26. In that passage Paul refers to the same two verses in Hosea. In verse 24 he refers to the work of God in effectually calling "not from the Jews only, but also from the Gentiles." He then goes on in verses 25-26 to prove that this is what the Lord said he would do. It is here that Paul then refers back to Hosea 1:10 and 2:23: "So it is with the Gentiles, once forsaken of God but later embraced in covenant love and favour" (John Murray, *Epistle to the Romans,* vol. 2, p. 38).

Questions for Discussion

1. How many Old Testament quotations are found in I Peter 2:9-10? What are the Old Testament references?

2. Review and give consideration to each of those references.

3. To whom were the original Old Testament references written and to whom did they apply?

4. To whom does Peter apply these references? What significance and meaning can we draw from Peter's use of these quotations?

5. What are the contrasting statements found in I Peter 2:10?

6. Discuss the covenant relationship described in the original Old Testament setting and how that relationship is carried over to the New Testament people of God.

7. How does Paul in Romans 9:24-26 apply these Old Testament words found in I Peter 2:10?

5

CONTINUITY OF THE COVENANT PROMISES TO ISRAEL

Exodus 6:1-9

Introduction

1. There is a continuity throughout Scripture of the promises given to Abraham in Genesis 17. This is especially true of the covenant promise "to be a God unto thee, and to thy seed after thee."

2. The purpose of this lesson is to show that this promise was carried forward and reaffirmed to the nation of Israel. That promise is included in our text found in Exodus 6:1-9.

The Historical Setting

a. The opening chapter of Exodus finds the nation of Israel in Egyptian bondage. Israel was an oppressed and an afflicted people. The Egyptians were hard taskmasters and made Israel "serve with rigour."

b. The historical situation of Exodus chapter one is precisely what the Lord had foretold Abraham as recorded in Genesis 15:13-18. He promised the following events:

Verse 13: Abraham's seed would be in a strange land for 400 years. They shall be afflicted.

Verse 14: God promises judgment to that nation and release for Israel.

Verse 16: The release is to come in the fourth generation. They are to return to the land promised Abraham.

Verse 18: The Lord made a covenant with Abraham promising him that his seed shall return to the promised land.

c. Exodus 2:24: "And God heard their groanings, and God remembered His covenant with Abraham, with Isaac and with Jacob."

As the time for their release from Egyptian bondage draws near, the Lord makes the necessary preparations. He prepares to fulfill His covenant promises made to Abraham and later confirmed to Isaac and to Jacob.

d. Exodus 3 records the call of Moses to lead Israel out of Egyptian bondage. In verse 6 the Lord introduced Himself as "the God of thy father, the God of Abraham, the God of Isaac, and the God of Jacob." This is the covenantal language expressing the relationship of God to His people. In verses 7-10 the Lord refers to Israel as "My people" and expresses His intentions and His plans to release them from bondage to bring them up to the land of Canaan.

e. At the end of chapter 5 Moses returned to the Lord in great discouragement. His words to Pharaoh to let the Israelites go had resulted in greater burdens being added. In verse 22 Moses prays "Lord, wherefore has thou so evil entreated this people? Why is it that thou has sent me?"

The Lord responds to those questions in Exodus 6:1-8.

Exodus 6:1-8:

Verse 1:

a. This verse contains the very message that a discouraged Moses needed. The Lord promises to show His power, and to deliver Israel from bondage. At this moment Pharaoh refuses to let Israel go but when the Lord deals with him he will "drive them out of his land."

b. Verse 1 gives us the end to be accomplished. That was the message needed by Moses but then the following verses 2-8 provide us with the reason or the basis on which the Lord promised deliverance. Why did the Lord deliver?

Verse 2: "And God spake unto Moses, and said unto him, I am Jehovah."

The verse stands out as significant. The Lord meant it to be. A momentous event in the history of revelation is about to unfold. We saw the same formula in Genesis 17:1 when the Lord appears to Abram and announces that He is El Shaddai, the Almighty God. It was in that context that the Lord enters into the formal covenant with Abraham.

Verse 3:

a. As we have previously seen, God's covenant name to Abraham, Isaac, and Jacob was El Shaddai. They needed a revelation of God as the Strong One, the All-Powerful One but now the historical situation is changed. Will God remember and keep His covenant which He made with Abraham 400 years previously?

b. The name "Jehovah" is calculated to answer "Yes" to that question.

    1. Meaning of Jehovah:

        a) "I am who I am"—see Exodus 3:14 (KJV: I AM THAT I AM)

        "I Who Am, Truly Am"—Vos, page 132, *Biblical Theology*

    2. The revelation of His character:

        a) Self-existence

        b) Independence

        c) Immutability

d) His sovereignty

e) Faithfulness

f) "Denotes the infinite fulness of the Divine Being, which is a pledge that He will fulfill all His promises."

Exodus 3:15: "This is My Name forever, and this is My memorial-name to all generations." Beginning with Moses and the Israelites "Jehovah" is the covenant name to succeeding generations.

Verse 4:

a. Though the Lord had not been known to Abraham, Isaac and Jacob as Jehovah, nevertheless He had established His covenant with them. Included in the covenant is His promise "to give them the land of Canaan."

b. At this point the Lord indicates to Moses that though He had established His covenant promise to give Abraham, Isaac and Jacob the land of Canaan, nevertheless they had been but pilgrims and strangers in that land.

c. What the Lord promises He always fulfills. But there seems to be the inference here that though He had established His promise to Abraham nevertheless up to that point the promise remained unfulfilled. That thought seems to be the introduction to what the Lord is about to say in the following verses.

Verse 5:

a. "I have heard." This is the first of two significant actions recorded in this verse. He had heard the groanings of the children of Israel caused by the oppression of the Egyptians. When God's children groan the Lord hears their cry. He is like a father. He is ever listening for the cry of His children. When they are in distress He flies to their relief.

b. "I have remembered" is the second significant action. It is a logical follow-up of the first activity. He remembers the covenant promise given to Abraham concerning the land of Canaan.

When the Lord hears and remembers it is an indication that He is about to act on the behalf of those who have cried unto Him.

Verse 6:

a. Verses 6, 7, and 8 record three great acts which the Lord promises to perform on the behalf of the children of Israel. Seven times in these three verses the Lord says, "I will." Clearly, it is to be the Lord's activity that is to fulfill the *three great promises*.

b. Deliverance Promised

"I am Jehovah." Israel is to learn of the covenant faithfulness of God. He is saying: "I am Jehovah. I'll attest My being and My faithfulness by My activity."

c. Three times He says, "I will" in this verse:

1. "I will bring you out." He will release them from their bondage imposed by the Egyptians.

2. "I will deliver you out." He will rescue them from their slavery.

3. "I will redeem you." He will redeem by His own mighty power and with mighty acts of judgment. Geerhardus Vos writes, "Finally, the term 'redemption' enters into religious use here. Its specific meaning (different from such general terms as 'to rescue,' 'to deliver') lies precisely in this, that it describes the loving reacquisition of something formerly possessed." Vos, page 129, *Biblical Theology.*

I suggest that this very thought is carried over into the two Old Testament passages, Exodus 19:5 and Deuteronomy 14:2, and the New Testament passage of I Peter 2:9, all of which we have previously studied. The English translates these passages as "a peculiar people," but we previously suggested that the better rendering is a "people for God's own possession."

Israel was God's own possession, chosen out of all the nations of the world to be "a holy nation." They were His by covenant relationship in Abraham. He was going to show His love for them and prove His covenant faithfulness by redeeming them by His mighty power and bringing them into their covenant inheritance.

Verse 7: "And I will take you to Me for a people, And I will be to you a God, And ye shall know that I am Jehovah your God, Who bringeth you out from under the burdens of the Egyptians."

a. Adoption Promised

This is the *second* great act which the Lord promises to perform.

1. "I will take you to Me." He will make them His own beloved people. By His own free sovereign grace He adopts them into His own family—children of God. He makes them His own possession.

2. "I will be your God." He binds them to Himself by giving Himself to them. Jehovah will forever be known as their God. He will demonstrate that He is their God by the act of delivering them from their slavery in Egypt. They will know Him by His acts on their behalf. Their release will unmistakenly be His work.

b. I trust you recognized the covenant language of Genesis 17:7 and Leviticus 26:12. "I will be your God. You shall be My people." He is therefore promising them the covenant blessings promised to Abraham, Isaac and Jacob. He is promising them union and communion with Himself.

Verse 8: "And I will bring you to the land which I swore to give to Abraham, Isaac and Jacob, And I will give it to you for a possession: I am Jehovah."

a. The Promised Land

This is the *third* great act which the Lord promises to perform. He had promised them deliverance from slavery. He had promised to make them His own people and now He promises to bring them into a land which shall be their own possession. "I will bring." It is the Lord's doing. He, it is, that brings them into the land. It is His sovereign power.

23

Notice also that it is a very special land. It's the land which He had promised to Abraham, Isaac and Jacob. He "swore" to give it to them. The word "swore" literally means "lifted up my hand." The Lord took an oath when He made those promises to Abraham, Isaac and Jacob that He would fulfill them. Genesis 15 bears for us the record of the Lord sealing His covenant promise with an oath.

"I will give it to you for a possession."

The promised land is a *gift* from the Lord to His people. They did not merit it in any way. The Lord dispossessed one people and gave it to His own people out of His own free grace.

"I am Jehovah."

Verse 2: The Lord opened His conversation with Moses with the introduction, "I am Jehovah."

Verse 6: The Lord's message to Israel was "I am Jehovah." It was Jehovah that gave His promise to deliver them from Egyptian bondage.

Verse 7: Through their deliverance from bondage they would know "I am Jehovah." They would know that Jehovah was their God and they His people.

Verse 8: Now the final words spoken to Moses in this conversation are, "I am Jehovah." He will bring them to the land which He has promised.

Is there some special meaning to this fourfold repetition? I think Jehovah is staking his whole claim to Israel as His people upon the promised fulfillment of the three promises which He has just made to them through Moses. His reputation is at stake.

But on behalf of the people He is calling them to trust in His word and His faithfulness to His promises. He is going to prove His covenant faithfulness to His people before the nations of the world.

Verse 9: "So Moses spoke thus to the children of Israel, but they did not listen to Moses on account of their despondency and cruel bondage" (NASB).

a. What a tragic verse. Moses faithfully gives them the Word of Jehovah. He brought them God's promises, words of deliverance and words of encouragement. The Lord was responding to their groanings.

b. What was *their* response? They continued their groaning. *They didn't hear* what Moses said. Their spirit of despondency crushed out the word of Jehovah. Moses brought the message of hope and release from despair but they failed to hear the message.

c. Don't we have the same problem today?

Fulfillment to Israel

a. We believe that the covenant promises given to Abraham in Genesis 17 were not only reaffirmed to the nation of Israel but that the Lord kept His promises and fulfilled them when He brought Israel into Canaan at the end of the 40-year wilderness journey. This belief is not shared by a great part of Christendom today. This is contrary to the teaching known as Modern Dispensationalism of which the Scofield Bible is an exponent.

b. In this regard, we want to refer you to two explanatory notes found in the Scofield Bible.

1. The first footnote is referred to in Genesis 12:1 and is quoted here, in part, as follows:

The Fourth Dispensation: Promise.

For Abraham and his descendents it is evident that the Abrahamic Covenant (Gen 15:18 note) made a great change. They became distinctively the heirs of promise. That covenant is wholly gracious and unconditional. The descendents of Abraham had but to abide in their own land to inherit every blessing. In Egypt they lost their blessings, but not their covenant. The Dispensation of Promise ended when Israel rashly accepted the law (Ex 19:8). Grace had prepared a deliverer (Moses), provided a sacrifice for the guilty, and by divine power brought them out of bondage (Ex 19:4): but at Sinai they exchanged grace for law. The Dispensation of Promise extends from Gen 12:1 to Ex 19:8, and was exclusively Israelitish. . . .

2. The second footnote is referred to in Exodus 19:8 and is quoted here in full as follows:

The Fifth Dispensation: Law

This dispensation extends from Sinai to Calvary—from the Exodus to the Cross. The history of Israel in the wilderness and in the land is one long record of the violations of the law. The testing of the nation by law ended in the judgment of the Captivities, but the dispensation itself ended at the Cross. (1) Man's state at the beginning (Ex 19: 1-4). (2) His responsibility (Ex 19:5, 6; Rom 10:5). (3) His failure (II Ki 17:7-17, 19; Acts 2:22, 23). (4) The judgment (II Ki 17:1-6, 20; 25:1-11; Lk 21:2-24).

c. Answer to above notes:

1. Exodus 19:8: Does this verse represent a change in God's dealings with the nation of Israel?

a) To hold that would indicate that the Lord tricked them for the people were simply responding to the words of the Lord. They responded in the way that the Lord desired.

b) It is perfectly evident from the opening chapters of Exodus that the Lord was preparing to fulfill His covenant promises made to Abraham. That is particularly true of such passages as Exodus 2:24; 3:6-10, 15-17. When Jehovah delivered Israel from bondage and eventually brought them into Canaan He did so in fulfillment of His promises to Abraham, Isaac and Jacob.

c) It is the law to which the dispensationalist takes exception. The law is presumed to be against grace. The law is recorded beginning at Exodus 20:2. Notice carefully the words: "I am Jehovah thy God, which have brought thee out of the land of Egypt, out of the house of bondage."

(1) "I am Jehovah thy God." Is not that the equivalent to God's promise to Abraham in Genesis 17:7, "And I will . . . be a God unto thee"?

(2) The words of Exodus 20:2 are referred to as "the preface to the ten commandments." The answer to the Westminster Shorter Catechism No. 44 says, "The preface to the ten commandments teacheth us, that because God is the Lord, and our God, and *Redeemer*, therefore we are bound to keep all his commandments."

(3) The words or the thought expressed by Jehovah in Exodus 20:2 is repeated again and again throughout the passages which set forth the law. It stands as a constant reminder of the *grace* and power of God present in their redemption from bondage.

d) Leviticus 26:9-13: It is obvious from these words that the Lord spoke them after the deliverance from Egyptian bondage, and after the events of Exodus 19:8 and yet the Lord repeats the promise of Genesis 17:7 (see Lev. 26:12).

e) Leviticus 26:40-46

(1) In verses 14-39 the Lord issues a series of warnings predicting judgments that would come upon the nation if they despise the Lord's ordinances. Included in these judgments is the warning that another nation would conquer them and carry them into captivity (vss. 32-39). Verses 40-46 are in response to that thought.

(2) Verse 40: If the people who are in captivity will turn to the Lord in confession of their sins and the sins of the nation:

Verse 41: *And* they acknowledge God's righteous judgments of their iniquities and humble their hearts:

Verse 42: *Then* will Jehovah remember His covenant with Jacob, Isaac and Abraham. He will remember His promise regarding the land.

Verse 43: During the captivity the land shall rest. It shall enjoy the sabbath's rest which they failed to give it (see vss. 34-35). The reference is to the commandment that the land was not to be worked each seventh year. It was a sabbath of rest unto the land (see Lev. 25:1-7).

Verse 44: Even while in captivity the Lord will not cast them away. He will not break His covenant with them for He is Jehovah their God.

Verse 45: He will remember His covenant which He made with them when He brought them out of Egypt: "I am Jehovah."

Verse 46: This is the record of the "statutes," "ordinances," and "laws" which the Lord gave to Moses on Mt. Sinai.

(3) Some observations of Leviticus 26:40-46.

(a) Without question this passage is included in the dispensation of Law as taught by the dispensationalists. Yet the predominant theme is God's *grace*. If they confess their sins the Lord will forgive and return them to the promised land again.

(b) According to verse 42, His gracious dealings even with the sinful nations is based squarely upon the covenant made with Abraham.

(c) Verse 45 apparently refers to the covenant entered into at Sinai. See Exodus 24. This according to the dispensationalist is the covenant of law and yet the Lord sees no antithesis between the covenant made with Abraham and that made with the nation at Sinai. "I am Jehovah their God" is equally applicable to both covenants.

(4) See Westminster Confession of Faith, chapter 7.

Questions for Discussion

1. How do we know that the Egyptian bondage for the nation of Israel was included in God's plan and purposes?

2. What caused God to remember His covenant promises? How should this encourage us?

3. What was the occasion that brought this revelation from God in Exodus 6:1-8?

4. What does the Lord promise Moses?

5. What is the meaning and significance of God's revelation of His name Jehovah?

6. What encouragement should it be to us when we read that the Lord "heard" and "remembered"?

7. What three great acts did God promise to Israel in verses 6-8? Is there any relationship in these events to the covenant promises made to Abraham?

8. How did Israel respond when Moses brought God's message to them? How do we respond today?

9. Discuss the significance of Leviticus chapter 26. What is the great theme of this chapter? What is the meaning of verse 42?

6

CONTINUITY OF THE COVENANT PROMISES TO THE NEW TESTAMENT CHURCH

II Corinthians 6:14 to 7:1

Introduction

1. We believe that there is a continuing re-affirmation of the covenant promise first given to Abraham. The study of Exodus 6:1-9 shows that the Lord had this promise in mind as He delivered Israel from Egyptian bondage. Israel's deliverance was in fulfillment of Jehovah's promises to Abraham.

2. But we further believe that the same covenant promises given to Abraham and confirmed to Old Testament Israel are also reaffirmed to the New Testament church. It is with that thought in mind that we want to study II Corinthians 6:14-7:1.

3. In II Corinthians 6:1 Paul had exhorted the church that they "receive not the grace of God in vain." He was concerned that in life they did not measure up to their profession as Christians. Their lives were so inconsistent as to constitute a denial of the gospel. It is to that situation that Paul speaks in this text.

Verse 14:

Be not yoked together with unbelievers: for what fellowship have righteousness with unrighteousness? Or what communion [fellowship] hath light with darkness?

a. *Separation from Unbelievers*

1. Believers are not to be bound together with unbelievers. Believers and unbelievers are not to be bound together with the same yoke. Paul is drawing the figure from an Old Testament prohibition set forth in Deuteronomy 22:10: "Thou shalt not plough with an ox and an ass together." Paul is applying that Old Testament principle to the relationship of believers to unbelievers. Two animals of a different nature, harnessed together in the same yoke, are a type of Christians having fellowship with unbelievers.

2. It is the Lord who demands that His children are not to be yoked together with unbelievers. He it is that established the division. The antithesis between believers and unbelievers creates an eternal separation between the two. There is

no reconciliation. That truth is brought out by a series of five questions.

3. What restrictions does this admonition put upon us in our daily contacts with unbelievers.? It must be obvious that we cannot withdraw from society. Neither the apostles nor the New Testament church established monasteries.

The following should help us as general guidelines in our contacts with society:

No unholy alliances. We should not in any way be bound together with an unbeliever in an entangling, intimate, voluntary association.

No compromise with our faith and life. In our contacts with society we must so speak and act that we do not in any way compromise the integrity of the faith, or in any way lower the high standards of Christian morality.

Propagate the faith. Our lives should be so ordered with the great objective of winning others to Christ, to glorify God.

The First Question: "What fellowship hath righteousness with unrighteousness?"

a. As we look at these five questions we should see two kingdoms, two systems of thought which are totally incompatible. These two systems are represented by biblical Christianity and paganism in whatever dress it may appear.

b. Righteousness is placed in antithesis to unrighteousness. The righteousness in view is God's righteousness which has been set forth for us in God's law. It is perfect righteousness. Unrighteousness is iniquity, sometimes translated "lawlessness." It is the transgression of God's law. I John 3:4: "for sin is the transgression of the law."

c. Righteousness and lawlessness stand as radical opposites the one to the other. This being true there can be no partnership or fellowship between them. There can be no bond of union between them.

Of Christ it is said in Psalm 45:7 and quoted in Hebrews 1:9, "Thou hast loved righteousness and hated lawlessness." That same statement should be said of every Christian. See Titus 2:14.

The Second Question: "What fellowship has light with darkness?"

a. No clearer expression of the antithesis could be found. There is universal knowledge that light and darkness do not mix. There is no way that they can be joined together.

b. Light is a representation of God's holiness. "God is light, and in Him is no darkness at all" (I John 1:5). *Light* is the figurative expression for truth and purity. *Darkness* is the symbol for error and wickedness. John 3:20: "For every one that doeth evil hateth the light, neither cometh to the light, lest his deeds should be reproved."

c. Light and darkness are expressions representing the kingdom of God and the kingdom of Satan. Colossians 1:13: "Who hath delivered us from the domain of darkness, and hath translated us into the kingdom of His dear Son.''

d. It is impossible to retain citizenship in both kingdoms. Because it is impossible to combine light and darkness, holiness and sin, happiness and misery—so should the Christian flee from voluntary, intimate fellowship with the world.

Verse 15:

And what concord hath Christ with Belial? or what portion hath a believer with an unbeliever?

The Third Question: "What concord hath Christ with Belial?"

a. Here we have the names of the rulers of the two kingdoms so clearly characterized in the two previous questions. They are the captains of the opposing forces which had been previously characterized as righteousness and unrighteousness and light and darkness.

1. *Christ*. The King of righteousness and the Light of the world.

2. *Belial*. A proper name for Satan "the adversary." The prince of lawlessness. His character is revealed in that he was a liar and a murderer from the beginning (John 8:44).

b. Between these two no harmony is possible, but only the deadliest antagonism. Nothing but discord—"for the devil sinneth from the beginning. For this purpose the Son of God was manifested, that He might destroy the works of the devil" (I John 3:8). Mortal combat—but Christ has the victory. Christ partook of our flesh and blood "that through death He might render powerless him who had the power of death, that is, the devil" (Heb. 2:14).

The Fourth Question: "What portion hath a believer with an unbeliever?"

a. "What does a believer have in common with an unbeliever?" (NIV)

b. In the prior question we dealt with the two kings and their kingdoms but here we deal with the *citizens* of those kingdoms.

The qualities of life and the possessions of the citizens of those two kingdoms brings an irreconcilable division between them.

c. *The believer has Christ*. In Him is pardon, light, righteousness, peace, salvation, life eternal, everlasting joy and an eternal inheritance secured by Christ. The *unbeliever* has none of these things. He has Satan as a hard taskmaster, darkness and anguish of soul and eternal miseries awaiting him. There can be no fellowship between those whose respective destinies are so different.

d. *See how the antithesis works out in life:*

1. The unbeliever's life is centered on self, whereas the believer's life is centered on Christ.

2. The treasures of one are here on earth, whereas the other looks forward to treasures in heaven.

3. The values of the one belong to this world, whereas the values of the other belong to heaven.

4. The unbeliever seeks the glory of men, whereas the believer seeks to glorify God.

e. The things which the unbeliever wants and loves are the things from which the Lord has separated us. What then does the believer have in common with the unbeliever? The answer is: Nothing! The two are essentially hostile to each other. They are enemies at war. The two can never live together in unity or harmony.

Verse 16a:

And what agreement hath the temple of God with idols?

The Fifth Question: "What agreement hath the temple of God with idols?" "What agreement is there between the temple of God and idols?" (NIV)

a. The climax is reached in this final question. It concerns the worship of God.

b. The temple of God is holy. The Old Testament temple is the place where God met His people in worship. The Lord Himself consecrated the temple with His own presence.

c. It is significant that the temple was completely free of images or idols. The second commandment provides that in the worship of God "Thou shalt not make unto thee any graven image." To introduce an idol into the temple was an abomination before God and a desecration of His House. When idols are introduced into the temple it then ceases to be the temple of God.

d. Paul had already written strong warnings against idolatry. I Corinthians 10:7 "Neither be ye idolaters, as were some of them." Again verse 14, "Wherefore, my dearly beloved, flee from idolatry." In I Thessalonians 1:9 Paul reminds the church at Thessalonica that they had "turned to God from idols to serve the living and true God."

e. You cannot serve God and idols. There is no agreement between the two. Rather there is total disagreement.

Verse 16b:

For ye are the temple of the living God.

a. Paul has firmly established his case for separation from unbelief by five rhetorical questions. But that is not the end of his argument. He now presses home the point with the most telling argument that he could use.

b. "For ye are the temple of the living God." What a tremendous statement! Can't you feel the weight that Paul was putting on this statement? A dwelling for the living God!

c. Who is "the temple" referred to here?

1. The language seems to refer to believers in their corporate form as they

are joined together and form the church of Christ. In this figure Paul boldly identifies the temple of the living God with the New Testament church.

Paul has previously used this simile of the temple in his earlier letter to Corinth. He used it in a twofold application:

Corporately and Individually

I Corinthians 3:16 reads, "Know ye not that ye are the temple of God, and that the Spirit of God dwelleth in you?"

a) There are indications in this text that Paul is referring to the corporate church as "the temple."

(1) The letter is addressed to "the church of God which is at Corinth" (1:2).

(2) In chapter 3 he is concerned by the divisions in the church.

(3) In verse 9 he refers to the church at Corinth as "God's building."

Verse 10-11 Paul is concerned that men take heed to build the church on no other foundation than Jesus Christ.

b) However beginning at verse 13 there appear to be references relating to individuals. It therefore seems best to refer the statement "ye are the temple" to the church but also to individual believers in their *organic connection to the church.* The whole church of Christ is the "temple of God," but so is every true congregation and every individual Christian (see also I Cor. 6:19-20; Eph. 2:19-22).

c) "Ye are the temple of the living God."

(1) Such a statement stretches the mind to its fullest capabilities. Every believer in Christ is God's habitation.

(2) Can there be any greater argument for separation from evil and evil associations? "Know ye not that your *body* is the temple of the Holy Spirit?" (I Cor. 6:19). You are holy. As a temple of God we have been consecrated to God by His presence and dedicated to His holy service and worship wherein no evil thing should enter.

As the Old Testament temple was not to be defiled because it was God's dwelling place, so neither is the body to be defiled because it is God's dwelling place.

(3) It is here that the antithesis comes to its clearest and fullest expression: Whoever is not a temple of God must be a temple of idols and of Satan.

Verse 16c:

as God said, "I will dwell in them, and walk in them; And I will be their God, And they shall be My People."

a. Where did Paul get this fantastic idea that we were "temples of the living God"? He got it from the Old Testament Scriptures. This portion of verse 16, plus

32

verses 17 and 18, is part of a series of quotations from the Old Testament Scriptures.

    b. "As God said" is a clear reference to Scripture. For the apostle Paul Scripture was the authoritative Word of God; it is what "God said." It is an appeal to that which is the absolute truth and which is not open to dispute.

    c. In the light of these words it seems appropriate to issue a warning to put us on our guard. In the 1920's and 30's the liberals in the church of Christ attacked the infallibility of the Bible. We were assured that the higher criticism studies showed that the Bible was not the infallible Word of God which we once thought it to be!

Today we must be aware of another attack upon the infallibility of the Bible. It is particularly dangerous because it comes from men who are looked to as evangelical scholars and even in the Reformed Churches.

Dr. Harold Lindsell, former editor of *Christianity Today*, has performed a notable service in the church in the writing of his book, *The Battle for the Bible*. Dr. Lindsell states that he left Fuller Seminary when it failed to continue its original position of infallibility.

Appeal is again being made to higher criticism. The word of scientists and historians is put over against the Bible. We are told that chapters 1 to 11 of Genesis are neither scientifically nor historically accurate. The language of Scripture is time-bound or is bound by the culture of that day so that it is not binding on us today. The place of women in the church is being attacked precisely on this basis.

But for the apostle Paul it was what "God said" in His Word that counted.

Leviticus 26:11-12

    a. To prove his case from Scriptures Paul cites Leviticus 26:11-12. From the context of this passage it is obvious that Paul considered the Old Testament citation to prove that God's people were indeed "a temple of the living God."

    b. 1. *Divine Presence*. The quotation "I will dwell in them, and walk in them" certainly expresses the presence of God. Because the Lord permanently manifests His presence in His people collectively and individually, He is said to dwell in all as His habitation and resting place.

Psalm 132:13-14 says, "For the Lord has chosen Zion; He has desired it for His habitation. This is My resting place forever; Here will I dwell, for I have desired it."

    2. *Paul's citation of Leviticus 26:11-12* appears to signal a New Testament advance in the fulfillment of this promise. The thought expressed in Leviticus is that God will dwell *among* you and walk *among* you. Those words came to expression as God dwelt in the tabernacle and in the temple. Paul renders the promise in the words, "I will dwell *in* them, and walk *in* them." What was symbolized in the temple ritual has now come to a fuller realization. The promise

now assures believers of the inward and spiritual presence of God within themselves (see I Cor. 3:16-17).

Jesus promised nothing less than that in His words recorded in John 14:23, "If a man love Me, he will keep My words: and My Father will love him, and We will come unto him, and make Our abode with him."

c. *The Lord sanctifies every believer* and makes him a holy temple by His presence within him. If you are a believer in the Lord Jesus Christ and His sacrifice on your behalf, then God dwells in your heart and all your affections and your acts *should* be determined and controlled by Him. His divine presence is ever with us. What a promise! What hope and encouragement that should give us!

d. And I will be their God, And they shall be My people.

1. As we continue the promise we learn that it not only includes the Lord's presence among and in His people but also fellowship between the Lord and His people.

2. On God's part there is the communication of Himself and the bestowal of the benefits of His salvation. He gives Himself to His people.

On the people's part there is fellowship in the presence of their divine redeemer and there is the enjoyment of His blessings.

The essence of this great promise can be described in the two words *union* and *communion*. The Lord *united* to His people and His people in *communion* with Him. Divine presence and divine fellowship.

e. This is the great covenant promise made with Abraham and recorded in Genesis 17:7. In accordance with that promise made to Abraham the promise has been renewed again and again with "thy seed after thee." Hodge comments: "It is one of the most comprehensive and frequently repeated promises of the Scripture." Now we find that it has significance for us as New Testament believers. Here in our text is the same promise given to Abraham, Isaac and Jacob, then to Israel and now to the New Testament church. The unity and the continuity of the covenant of grace in all ages cannot be denied.

f. The promises of God are far greater and far more comprehensive than we realize. Hodge: "The promise that the nations should be blessed in the seed of Abraham, as unfolded in the New Testament is found to comprehend all the blessings of redemption."

How small is our view of God's promises and how totally inadequate is our conception of God.

Do you have Jehovah as your God? If so, then

1. You have an infinite protector and benefactor.
2. You have the infinite presence of God.
3. You have an infinite object of love and confidence.
4. You have an infinite source of knowledge and holiness.
5. You are the object of divine love.

6. You have a divine redeemer.

7. You are God's own possession and His temple.

Verse 17:

Therefore, come out from their midst and be separated, saith the Lord. Touch no unclean thing (Isa. 52:11). And I will receive you (Ezek. 20:34).

a. This is a case of adding Scripture to Scripture. He is supporting Scripture with Scripture. He is supporting his quotation found in verse 16 with additional scriptural support found in verses 17-18.

b. The first two lines of verse 17 represent a free citation from Isaiah 52:11 and the last line from Ezekiel 20:34. Paul renders their meanings by his quotation.

c. These Old Testament passages were originally addressed to God's people who, because of their sin and idolatry, had been carried into the Babylonian captivity. The citation from Isaiah is God's warning to those who returned from exile to leave everything that was unclean behind them in Babylon. Now in its New Testament setting it is repeated and applied to the church at Corinth, to those who had been delivered from their sins and idolatry.

d. Paul was deeply concerned that through either carelessness or compromise the church may be carried away into paganism. So it is that as an ambassador of Christ he pleads with them ''not to receive the grace of God in vain'' (II Cor. 6:1). In his salutation in the epistle to the Galatians Paul writes of Christ: ''Who gave Himself for our sins, that He might deliver us from this present evil world'' (Gal. 1:4). As God's redeemed people we are no longer in the bondage of sin. It is therefore incumbent upon us that we should not be ''bound together with unbelievers.'' As God's people, His own possession, we are to be separated from all heathen practices which would defile us as God's temple.

e. ''And I will receive you.'' If there is to be a break in these verses, I am inclined to think that this clause belongs with verse 18. It's a part of the complete thought which is there expressed.

Those whom the Lord has separated He receives. Such separation is the necessary preparation for fellowship with God. Does this mean that we are the poorer for this separation? Not at all, for we are the richer. We are separated from the world that we may enjoy fellowship with God together with that great company washed in the cleansing blood of Jesus Christ.

Verse 18:

And I will be a Father unto you. And ye shall be My sons and daughters saith the Lord Almighty.

a. This verse is a continuation of the Old Testament promises begun in verse 16. Which passage Paul had in mind is not clear. Some believe the citation to be from Isaiah 43:6, and others, II Samuel 7:14.

b. "I will be a Father unto you, Ye shall be My sons and daughters." That's nothing less than the promise of adoption—adoption into God's holy family. Larger Catechism—No. 74 What is Adoption?

"Adoption is an act of the free grace of God, in and for His only Son Jesus Christ, whereby all those that are justified are received into the number of His children, have His name put upon them, the Spirit of His Son given to them, are under His fatherly care and dispensations, admitted to all the liberties and privileges of the sons of God, made heirs of all the promises, and fellow-heirs with Christ in glory."

Those adopted are not servants in the house, but sons and daughters of the Lord Almighty—children of the heavenly King. To be His sons and daughters brings with it a majestic dignity and a heavenly blessedness before which all earthly honors and worldly goods should pale into utter insignificance.

We should count it no common honor to be reckoned among the sons of God. What an affront it is to God that He should call us His children and then we defile ourselves by being joined together with unbelievers and their sinful practices.

Chapter 7:1:

Therefore, having these promises, dearly beloved, let us cleanse ourselves from all defilement of flesh and spirit, perfecting holiness in the fear of God.

a. This is Paul's exhortation based on the previous verses. "*Therefore,* having these promises. . . ." *Because* we have these promises we should make a complete break with every compromise with sin. This is the logical consequence of having such promises.

b. "These promises": Paul has referred not to vague generalities but to specific and very wonderful promises attached to God's everlasting covenant. It is very clear that Paul believes that these Old Testament promises belong to us as believers in Jesus Christ. The promises had been given to the whole body of the church, namely God's covenant people in every age.

c. Therefore, because we have these promises of intimate relationship and fellowship—union and communion—with God and the assurance of His love, "let us purify ourselves from every defilement." So it is that Paul stresses the privileges in order to enforce the obligation of obedience. The full realization of these promises requires a complete renunciation of everything inconsistent with the Divine holiness, together with an earnest pursuit after perfect holiness. We must strive against sin and for purity.

If God is our heavenly Father, and we His children then we ought to have the desire for true holiness for it is God that creates such desires within us. "Continue to work out your own salvation with fear and trembling, for it is God who works in you to will and do what pleases Him" (Phil. 2:12-13).

d. "From all defilement of flesh and spirit." There are two classes of sin here recognized; those of the flesh, and those of the spirit. The whole man belongs to God; the body and the soul. The body and the soul are the subjects of holiness. Christ redeemed the whole man.

We are to cleanse ourselves from all that defiles, both external and internal, both seen and unseen, both public and private whether of the body or the spirit.

Hebrews 6:1 tells us that we are to "press on to perfection." Because we have these glorious promises we are to be earnestly engaged in the work of purification. We purify ourselves by "perfecting holiness." It is the great purpose of the Christian to complete the work of holiness, to be fully consecrated to God. That work was begun in faith but it is now to be actualized, developed and perfected during the whole of life. Those who are unwilling to cleanse themselves from every stain of sin only show that they have not been cleansed from the guilt of sin.

e. That striving unto perfection is to be done "in the fear of God." Here is our motivation. It is to be done because of our reverence of God who has made us His own dear children. We are to serve Him in supreme love and devotion. Our motivation for purifying ourselves is not regard to the good of others, nor our own happiness, but reverence for God. We are to be holy because He is holy (Hodge). I Peter 1:15-16 reads, "But as He which hath called you is holy, so be ye holy in all manner of conversation: Because it is written, Be ye holy; for I am holy."

Conclusion:

There can be no doubt that Paul writing to the church at Corinth is applying to them the same convenantal promises given to Abraham in Genesis 17 and to Moses in Leviticus 26.

The study of II Corinthians 6:14-18 forces us to the conclusion that New Testament Christians are one with the Old Testament People of God. They are bound together with God and with one another through the gracious covenant promises. The burden of Paul's argument is that the New Testament church, like the Old Testament church has the same covenant promises and the same covenant relationship with God.

The Lord demands holiness of His adopted children. That demand is based on our covenant relationship to our Heavenly Father. Covenant blessings also bring covenant responsibilities.

Questions for Discussion

1. What was Paul's concern as he wrote II Corinthians chapter six? Would Paul have the same concern today?

2. In what ways do we let today's culture cause us to make unholy alliances and compromise our faith?

3. What kingdoms and life styles are presented in the five questions presented in our passage? Are they still in existence?

4. What is the purpose of the five questions?

5. What do you think is Paul's greatest argument for the Christian's separation from evil?

6. What Old Testament passage does Paul quote to prove that the Christian is a temple of God?

7. What relationship does Paul's argument have to the covenant of grace made with Abraham in Genesis 17?

8. How does that relationship relate to the promise of II Corinthians 6:18?

9. What is Paul's exhortation? Do we have the same promises? What then is our responsibility?

10. Discuss the significance of the application of the Old Testament covenant promises to the New Testament church and New Testament Christians.

11. How does this teaching on separation affect our work of evangelism? What was Jesus' attitude when He ate with sinners?

12. How does this teaching on separation affect marriage? What difficulties arise for Christian young people?

7

THE COVENANT'S FINAL FULFILLMENT

Revelation 21

Introduction

1. We have been insisting that the promise made to Abraham in Genesis 17: "to be a God unto thee, and to thy seed after thee" applied successively to Abraham, Isaac, and Jacob, to the people of Israel and equally so to the New Testament church. We have appealed to passages in both the Old Testament and the New Testament to support this position.

2. On the basis of these passages we have maintained that the unity and the continuity of the covenant of grace is equally appropriate to all ages. Finally, we have maintained that the essence of the covenant is God's relationship to His people in union and communion.

3. We believe that Revelation 21 confirms what we have tried to maintain and that this passage reaches the climax in the fulfillment of the covenant promises.

Verse 1: The New Heaven and the New Earth.

It is a picture of the consummation. The new world unfolds in all its glory. All things are new. John sees the appearance of the new heaven and the new earth.

From II Peter 3:7-13 we find that, verse 7, "the present heavens and earth are reserved for fire, being kept for the day of judgment." Verse 12: "That day will bring about the destruction of the heavens by fire, and the elements will melt in the heat." Verse 13: "But in keeping with His promise we are looking forward to a new heaven and a new earth, the home of righteousness."

Out of this great conflagration a new universe is born. But the "new" is the same heaven and earth having passed through the cleansing fires. The "new" has fully come and the "old" has vanished.

Verse 2: The Holy City Appears.

a. The Holy City, the New Jerusalem, now descends from God out of heaven.

It is called "holy" because it has been separated from sin and completely consecrated to God. It is called "new" probably in contradistinction to the earthly Palestinian Jerusalem. The city is described as "a bride adorned for her husband."

b. Whom or what does the Holy City symbolize? One does not have to look far for the answer (Rev. 21:9-10). These verses tell us that the angel is showing John "the bride, the Lamb's wife." Verse 2 had referred to the Holy City as being "prepared as a bride adorned for her husband." To what did the angel point when he showed John "the Lamb's wife"? John describes this scene in verse 10 when he says that the angel "showed me that great city, the Holy Jerusalem, descending out of heaven from God."

So it is that the *two symbols,* the *bride* and the *city* are identical. They both indicate the church of God. Speaking in Ephesians 5:24-33 Paul uses the relationship between husbands and wives as an example of the relationship of Christ to His bride. Verse 32: "This is a great mystery: but I speak concerning Christ and the church."

The symbol of the bride representing the church can only speak of that glorious, holy fellowship between Christ and His church. The symbol speaks of love, the love of Christ for His church and the love of the church for Christ. So great is Christ's love that He gave Himself for it that it might be spotless, pure and holy (see Eph. 5:25-26).

Verse 3: "And I heard a great voice from the throne, saying:
Behold the tabernacle of God is with men, And He shall dwell with them, And they shall be His people, And God Himself shall be with them and be their God" (see vss. 5-6).

a. The voice is the voice of Christ from His throne announcing His marriage to His bride, the church, but significantly this announcement is in the form of the *final fulfillment of the covenant* promises.

b. It is the climactic event of the ages. "The tabernacle of God is with men." God's dwelling place, His temple, is with men. The symbol of God's presence or dwelling, namely the Old Testament tabernacle and later the temple at Jerusalem, now is completely realized. All the types and symbols of both the Old Testament and the New Testament give way to reality.

"He shall dwell with them." With the marriage supper of the Lamb the Lord comes to abide with His people. This relationship is eternal. This is the eternal state of communion between the Lord and His people. The provisional element is past for this is God's redeemed humanity. All "have washed their robes and made them white in the blood of the Lamb" (Rev. 7:14. See Lev. 26:11). Here is its fulfillment.

c. John continues with the words and thought of Leviticus 26:12. These people are His covenant people and so shall they ever be His people. He will ever be with them: He is their God and they dwell within the security of His tabernacle. Here is the eternal fellowship between God and His people.

The covenant relationship which the Lord established here and now will then be brought to perfection in the new heaven and the new earth. The hearts of His people shall forever be filled with love, honor, and delight in God. Here they shall find perfect holiness. The Lord in their presence shall fully manifest His love for them and crown them with glory and perfect happiness.

d. We ought now to see something of the importance of the covenant promise, "I will be your God, and you shall be My people." We receive its blessings in this life but they are carried on to perfection in the next. Hendriksen says, "It is THE promise, for it includes all other promises" (*More than Conquerors*, p. 242).

Verse 4: "And He shall wipe away every tear from their eyes. And there shall be no more earth; Neither mourning, nor crying, nor pain, any more: The old order has passed away."

All the effects and consequences of sin shall be done away with. All the trials and tribulations which we are heir to in this life are forever past. "He shall wipe away every tear": In those words we see the tenderness and compassion of our Heavenly Father. He wipes every tear dry.

All the causes of future sorrow shall be forever removed. No more death. Christ has vanquished death our great enemy in this life. Separations and divisions caused by death shall be forever done away with.

Death, mourning, crying, and pain are elements which we encounter in this life. but they are intrusions into God's perfect creation. They are the judgments of God upon sin. The curse passed upon men because of disobedience.

But Christ has appeared upon the scene of history. By His cross He has intervened to pay the price of sin and to make reconciliation for His people.

"The old order has passed away." Isaiah in prophetic vision saw that the days of sorrow would end and a new day would dawn as recorded in 51:11, "Therefore the redeemed of the Lord shall return, and come with singing unto Zion; and everlasting joy shall be upon their head: they shall obtain gladness and joy; and sorrowing and mourning shall flee away."

The old order, things present in the "first heaven and the first earth are passed away" and the new order, the "new heaven and the new earth" appear. With this new order there is "everlasting joy." There is joy and gladness without end. The *presence* of *God* is there *without interruption.* So the picture of Revelation 21 is *eternal presence, eternal communion, eternal fellowship* between God and His redeemed people.

It is the full and final glorious fulfillment of the covenant promises made to Abraham and secured for us in Jesus Christ.

For the purposes of this study we shall confine our lesson to only three more verses in this chapter, namely 12-14.

Revelation 21:12-13: The Twelve Gates.

The Holy City is described in verse 12 as having "a wall great and high, and had twelve gates, and at the gates twelve angels; and names were written on them, which are those of the twelve tribes of the sons of Israel."

1. The Holy City has "a wall great and high." City walls were for protection, safety, and security. Hence, the *symbolical* meaning of this wall is that there is security for the church in the presence of God.

2. But walls have gates for access into the city. The four walls of this city are described as having twelve gates, three on each side of the city, and each gate with a name written on it. Each gate had a name of one of the twelve tribes of Israel.

3. Ezekiel closes his prophecy with a picture similar to that which is described by John in Revelation 21:12-13 (see Ezek. 48:30-35). In Ezekiel's prophecy the 12 tribes were to return to the land. The land is then divided among the tribes. But in the middle of the land a portion was to be reserved "for the prince" (verse 21). In a special city described by Ezekiel a sanctuary is located in the midst of it. It is this city which is referred to in verses 30-35. The city is square, the four sides of the city being of equal length. Each side of the city has three gates. Each gate is named after one of the twelve tribes. In verse 35 the city is given a name. It is called, "The Lord is there."

There is a marked similarity between the passage in Ezekiel and that in Revelation 21. Ezekiel is obviously describing the Holy City of Revelation 21. "The Lord is there."

Ezekiel sees Israel as God's covenant people with access into the Holy City from the north, south, east, and west. The gates named for each one of the tribes was their invitation to enter. This was a fulfillment of the covenant promise related in Ezekiel 37:26-28 where God had promised to "set My sanctuary in their midst forever. My dwelling place also will be with them; and I will be their God, and they will be My people."

So the gates symbolize the invitation and the entering in of God's covenant people into the Holy City. It is significant that John sets forth the covenant promise in Revelation 21:3 as Ezekiel did in 37:26-28.

But now we know that the names of the twelve tribes of Israel represent the whole of the redeemed church, the Lamb's bride. The redeemed are being gathered from the north, south, east, and west—from all nations and peoples. The picture before us is the fulfillment of God's promise to Abraham in Genesis 22:18: "And in thy seed shall all the nations of the earth be blessed." It is the teaching of these scriptures, as well as Galatians 3:14 and 29, that in the Holy City we're all children of Abraham. Both Old and New Testament believers are heirs of the covenant promises. Both Jews and Gentiles constitute the Lamb's bride.

Revelation 21:14: Twelve Foundations.

"The wall of the City had twelve foundations, and on them the names of the twelve apostles of the Lamb."

a. The twelve foundations are symbolic of the truth that the Holy City is grounded upon the evangelical foundations of the twelve apostles.

b. In Ephesians 2:20 Paul, writing about the church, says: "And are built upon the foundation of the apostles and prophets, Jesus Christ Himself being the chief cornerstone."

c. The apostles were ambassadors extraordinary. In the history of the church they occupy a unique position. None can take their place. *Our Faith rests upon their testimony of Christ,* His words and His work. In I John 1:3, referring to the apostles, John says to the church, "That ye also may have fellowship with us," and then he adds "and truly our fellowship is with the Father, and with His Son Jesus Christ." Their significance is not transient and temporary, but permanent and includes the whole church.

d. Their place and the importance to the church certainly warrants the symbolic expression "twelve foundations."

Conclusion

1. In the light of this text it appears indisputable that the church of Christ is made up of believers from both the Old and the New Testaments.

2. Paul clearly teaches the unity and continuity of the covenant promises of the Old and New Testaments in Ephesians 2:11-22. In verse 15 Jew and Gentile become "one new man."

3. Revelation 21 sets forth for us the highest possible conception of union and communion of God with His redeemed church.

Questions for Discussion

1. What relationship does the present world have to the new heaven and new earth of Revelation 21?

2. Who are the bride and the holy city?

3. What does the symbol of a bride, in this context, convey to us?

4. What is the significance of the marriage announcement?

5. How is Leviticus 26:11-12 fulfilled in the scene presented in Revelation 21?

6. What do we have today that will be missing in the holy city?

7. How has God shown His compassion to men?

8. What is the difference between God's presence now and in eternity?

9. What is the meaning of the twelve gates?

10. What is the meaning of the twelve foundations?

11. What is the significance of both the twelve tribes and the twelve apostles being included in the structure of the holy city?

8

THE PROMISED LAND

Genesis 17:8

And I will give unto thee, and to thy seed after thee, the land wherein thou art a stranger, all the land of Canaan, for an everlasting possession; and I will be their God.

In the prior provisions of the covenant God had promised Abraham (1), verses 4-6, that he would ''be a father of many nations,'' (2) verse 7 that the covenant was ''between Me and thee and thy seed after thee, and (3) that He would ''be a God unto thee and to thy seed after thee.''

Now we come to the fourth and last promise. This promise concerns the ''land of Canaan.'' It is included in the covenant promises even though the Lord had promised Abraham this land on three prior occasions:

1. Genesis 12:7: ''The Lord appeared unto Abram and said, Unto thy seed will I give this land.''

2. Genesis 13:15: ''For all the land which thou seest, to thee will I give it, and to thy seed for ever.''

3. Genesis 15:18: ''Unto thy seed have I given this land, from the river of Egypt unto the great river, the river Euphrates.''

The Problem of the Land

a. It is no secret that the Lord's promises concerning the land of Canaan and its possession by the Jews has caused a great deal of conflict throughout the history of the New Testament church. For some Christians today the return of the Jews to Palestine is a cardinal doctrine of faith.

b. There appear to be but two alternatives:

1. The literal understanding of the promises, meaning, the return and everlasting possession of the land by the Jews. Ultimately this involves the conversion of the nation of Israel.

2. The spiritual understanding, meaning, that Israel is the people of God, the church of Christ composed of believing Jews and Gentiles. The land of Canaan then becomes either, or both, the earth or the heavenly abode.

The Dispensationalist View

a. For the modern dispensationalist the return of national Israel is extremely important. It is a part of God's plan for the ages.

   b. One quotation from the Scofield Bible will highlight the importance placed upon the land of Canaan. The note is related to Deuteronomy 30:3. Scofield says that this is the "Palestinian Covenant." This footnote is as follows:

(Page 250) The Palestinian Covenant gives the conditions under which Israel entered the land of promise. It is important to see that the nation has never as yet taken the land under the unconditional Abrahamic Covenant, nor has it ever possessed the whole land (cf. Gen. 15:18 with Num. 34:1-12). The Palestinian Covenant is in seven parts:
(1) Dispersion for disobedience, verse 1 (Deut. 28:63-68, see Gen. 15:18 note).
(2) The future repentance of Israel while in the dispersion, verse 2.
(3) The return of the Lord, verse 3 (Amos 9:9-14; Acts 15:14-17).
(4) Restoration to the land, verse 5 (Isa. 11:11-12; Jer. 23:3-8; Ezek. 37:21-25; see verses 26-27).
(5) National conversion, verse 6 (Rom. 11:26-27; Hos. 2:14-16).
(6) The judgment of Israel's oppressors, verse 7 (Isa. 14:1-2; Joel 3:1-8; Matt. 25:31-46).
(7) National prosperity, verse 9 (Amos 9:11-14).

   c. Without spending a great deal of time on this quotation, let us look briefly at two or three items mentioned.
      1. Is it true, as Scofield says, that Israel "has never as yet taken the land under the *unconditional Abrahamic Covenant*"?
   According to the Bible this simply is not a true statement. I refer you to a passage that we previously considered, namely Exodus 6:1-6. See also Exodus 2:24; 3:8; Deuteronomy 4:36-40.
   It is clear that Scofield's note tries to distinguish between *two entrances* into the land of Canaan: a conditional one under the "Palestinian Covenant" and one under an "unconditional Abrahamic Covenant." But the Scriptures know nothing of any such division. Stephen in Acts 7 made his defense before the Sanhedrin. In that defense he rehearsed the history of God's people, the nation of Israel, beginning with Abraham. In verse 17 he said, "But when the time of the promise drew nigh, which God had sworn to Abraham, the people grew and multiplied in Egypt." He specifically clarifies which promise. It was that "which God had sworn to Abraham." Stephen then goes on to recount the deliverance from the Egyptian bondage and entrance into the land of Canaan. Stephen believed that God performed these acts in accordance with the promise "sworn to Abraham."
      2. Is it true as Scofield says, that Israel has never "ever possessed the whole land"?
   We refer you to one short passage: Joshua 21:43-45. Verse 43: "And the Lord gave unto Israel all the land which he swore to give unto their fathers; and they possessed it, and dwelt therein." It is obvious that Joshua believed that the

45

Lord had fulfilled His promise to their fathers and they possessed it, and dwelt in it.

See also II Chronicles 9:26. It is there recorded of Solomon: "And he reigned over all the kings from the river even unto the land of the Philistines, and to the border of Egypt." The marginal note in the Scofield Bible is as follows:

"The 'river', i.e., Euphrates, to the border of Egypt, but not to the 'river of Egypt'. Cf. Genesis 15:18 yet to be fulfilled." Map no. 4 in the Scofield Bible shows the borders of the land under David and Solomon. That map shows the southern boundary reaching to the river of Egypt in accordance with the promise in Genesis 15:18.

I Kings 8:65-66 records a gathering of Israel under Solomon. They came from Hameth in the north to "the river of Egypt" in the south.

The Land Limited

Is there any significance to the predetermination of the boundaries of the land which the Lord appointed to Israel?

I think that there may be at least two reasons for specific boundaries under God's promise:

1. That was the land allotted by the Lord. It was a specific land which the Lord gave to Israel. It was the Land of Promise but it was also the land to be acquired. Israel was to possess it by faith. It was not to rest until it had completed the task of conquering the land. Every enemy was to be eradicated from within its borders.

2. But the Promised Land was limited. Only that territory was consecrated by God's promise. It was thereby restricted and forbidden from endeavoring to become a world empire like its neighbors. Was this what David, the warrior, had in mind when he ordered the census of the people in II Samuel 24? See verse 10. David had sinned. The glory of Israel was to be attained within the land consecrated by God.

The Promise Understood Spiritually

a. From our discussion thus far I believe we have shown that the dispensationalist view of the Land of Canaan is in error. However, the question still remains, can we from Scripture establish a better view?

b. The Theocracy

When the Lord confirmed the promise to Abraham in Genesis 15:18, He was looking forward 400 years to the establishment of Israel as a nation. He undertook to establish a theocratic nation among the other nations of the world. It is therefore only fitting that He should also establish such a nation within the confines of its own land. It therefore appears that the land was a necessity to carry out God's program.

Now, the Lord knows that a nation has to be fed and clothed. It is for this reason that the Old Testament promises speak of the provision of physical blessings. Herein Israel was to be the *one nation* of the world to function as a theocracy. The Lord provided them a land flowing with milk and honey. The Lord would provide for them and keep them. He would be their Shield. He was their King. The nations of the world would watch as they beheld Jehovah watching over and protecting this small nation: His own possession.

But what the dispensationalist and the Zionist movements forget is that the *external privileges flow from the covenantal relationship.* It is that covenantal relationship which is secured for both Jews and Gentile in Jesus Christ. It is precisely this that Paul teaches us in Galatians chapter three. The promised covenant blessings made to Abraham are fulfilled in Christ and thereby flow to the covenant people, both Jew and Gentile. Verse 14: "That the blessings of Abraham might come on the Gentiles through Jesus Christ." Verse 21: "Is the law then against the promises of God? God forbid." True faith in Christ issues in true obedience. The prophetic message of the Old Testament is that you cannot have the spiritual and physical blessings of the covenant unless you walk in *obedience* to the demands of the covenant. That means true holiness before God (see Deut. 10:12). The requirements of the Lord: (1) to fear the Lord, (2) to walk in all His ways, (3) to love Him, and (4) to serve Him with all the heart and soul.

But the requirements are based on the love and grace of the covenant God, as is abundantly clear from Deuteronomy 10:15. The Lord loved their fathers, "and He chose their seed after them, even you above all people, as it is this day." These are the words to the nation of Israel as they stood at the Jordan river ready to enter into the promised land.

The Lord was fulfilling His promises made to Abraham 400 years earlier.

c. The Promise to Abraham

1. The covenant promise to Abraham concerning the land of Canaan was "I will give [it] unto thee." This is the promise given in our text and Genesis 13:15.

Did Abraham ever literally possess the land of Canaan?

a) Genesis 23 records the death of Abraham's wife Sarah. Abraham seeks a place to bury Sarah. Verse 3, he came to the sons of Heth. Verse 4: I am a stranger. He asks them for a burying place. Verse 16, he bought a field with a cave in it for 400 shekels of silver. Verse 19: He buried Sarah "in a cave of the field of Machpelah before Mamre: the same is Hebron in the land of Canaan."

b) Read Genesis 49:29-33—the death of Jacob in Egypt. He charged his sons that he was to be buried "in the cave that is in the field of Machpelah, which is before Mamre, in the land of Canaan, which Abraham bought." Verse 31: first Abraham, then Isaac, and now Jacob.

c) It is apparent from these two passages that the only part of Canaan that Abraham owned was a field with a cave in it that he and Sarah might be buried there. And even that he had to buy. From Genesis 49 we also discover that neither

Isaac nor Jacob acquired any additional land and that they also were buried there.

d) The New Testament confirms that Abraham did not receive possession of the promised land. Again we refer you to Stephen's defense before the Sanhedrin in Acts 7:5: "And He gave him none inheritance in it, no, not so much as to set his foot on; yet He promised that He would give it to him for a possession, and to his seed after him, when as yet he had no child.

Now if I maintained that the Bible *always* must be understood literally those verses, Genesis 13:15, 17:8, and Acts 7:5 would certainly cause me a lot of trouble. God's literal promise was that He would give the land to Abraham, but the sacred records shows that he did not literally possess it. In my mind that would raise a very serious problem: "Did God fail to keep His promise?" There is no other answer for the literalist. That should force us back to the Bible to find a better answer if there is one.

e) How Is the Promise to Be Understood?

Acts 7:5. We should notice that though Stephen quotes the promise that God would give Abraham the land, he also states very clearly that, "He gave him none inheritance in it." But notice that *Stephen is not troubled by this.* I think he pointed to the presence of the Sanhedrin in verse 4, "into this land, wherein ye now dwell" as the fulfillment of the promise.

But what is the real significance of Acts 7:5? Stephen says that though Abraham did not physically possess it, "*yet* He promised that He would give it to him for a possession, *and* to his seed after him, *when* as yet he had no child."

When Abraham received the promise of the land that he might give as an inheritance "to his seed after him," Stephen says, "as yet he had no child." I think Stephen is saying to the Sanhedrin: Look, Abraham didn't need an inheritance at the time of the promise because he didn't have a son. He had no one to leave it to. He was reminding his hearers that *both* the possession of the inheritance of the *land and* also the birth of an *heir* depended entirely on God. Both were the free gifts of God's grace. When Abraham received these promises he had no tangible object in which to trust, but he believed the word of God. By faith he received the son of promise at the age of 100. The birth of Isaac was *God's pledge* that He would also provide the land of promise as an inheritance to Abraham's seed in God's appointed time.

f) Genesis 13:14-18

Let us take another brief look at this passage.

Verse 14: "Lift up now thine eyes and look." He was camped at Bethel near the center of the land. He was to survey the land, north, south, east, and west.

Verse 15: God promised him all the land which he could see.

Verse 16: The promise of an innumerable seed.

Verse 17: God's commandment: "Arise, walk through the land in the length of it and in the breadth of it: for I will give it unto thee.''

Verse 18: Abraham's response: ''then Abraham removed his tent,'' he traveled southward to Hebron ''and built an altar unto the Lord.''

Note the progressive nature of the events. Lift up your eyes and behold the land. That's what God promised him, together with an abundant seed. Then came God's commandment to ''arise, walk through the land.''

By faith he beheld the land, and God gave it to him. He secured to him the land and to his seed. God gave him title to the land. By faith he arose and walked through the land. By faith he possessed it.

And Abraham ''built an altar unto the Lord.'' What a beautiful climax to a magnificent chain of events. *He worshiped God.* He expressed his faith in God's promises. He blessed the Lord for all His blessings. He thanked God for His grace and gave God the glory.

Conclusion

1. By God's grace Abraham received the promises of a land and a numerous seed. By faith he walked through the land and possessed it. By faith he received a son. By faith he looked forward 400 years when God in His own time brought together the seed of Abraham in a theocratic kingdom in the land of promise.

2. When God gives promises He *always* fulfills them but *always* in His own time and in His own way.

Questions for Discussion

1. Why is Palestine referred to as the promised land?
2. What problems does the land of Palestine present us today?
3. What information does Stephen give us about the land of Palestine in Acts 7?
4. Has Israel ever possessed the whole of the promised land? What are the Old Testament references?
5. What was the relationship of the Old Testament theocracy to the land of Palestine? Is Israel a theocracy today? Is there a theocracy today?
6. What was the promise to Abraham concerning the land of Palestine? When was this promise fulfilled? How much of Palestine did Abraham own before his death? What problems does this raise?
7. Does Genesis 13:14-18 help resolve some of these problems? What about Acts 7?
8. Is the present state of Israel keeping the Old Testament demands for worship and righteousness?

9

THE PROMISED LAND IN THE NEW TESTAMENT

Hebrews 11:8-16 and Hebrews 3 and 4

Introduction

1. The covenant promise of Genesis 17:8 is to the effect that God would give to Abraham and his seed the land of Canaan, for an everlasting possession.

2. We have tried to show from Scriptures that under King David, and his son, Solomon, the whole of the promised land was possessed by the kingdom of Israel.

The land of Canaan was important in God's plans for it was there that He established the only theocratic state that the world has ever known.

3. As Christians now with the complete revelation of the New Testament we should know that the New Testament writers had something to say about God's promise concerning the land of Canaan. Hebrews 11:8-16 is related to the faith of Abraham with the chief topic in these verses being the promised land.

Verse 8:

By faith Abraham, when he was called, obeyed to go out unto a place which he was to receive for an inheritance; and he went out, not knowing whither he went.

The Bible presents Abraham as the classic example of one who lived by faith. It is therefore fitting that he should be included in the heroes of faith in Hebrews 11.

In Genesis 12:1, God calls Abraham to leave his kindred and to go out into another land. God did not name the land of his destination. He simply described it as ''a land that I will shew thee.'' Note the future tense. He was to receive it ''for an inheritance.''

''By faith Abraham obeyed.'' Abraham responded to God's call to live a life of faith. He displayed his faith by his willingness and readiness to get up and go at God's call. Genesis 12:4: ''So Abram departed, as the Lord had spoken unto him.'' There appears to have been no questioning or any undue delay.

Faith and obedience are inseparable in our relationship to God. Abraham believed God therefore he obeyed. His obedience was the outward evidence of his inward faith. Abraham knew not whither he went, yet he knew who had called him and that was enough.

Verse 9:

By faith he sojourned in the land of promise, as in a strange country, dwelling in tents with Isaac and Jacob, the heirs with him of the same promise.

He lived by faith. He was a wanderer living in tents. He lived like a stranger in a foreign country; never settling down. He established no cities. But he lived in the light of God's promise knowing that this was "the land of promise." He became known among the inhabitants as a "prince of God" (Gen. 23:6).

Though by faith in God's promises he knew that this was the land promised to him as an inheritance, nevertheless, he did not grow impatient. He waited for God's time of fulfillment.

Though the promises were also given to Isaac and Jacob, they too lived like Abraham dwelling in tents.

Verse 10:

For he was looking forward to the city with foundations, whose architect and builder is God (NIV).

What was the secret of Abraham's patience?

His hopes were set on an eternal city. The City of God. He was not looking for a temporal city. He was looking for a city which had eternal foundations; such a city that only God could build.

The text is saying that Abraham looked *beyond the earthly* land of Canaan. Abraham saw in the promise of the earthly Canaan the *underlying promise* of a far greater and richer promise that included an eternal inheritance.

According to Hebrews 12:22 that eternal inheritance is the "heavenly Jerusalem." It is "the city of the living God." By faith we have become citizens together with Abraham, of "the city of the living God." According to Hebrews 11:10 it is the city that Abraham sought by faith. By faith it is the same city which we ought to be seeking.

Hebrews 13:5: Be content with God's providence. His promise is: "I will never leave thee nor forsake thee." This is the same promise given to God's people in the Old Testament in Deuteronomy 31:6 and now repeated for God's people in the New Testament.

Verse 13:

These all died in faith, not having received the promises, but having *seen* them afar off, and *embraced* them, and confessed that they were strangers and pilgrims on the earth.

a. "These all died in faith" is referring to Abraham, Sarah, Isaac, and Jacob. They had received the promises concerning the land and the innumerable seed. But

51

they did not see them literally fulfilled.

But as they had lived by faith, they also died by faith. They had the firm conviction and assurance that God would fulfill the promises which He had given them.

b. "But having seen them afar off and embraced them." They saw the fulfillment in the future. So certain were they of the future fulfillment that they "embraced them." Some modern translations put it this way: "having seen them and having welcomed them from a distance." They counted the fulfillment of the promises as a certainty and they staked everything on its certainty. They believed God and His promises.

Hebrews 6:15 says, "And so, after he had patiently endured, he obtained the promise." The specific reference is to Abraham receiving the promise that his seed shall be "as the stars" and "as the sand which is upon the sea shore" (Gen. 22:17). He saw the fulfillment of that promise in his son Isaac, who was indeed the son of promise.

c. Even though they looked forward to the fulfillment of the promises, nevertheless they lived as sojourners in the land. In Genesis 23:4 Abraham refers to himself as "a stranger and a sojourner." In Genesis 47:9 Jacob refers to his life as: "The days of the years of my pilgrimage."

There was a conscious recognition by Abraham, Isaac, and Jacob that they were pilgrims on the earth. They recognized and accepted that status. Because they put their trust in God's word, they lived by faith and they died by faith. The verse is a picture of contentment. They were content to live as pilgrims for by faith they saw the eternal reward.

Verse 14:

For those who say such things make it clear that they are seeking a country of their own (NASB).

a. The closing words of verse 13 had been said in anticipation of these words in verse 14. There is a continuity of thought. "For those who say such things" is a reference to verse 13 and the fact that they lived and died as pilgrims on the earth.

b. The patriarchs made it clear that the land of their sojourning was not their home. Their lives testified to that.

Verse 15:

And indeed if they had been thinking of that country from which they went out, they would have had opportunity to return.

a. The verse is a clarification of what might have been drawn from the previous verse from the words, "they seek a country." That country which was in their minds was not the country which they had left. As the verse points out, if that had been the country which they sought, they could have returned. But the fact that they didn't shows that they did not count that as their homeland.

b. Is it not significant that when Abraham's servant suggested that Isaac might have to go to Mesopotamia to persuade his bride to accompany him to Canaan, Abraham warned him: "Beware thou that thou bring not my son thither again" (Gen. 24:6). There was to be no return.

Verse 16:

But now they desire a better country, that is a heavenly one. Therefore God is not ashamed to be called their God; for He has prepared a city for them.

a. "A better country": It is quite clear that their true homeland was not on the earth at all. Their heart's desire of a better country was the heavenly country.

The earthly Canaan was but the object-lesson pointing to the heavenly country. The earthly Jerusalem pointed to the true City of God, the New Jerusalem. These were but types and symbols of the eternal reality.

b. Because they had faith in God's promises, and because they displayed their faith by living as pilgrims, "God was not ashamed to be called their God." Here indeed is the fulfillment of the *covenant promise* to Abraham in Genesis 17:7, "to be a God unto thee, and to thy seed after thee." And (17:8) by God's grace they were His children and He was their God. The Lord Himself acknowledged them as such. In Exodus 3:6, He introduces Himself to Moses as "the God of Abraham, the God of Isaac, and the God of Jacob."

Hebrews—Chapters 3 and 4

a. Chapters 3 and 4 of Hebrews are a New Testament meditation and application of Psalm 95.

Psalm 95, especially verses 7-11, is reflecting on the events of the 40-year wilderness journey.

b. When, in chapter 3, verse 1, the writer exhorts us to consider the "heavenly calling" in Jesus Christ, he introduces us to the antithesis which is present throughout this epistle. This is important to the understanding of the epistle. The antithesis is between the world, that which is temporal on the one hand, and heaven, that which is eternal on the other.

c. Verses 2-6 contain a discussion about a household. It speaks of but *one* household. *Moses* was a faithful servant *in the house;* But *Christ* is a son *over the house,* "whose house are we." The meaning can only refer to the church in *both the Old and New Testaments.* In Christ there is the spiritual continuity between the period of promise and the age of fulfillment.

d. Verses 7-19 is a consideration of the wilderness journey with dependence upon Psalm 95. In fact verses 7-11 of Hebrews 3 is a verbatim quotation of Psalm 95:7-11. Hebrews 3:13-19 is the exhortation and application to the readers of this Epistle.

Some teachings of verses 13-19 (chapt. 3)

Verse 13: We are urged to encourage one another to strive against sin lest we be hardened by sin's deceitfulness.

Verse 14: Be steadfast in Christ.

Verse 15: Hear and obey God's Word Today.

Verse 16: All who came out of Egypt did not enter into Canaan. They heard the voice of God at Sinai but they tempted God and rebelled.

Verse 17: The consequences of Israel's sin: they died in the wilderness.

Verse 18: God's judgment to those who did not believe: they were excluded from entering into His rest.

Verse 19: The conclusion: They failed to enter because of unbelief. Unbelief deprives men of any right to God's promises. Because of unbelief they died in the wilderness and so failed to enter the promised land of Canaan.

Chapter 4 of Hebrews. A Sabbath rest for the people of God—Verses 1-11

Verse 1: We have a promise of entering into His rest. Take heed lest we also fall short and fail to enter into His rest.

Verse 2: The gospel was preached unto us just as it was to those who traveled in the wilderness. They heard it, but it was of no value to them because they did not believe it.

Verse 3: Those who believe enter into God's rest. This is the rest that God entered when He finished the work of creation.

Verse 4: Verse 4 identifies God's rest as symbolized by the Sabbath-rest.

Verse 5: Verse 5 identifies that rest of God referred to in Genesis 2:2 as the same rest which those who died in the wilderness failed to enter into.

Verses 6 and 7: Though some failed to enter into God's rest nevertheless the gospel invitation is still being issued. "Today" is now.

Verse 8: This is an important verse. Entering the land did not mean entering God's rest. Under Joshua's leadership the second generation of those coming out of Egypt did enter into the land of Canaan. But it is clear from this verse that those who entered into the land of Canaan did not possess the true rest of God. Canaan was but a shadow. The rest of Psalm 95:11 is not the earthly Canaan. Psalm 95 was originally addressed to those who were living in the land of Canaan but they also received the invitation to enter into God's rest: "Today if you will hear His voice."

Verse 9: The *same invitation* to enter into the *same rest* is here issued to the New Testament church. It is here called "a sabbath rest" and is therefore symbolized by the weekly sabbath.

Verses 10 and 11: We enter into that rest by faith even as the Old Testament saints. The "rest" is the *heavenly Canaan* toward which all God's people are traveling. It is the same rest which Christ promised when He said: "Come unto me, all ye that labor and are heavy laden, and I will give you rest" (Matt. 11:28).

Conclusions

1. The Forward Look

a. The book of Hebrews was written to New Testament believers and more particularly to Jewish Christians. No conclusions regarding the land of Canaan can be considered valid without at least some consideration of Hebrews 3, 4, and 11.

b. We have seen that Psalm 95 and Hebrews 3 and 4 speak of the *rest* of Canaan. But as we have seen the idea *rest* is consistently eschatological. It looks forward to the true rest which is to come in the future.

c. The "rest" of God in Hebrews 3 and 4 presents for us the eternal side of the promises of God. Vos says: "The author instructs the readers that they must rely *less upon the fulfillment than upon the promise.* What they need is an eschatology of faith, not an eschatology of imagination." Fulfillment is God's work; faith in the promise is ours.

d. Specifically from Hebrews 3:11, 17-19 we see that those Old Testament unbelievers who died in the wilderness were excluded from the rest of Canaan, but from the whole context of Hebrews 3 and 4 we conclude that they were *also excluded from the absolute rest,* that is, from the *eternal rest.* They not only lost the inheritance of the earthly Canaan, but also they were eternally lost. God took their *faith or unbelief as having eternal and final consequences.*

e. Oswald T. Allis, *Prophecy and the Church,* p. 101: "In Hebrews as in Romans, we find nothing about a return to the land of Canaan. On the contrary, the writer stresses the *heavenly* character of the hope which the patriarchs cherished. It was not an earthly *land,* but a home ('A country of their own') which is not earthly, but heavenly, a city 'whose maker and builder is God.' The whole emphasis in this great faith chapter in Hebrews is that the faith of the Old Testament worthies was not earthly but heavenly."

2. It is also clear from Hebrews that there is but one rest of God, but one heavenly city. It is significant that after referring to the Old Testament people Hebrews 4:11 records, "Let us labour therefore to enter into that rest." There is but one rest for both Old and New Testament saints. The heavenly Canaan is the object of all saints of all dispensations.

3. Faith the Essential Element

Hebrews 11 records events and history from Abel in verse 4 through "David, Samuel and the prophets" in verse 32. That period of time covers the events of history from Genesis 4 onward throughout the whole of the Old Testament.

It seems to me tremendously important to observe that *one* essential characteristic is mentioned in connection with every event recorded during this period of time. Their exploits for God were accomplished by *faith*. It is the roll call of the heroes of *faith*, all from the Old Testament, passing in review.

These were all commended for their faith, yet none of them received what had been promised. God had planned something better for us so that only *together with us* would they be made perfect (Heb. 11:39-40 NIV).

a. All these heroes of faith died looking forward to the coming of the Messiah. They did not see His day though they looked for it. But now the promised Messiah has come. Now because the perfect sin-offering has been sacrificed in Christ's body and blood therefore those Old Testament saints "together with us" are made perfect by *faith*.

b. We together with them tread the same path of faith and "look for a city with foundations whose architect and builder is God" (vs. 10). It should be clear to us now that all the Old Testament saints share in the *same inheritance* of glory as is promised to believers in Christ of New Testament times.

So we see again from Hebrews 3, 4, and 11 the unity and the continuity of the covenant promises to all God's people in all ages of history. The essence of the covenant is summarized in Genesis 17:7: "To be a God unto thee and to thy seed after thee."

"Your father Abraham rejoiced to see my day: and he saw it, and was glad" (John 8:56).

Questions for Discussion

1. What, if any, is the relationship of works to faith?
2. Why is Abraham known as the father of the faithful? (Gal. 3:7).
3. How did Abraham show his faith?
4. What land was Abraham looking for?
5. What was the secret of Abraham's patience?
6. What land are we looking for? Have we learned to be patient like Abraham?
7. In what sense did Abraham obtain God's promises?
8. What is the "better country"? Who has prepared it?
9. Discuss the relationship of Moses and Christ to the symbolism of the house in Hebrews 3:2-6.
10. Discuss the rest of Genesis 2:2, Psalm 95:11, and Hebrews 4:1-11. What is the meaning of the rest? How many places of rest are referred to in the passages?
11. What is the relationship of the land of Canaan to the rest being referred to?
12. Discuss the meaning and the importance of Hebrews 11:39-40. Relate to the unity of the Old and New Testaments.

10

THE SIGN OF THE PROMISE IN THE OLD TESTAMENT

Genesis 17:9-14

Introduction

1. We believe from our study of Genesis 17:1-4 that these verses represent the formalizing of the covenant of grace. Recent studies have indicated that the structure of the covenant represents a treaty similar to that imposed by victorious kings upon those whom they had vanquished.

2. In keeping with the treaty format, we see from verses 2-8 that it is Jehovah, the almighty God, the sovereign Lord of heaven and earth, who enters into the covenant relationship with Abraham and dictates all the terms. In these same verses we have seen what God covenanted to do. The covenant provisions include:

a. Verse 4-6: Abraham would "be a father of many nations."

b. Verse 7: The covenant was between Jehovah and Abraham and extended on to "thy seed after thee."

c. Verse 7: The Lord promises to "be a God unto thee and to thy seed after thee."

d. Verse 8: He gives to Abraham and his seed the land of Canaan for an everlasting possession.

We have tried to show from Scripture that the promises are far greater in the magnitude of their provisions than anything contemplated by Abraham or his immediate posterity. We have tried to show that the promises are carried over into the New Testament and that their fulfillment is in Christ. The unity of the Old and New Testament church is thereby established.

3. In Genesis 17:9-14 Jehovah, the Sovereign God, sets down the treaty provisions required of Abraham and his seed.

The Lord introduces His treaty obligations to Abraham in a twofold manner:

a. Verse 2:"I will make My covenant between Me and thee."

b. Verse 4:"As for Me, behold My covenant is with thee."

We find two corresponding references to Abraham's treaty obligations:

    a. Verse 9:"Thou shalt keep My covenant."

    b. Verse 10:"this is My covenant, which ye shall keep."

Not only the *authority* of the sovereign God but also the *grace* of God is seen in these introductory statements to the provisions of the covenant. His *grace* is seen in the fact that *God chose* Abraham to be the recipient of His covenantal promises. His authority is seen from a twofold aspect. First, His sovereign ability to bring His promises to pass. Secondly, in His demands that Abraham keep the covenant obligations which God requires of him.

1. The Covenant Obligations

    a. When you look for the covenant obligations in verses 9-14 which were placed upon Abraham and his seed, you find something very strange. Verses 10-14 speak of *only one item,* namely, circumcision. This being true we should be immediately alerted to the *great importance* of this rite.

    b. Verse 10: "This is My covenant, which ye shall keep. . . . Every man child among you shall be circumcised."

    Verse 13: ". . . and My covenant shall be in your flesh for an everlasting covenant."

    c. All the treaty obligations were to be seen by Abraham and his seed in the rite of circumcision. This is true because circumcision is a *sacramental ritual.* The ritual was designed by God to point to the teaching of the *ethical and spiritual truths* contained in the sacrament.

    d. Let us look first at *who* were to be circumcised and *then* the *meaning of the rite.*

2. To Whom Administered

    a. Who were to receive the rite of circumcision? As we look at the text that question appears rather significant because it is answered is such detail. The Lord's instructions are detailed and clear.

    Verse 10: "*Every man child* among you shall be circumcised." The instruction is comprehensive. None were to be excluded.

    Verse 12: "And he that is eight days old shall be circumcised among you, every man child in your generations, he that is born in the house, or bought with money of any stranger, which is not of thy seed."

The text identifies those *infants* who are to be circumcised when eight days old. Two classes of infants are mentioned. First, those "born in the house." Second, those "bought with money of any stranger." Two categories of infants are mentioned: (1) Those born of the natural seed *within* the household, meaning the posterity of Abraham. (2) But it also includes the children of the *servants residing* in the household. To be sure that there was no misunderstanding the words "which is not of thy seed" are added to clearly identify the second group.

Verse 13: "He that is *born* in thy house, and he that is *bought* with thy money, *must* needs be circumcised."

Again I believe the text speaks of two categories of persons to be circumcised. (1) The first group are children "born in thy house." I believe that this refers to the two groups of infants mentioned in verse 12. (2) The second group includes adult male servants who have been bought.

This verse then is all-inclusive as to who are to be circumcised. But I think we should note that the commandment to circumcise is stated in the imperative mood. They "*must* needs be circumcised." This was God's commandment. It was *not* a *matter of choice*. This was the covenant obligation.

c. Exodus 12:41-49 relates the establishment of the passover feast. Note the *relationship of circumcision to the Passover*. *Only* those males who had been circumcised could participate with the family in the Passover meal. This included servants who had been purchased (vs. 44) and aliens living with them at the time of the feast (vs. 48). "No uncircumcised person shall eat thereof." The two Old Testament sacraments are thus bound together by God's commandment. The holiness of the sacraments in God's sight has thus forever been established.

3. The Meaning of Circumcision

a. Can we firmly establish that the rite of circumcision does have meaning beyond the performance of a physical act?

In verse 11 circumcision is spoken of in this manner: "and it shall be a token of the covenant betwixt me and you." NASB: "and it shall be the sign of the covenant between Me and you."

So, circumcision is not the essense of the covenant, *it is the sign of the essence of the covenant*. It points to the covenant. The sign has been given meaning by God in His revelation. Sometimes in Scripture the sign or the elements of the sacrament have been given the name of the object to which the sacrament points. In reference to the rite of circumcision, the Lord in Genesis 17:10 says, "This is My covenant." Actually circumcision was the rite which pointed to the covenant promises which the Lord had made to Abraham. We have a classic example of this, in Matthew 26:26-28, in the institution of the Lord's Supper. Jesus gave bread to the disciples and said, "Take, eat; this is My body." Then He took wine and gave it to them saying, "Drink ye all of it; for this is My blood of the covenant, which is shed for many for the remission of sins." In that situation it should be obvious that the bread and wine only represented the body and blood which Jesus *was soon to offer* for the sins of His people. Again an unwarranted literalism has led many people astray.

b. Paul directs us to the meaning of circumcision in Romans 4:11, "And he [Abraham] received the *sign* of circumcision, a seal of the righteousness of the faith which he had while being circumcised. . . ."

It was precisely this text which was in the minds of the framers of the Shorter Catechism when they answered question no. 92, What is a sacrament? ''A sacrament is a holy ordinance instituted by Christ; wherein, by sensible *signs,* Christ and the benefits of the new covenant are *represented, sealed* and *applied* to believers.''

A Sign

a. A sign points to the reality. A sign points to the existence of that which it signifies. So circumcision was a ritual involving the physical body but it pointed to a spiritual truth. Therefore the Lord said in Genesis 17:13, ''My covenant shall be in your flesh for an everlasting covenant.'' The rite of circumcision cannot be separated from the covenant because it was a *physical sign* representing the *spiritual meaning* of the covenant.

b. Circumcision was a sign of *inward purification.*

1. It was a sign intended to show the necessity of purity of heart. It taught men that such purification was needed and that this spiritual blessing was promised to those faithful to the covenant.

2. A number of passages in the Old Testament testify quite clearly that circumcision pointed to inward cleansing and the removal of defilement.

a) Exodus 6:30: ''Moses said before the Lord, Behold, I am of *uncircumcised lips,* and how shall Pharaoh hearken unto me?

b) Leviticus 26:41-42: ''And that I also have walked contrary unto them, and have brought them into the land of their enemies; if then their *uncircumcised hearts* be humbled, and they then accept of the punishment of their iniquity: Then will I remember My covenant with Jacob . . . Isaac . . . Abraham.''

c) Deuteronomy 10:16: ''*Circumcise* therefore the foreskin of *your heart,* and be no more stiffnecked.''

d) Deuteronomy 30:6: ''And the Lord thy God will *circumcise* thine *heart,* and the *heart of thy seed,* to love the Lord thy God with all thine heart, and with all thy soul, that thou mayest live.'' Note that there circumcision takes on the form of a promise of the work which God will do. This is the true circumcision. See Romans 2:28-29.

A Seal

a. A seal is something applied to an agreement or a covenant to establish or confirm it. In a sacrament a seal authenticates, confirms, and guarantees the genuineness of that which is signified.

The term ''a seal'' refers to the ancient use of a signet ring or cylinder, engraven with the owner's name or a design. The seal of a king applied to a document indicated that it was of royal authority. Sometimes a seal was stamped to the document as a substitute for one's signature. Sometimes documents were sealed on the outside by a seal thereby showing that it was the authoritative document and that its contents were unchanged. This is in view of Revelation 5:1: ''And I saw in the right hand of Him who sat on the throne a scroll written inside and on the back, *sealed up with seven seals.''*

b. Within this definition of a seal we now understand that by the sacrament of circumcision *God authenticated* and confirmed His covenant promises. It was *God's signature* whereby He bound Himself to execute the covenant promises.

c. But we must now take another look at Romans 4:11, ''and he [Abraham] received the sign of circumcision, a seal of the righteousness of the faith which he had yet being uncircumcised.'' In verse 3 Paul quotes Genesis 15:6: ''Abraham believed God, and it was counted unto him for righteousness.'' Paul is simply making the point that Abraham was justified before God not by works but by faith. He believed God. He believed that God would keep His word.

It is abundantly clear that in this chapter Paul is reflecting on the covenant promises made to Abraham.

Verse 13: ''The promise, that he should be heir of the world.''

Verse 16: ''To the end the promise might be sure to all the seed.''

Verse 17: ''I have made thee a father of many nations.'' Quoted from Genesis 17:5.

Verse 18: ''So shall thy seed be.'' See Genesis 15:5.

Abraham was justified by faith *before* he was circumcised. But God in His grace stooped to his need. He added the divine authentication by assuring Abraham that by his faith in God's promises, he had been accounted righteous. As the sign and seal of the covenant it was *also* the seal of that faith and of the justification by faith apart from which the covenant is meaningless. We cannot think of the covenant promises in abstraction from the faith elicited by them, *nor* can we think of the faith in abstraction from the disclosures of promises and purposes to which the faith of Abraham was directed. It is the impossibility of abstraction that renders harmonious the two facts that circumcision was *both* the seal of the covenant *and* the seal of faith. See John Murray's *Commentary on Romans,* chapter 4, vol. 1, p. 138.

So we see that circumcision was a seal of the righteousness which God accounted to him because of his faith in God's covenant promises.

d. Is there still some mystery regarding circumcision being a seal of the covenant promises? I have tried to remove some of the mystery by our prior discussion. I have pointed out that to seal something is to the effect of giving a pledge that the prescribed terms will be carried out. Our signature on a contract is our pledge that we will abide by the agreement.

At least some of the difficulty comes because it is difficult for us to keep clearly in mind that circumcision is *God's* sign and seal of the covenant. Circumcision is *God's signature* to the covenant. By the rite of circumcision God seals His promises to us. He binds Himself to fulfill His covenant.

I think that if we look at two other Old Testament passages it will help us understand that circumcision is God's sign and seal.

Genesis 9:8-17 is the record of the covenant made with Noah after the flood.

Verse 13: God sets the bow in the sky as a sign and seal of His covenant.

Verses 14-15: When the bow is *seen* in the cloud, "*I will remember* My covenant which is between Me and you."

Verse 16: "When the bow is in the cloud, then I will *look* upon it, to *remember* the everlasting covenant."

Verse 17: "This is the sign of the covenant which *I have established* between Me and all flesh. . . ." The Lord is saying, "This is My signature to the covenant."

Note carefully, the bow is set in the clouds so that *the Lord may see it*. When *He sees it*, He remembers His covenant to men. *Our* seeing it is a *secondary* purpose, but from it we receive comfort knowing that God will keep His covenant. But when He sees it, it is a reminder of His word which He has pledged to keep.

Exodus 12:1-14 is the record of the institution of the Passover.

Verses 3–6: The instructions regarding the selection of a lamb which was to be slain on the evening of the 14th day.

Verse 7: The blood was to be put on the two doorposts and on the lintels of the houses in which they did eat.

Verses 8-11: Instructions for the eating of the lamb. The 11th verse closes with the words: "It is the *Lord's Passover*."

Verse 12: The Lord promises judgment against the Egyptians.

Verse 13: The blood was their sign of security for He says, "*When I see* the blood, I will pass over you, and the plague shall not be upon you to destroy you."

Again note carefully, "When *I see* the blood, I will pass over you." The sign of the blood was primarily for *God's view*. It was a reminder to Him as He executed judgment. The blood was *His signature* to His Word of promise. *It sealed His covenant to them.* The blood was secondarily for the people. In faith they believed God's word. So, in faith, they struck the doorposts and lintels with the blood. They had God's word that He would pass over them. The *blood* was the *visible representation* of *His* words and *His promises*.

Conclusions

1. John Murray, in his book, *Christian Baptism,* (pp. 50-51) has clearly pointed out that circumcision is the sign and seal of the covenant of grace, which finds its highest meaning in the words, "I will be your God and ye shall be my people" (Lev. 26:12). Therefore circumcision carries with it the three notions— (1) union and communion with God, (2) the removal of defilement, and (3) the righteousness of faith. These three are not antithetical but are mutually complementary.

Circumcision was a sign that the recipient was in covenant relationship with

God. It was a sign of *communion with God* and *separation from the world*.

2. In the rite of circumcision we see very clearly that God binds Himself by an action of man which He himself has commanded to be done. There are times in Scripture that God directs men to act on His behalf. The act which He commands men to do He accounts to Himself. We find such an example in Genesis 15:9-17. Here the Lord cut the covenant, but He did so with the animals which He had commanded Abraham to divide. It is for this reason that we are able to say that circumcision was God's signature to the covenant. So it was that the covenant people could remind God of His covenant obligations. They had His signature to the promises.

3. Luke 1:67-79.

a. In this hymn of praise by Zacharias we learn of the close association of the birth of Christ with the covenant promises to Abraham.

b. In chapters 1 and 2 of Luke, the historian relates the intimate details concerning the events leading to Christ's birth and the birth itself. These chapters speak of prophecies old and new but also of fulfillment.

c. Verses 68-75: These verses refer to Christ as the strong One being raised up in the house of David.

Verse 68: The purpose of His coming: to redeem His people. He comes as a Savior from the power of sin.

Verse 70: This is in accordance with God's promises through the prophets.

Verse 71: They proclaimed the message of salvation from their enemies.

Verse 72: It was the message of the mercy of God. The prophetic message proclaimed God's covenant promises to His people. He will remember.

Verse 73: It is the *same covenant* that *He swore to Abraham*.

Verses 74-75: Zacharias sees the *essence of the covenant* as:

1. Deliverance from our enemies.
2. To serve and worship God in the freedom given.
3. To walk before Him in holiness and righteousness.

Verses 76-79 refer to John's work. He was to prepare the way for the coming of the Most High. John points to the redeeming work of the Most High. He brings the knowledge of salvation and forgiveness of sins.

Conclusion: The *spiritual character of the covenant* is clearly seen in this passage. The Most High came to redeem His covenant people from their sins.

Questions for Discussion

1. What do the introductory statements to Abraham's treaty obligations teach us?

2. How many obligations does the Lord place upon Abraham? What were those obligations?

3. Who were designated to receive the rite of circumcision?

4. Was there any connection between circumcision and the Passover Feast?

5. What did Jesus mean when He stated, "Take, eat; this is My body"? "Drink ye all of it, for this is My blood of the covenant, which is shed for many for the remission of sins"?

6. In what way is circumcision a sign?

7. What did the sign of circumcision represent? Support your answer from Scripture.

8. What is the meaning of a sacramental seal?

9. What New Testament passage refers to circumcision as a sign and seal? What is the meaning of this passage and its context?

10. What is one difficulty in understanding a sacrament as a seal? What two Old Testament passages help us clarify this problem?

11. What is the significance of Genesis 15:9-17?

12. What did Christ's coming have to do with the covenant made to Abraham?

11

THE BROKEN COVENANT

Genesis 17:14

Introduction

1. We have seen from our study of Genesis 17:9-13 that the Lord commanded that circumcision was to be a sign of the covenant which He had just formally announced to Abraham.

2. We have seen that inasmuch as circumcision was a sacrament it was a physical sign of a spiritual relationship established by the Lord. Inasmuch as circumcision was the outward token of the covenant, Stephen in Acts 7:8 refers to the covenant of Genesis 17 as "the covenant of the circumcision." The one obligation of Abraham, imposed by God's command, was the rite of circumcision.

3. We believe that all this points to the great importance of this rite in God's sight. Verse 14 clearly emphasizes the importance of the rite.

Verse 14:

> But an uncircumcised male who is not circumcised in the flesh of his foreskin, that person shall be cut off from his people; he has broken my covenant (NASB).

a. The importance of receiving the sign of the covenant is here seen in the light of the *judgment* which the Lord pronounced. God here reveals His great displeasure with those who refuse *or neglect* the administration of the sign of the covenant.

b. The penalty for failing to receive the sign of the covenant is that "that person shall be *cut off from his people.*" What precisely is the meaning of the term "cut off"?

1. Some understand the term to mean the cutting off from the people through the execution of the death penalty. Such a penalty under the theocracy would be the ultimate excommunication from the sacred community of God's people. The term carries precisely that meaning in Exodus 31:14: "Ye shall keep the sabbath therefore; for it is holy unto you: everyone that defileth it shall surely be *put to death*: for whosoever doeth any work therein, that soul shall be *cut off from among his people.*" It is quite clear from verses 12-17 that the sabbath is here

65

referred to as a sign of the covenant and therefore the observance was obligatory upon penalty of death to those who defiled the sabbath day.

However, we are not sure that the clause, "that soul shall be cut off from among his people," is in Genesis 17:14 equivalent to the death penalty. It should be noticed that the passage in Exodus 31:14 has specifically stated that the "soul shall be cut off from among his people" is to be done by death. However, Genesis 17:14 does not contain the word death and I have found no other passage which decrees physical death due to failure to receive the rite of circumcision, which judgment is to be carried out by the people.

2. On the other hand some understand the term "cut off" to be equivalent to exclusion from all the blessings and the final state of salvation promised to the covenant people.

3. It is interesting that Psalm 37 uses this term five times. See verses 9, 22, 28, 34, and 38. See also verse 2 which uses the term "cut down." The psalm is an exhortation not to be fretful because of the prosperity or the works of evil doers. God's people are exhorted to: verse 3—trust in the Lord; verse 4—delight thyself also in the Lord; verse 5—commit thy way unto the Lord; and verse 7—rest in the Lord. As far as the wicked are concerned, God's people are to trust in God's righteous judgments. It is the Lord who shall cut off the evil doers. In verses 12-13, we see the Lord laughs as the wicked plot against the just, for He sees that their day of judgment is coming. The righteous are to rest in God's providence knowing that He has also set the day of judgment for the wicked when "the transgressors shall be destroyed together: The end of the wicked shall be cut off" (verse 38).

4. The Psalm teaches us that the righteous receive the blessings of God. Verse 39: Salvation is of the Lord. However, the wicked receive their reward in judgment. They are cut off from God's blessings. Their end is not only physical death but eternal death. They are cut off from God in the ultimate sense. This appears to be the sense in which the term "cut off" is used in Genesis 17:14. Note the contrast in Psalm 37 between "inherit the earth" and "cut off."

c. "He Hath Broken My Covenant"

In these words the Lord tells us why it was so serious to neglect the rite of circumcision. The one who rejected the covenant sign rejected also the covenant. *To despise the sign was to despise the covenant.* God says if you refuse and neglect the sign, you have broken my covenant.

To reject the covenant sign is to deny God's covenant claim.

At this point it is extremely important to recall that God's requirement was that "every man child among you shall be circumcised, . . . and he that is eight days old shall be circumcised among you." It is an undeniable fact that infants were under God's commandment to receive the sign of the covenant. Therefore to refuse the sign of the covenant to children is to deny God's covenant claim upon them, and so withhold from Him those who are rightfully His.

To hold the rite of circumcision in contempt was equivalent to holding the covenant of God in contempt. It was to break God's covenant and provoked God's anger.

Exodus 4:24-26

1. This is a difficult and mysterious text yet it clearly speaks to the subject of breaking the covenant.

2. Moses, his wife, and sons were traveling from Midian toward Egypt. After 40 years of service to Jethro, his father-in-law, the Lord had called him to go up to Egypt to lead His people out of bondage.

But verse 24 tells us that as Moses was on this journey, in obedience to God's instructions, there was a sudden turn of events. The Lord ''sought to put him to death.'' It is plain that God's anger was kindled against him.

The sin of Moses is not specifically stated. However, we are led to understand by the events recorded in verse 25 that his sin was the neglecting to circumcise his son. Zipporah was a Midianite and probably opposed the rite of circumcision to her sons, hence one of the sons had not received the rite. The text states that it was Zipporah that took the sharp stone and performed the circumcision, after which she shows her displeasure by saying, ''A bridegroom of blood art thou to me.''

It has been suggested that an angel with sword in hand sought to slay Moses, and it was therefore a case of necessity that Zipporah perform the act. It was somehow made clear to them that the omission of the circumcision was the cause of God's anger.

From verse 26 we learn that upon the performance of the rite, the Lord let him go. The text conveys the impression that upon his release Zipporah again exclaims, ''A bridegroom of blood thou art.''

From this event recorded in Exodus we learn:

a) That the Lord is angry with His people and He brings judgment upon them when they neglect the duties required by His Word, particularly when we neglect the seals of His covenant.

b) When the Lord strives against us, only obedience and a speedy performance of the neglected duty will avail with God.

c) By the act of circumcision Zipporah set the sign of God's covenant ownership on the child. But notice carefully, that by obedience to God's covenant obligation, she also spared the life of her husband. The lesson should be clear to us: the performance of our covenant obligations is important and should not be trifled with.

Conclusions

1. From these passages we should be impressed with the necessity of obedience to God's commandments. This is particularly true of His sacraments. They are

sacred in His sight. We disobey at the peril of judgment and being cut off from His covenant blessings.

2. To refuse God's covenant sign is to refuse God's covenant claim. The lesson from Exodus 4 is that we cannot withhold from God that which is His—that includes our children.

3. You can't have the covenant blessings without the sign of the covenant, for to reject the sign is to deny the covenant and walk in disobedience. Even Moses was not exempt.

Questions for Discussion

1. How does the Lord teach us the importance of administering the signs of the covenant?

2. What is the meaning of the words ''cut off'' in Genesis 17:14? Is the cutting off physical or spiritual? How does Psalm 37 help us to understand the words ''cut off''?

3. How does God characterize the failure to keep the sacrament of circumcision?

4. What is the significance of God's declaration regarding the covenant?

5. What event in the life of Moses teaches us the significance and importance of Genesis 17:14? What saved Moses' life?

6. What are the lessons which we should learn from this even in the life of Moses?

12

PROMISED TO WHOM?

Genesis 17:1-4

Introduction

1. In our study of Genesis 17 we have repeatedly stated that this is the formalizing of the covenant of grace with Abraham and that the essence of the covenant is found in the words "to be a God unto thee, and to *thy seed* after thee" (vs. 7). We have referred to Leviticus 26:12 as having the fuller form of the promise: "And I will walk among you, and will be your God, and ye shall be My people."

2. But now that we have completed our study of the first 14 verses, we must ask "To whom were the promises given?" We previously traced the covenant promises through the New Testament and their final fulfillment in Revelation 21 but here we want to look now at *people* and their relationship to the promises. This question might be variously stated as:

"Who are the seed of Abraham?"

"Who are the children of Abraham?"

"Who are the people of God?"

Because this question divides the Christian church today it is important to prayerfully seek the biblical answer.

The Language of Genesis 17

a. It was in Genesis 12:1-3 that Jehovah called on Abraham to leave his kindred in Haran to seek the land of promise. On that occasion the Lord promised Abraham that He would make of him a great nation and that through him all families of the earth would be blessed.

b. These promises are incorporated in the covenant promises of Genesis 17. Let us look again at the language of Genesis 17.

Verse 2: "I will . . . multiply thee exceedingly."

Verse 4: "Thou shalt be a father of many nations."

Verse 5: "For a father of many nations have I made thee."

Verse 6: "I will make nations of thee, and kings shall come out of thee."

c. It is clear that the Jews understood these promises in a literal sense. They were indeed the physical descendants of Abraham. They restricted the covenant promises to themselves as lineal descendants. They considered themselves *alone* as being Abraham's seed.

d. But in John 8:32-47 Jesus challenged precisely this understanding of the covenant. The discussion: Whose children are they?

In verse 32 and the prior verse Jesus invites the Jews to believe in Him so that they might be free.

Verse 33: The Jews couldn't understand Jesus' invitation to set them free. So their response: "We be Abraham's seed, and were never in bondage to any man."

Verse 37: Jesus responds: "I know that ye are Abraham's seed; but ye seek to kill me, because my word hath no place in you."

Verse 39: Contains the Jews' claim: "Abraham is our father," and Jesus' response: "If ye were *Abraham's children,* you would do the works of Abraham."

Verses 40-42: Jesus proceeds to show them that they were *not the children* of Abraham because they seek to kill him, *neither* were they children of God otherwise they would love him. To be Abraham's seed was equivalent to being a *child of God.* It was and is a spiritual relationship.

In verse 44 Jesus draws the conclusion for them. He begins by the indictment: "Ye are of your father the devil."

e. Here then were Jews, lineal descendants of Abraham, circumcised the eighth day, and yet Jesus says to them: "You are not Abraham's seed." They were not really covenant children. They were "children of the devil." What was wrong?

f. Jeremiah tells us what was wrong. The prophet is describing the spiritual conditions in Judah immediately before the Babylonian captivity. Jeremiah speaks of their condition. Notice how their condition is related to circumcision in each passage.

1. Jeremiah 4:1-4: The Lord entreats the people to repentance, to put away their *idols* and to return to Him. In verse 2 He calls on them to pledge their allegiance to Him. In verse 4 the Lord warns them of His deep anger because of their sins. He calls upon them to consecrate themselves to Him if they are to escape fiery judgments. NEB—"Circumcise yourselves to the service of the Lord. Circumcise your hearts."

2. Jeremiah 6:8-10: Again the Lord speaks to the people. He calls on them to be instructed. "Hear My words lest I depart from thee." If they fail to *hear* and respond to His pleas, He will separate Himself from them and will bring the land into a state of desolation. In verse 10 the Lord laments their condition. They will not hear His words. They were deaf. They couldn't hear. "Behold, their *ear is uncircumcised,* and they cannot listen." They have rejected the Word of the Lord. They despise it. They refuse to hear God speaking to them.

3. Jeremiah 9:23-26: Again the Lord speaks to His people. He calls on them

to cease trusting in their own wisdom, their own strength or their own riches. Rather should they trust in knowing the Lord. They should know that He rules with loving kindness, justice and righteousness. (NASB) In verse 25 He declares, "Behold the days are coming, that I will punish all who are *circumcised* and *yet uncircumcised.*" And in verse 26: " All the house of *Israel are uncircumcised* in the *heart.*"

4. Three times the Lord speaks to Judah and three times the Lord rejects them as His people. Yes, they were the physical descendants of Abraham. Yes, they had received circumcision, the sign of the covenant. But *spiritually* they were not the seed of Abraham. They worshiped idols, they refused to hear the word of the Lord as He entreated them to return to Him. They trusted in their own wisdom, strength, and riches. They didn't know the Lord and they refused His rule.

Their *hearts* were *uncircumcised.* Their *ears* were *uncircumcised.* They were spiritually an uncircumcised nation. Abraham was not their father; they were not the people of God. *They were not the covenant seed of Abraham* even though they had received the sign of the covenant. As Jesus said, they were of their father the devil.

g. But we can rejoice that the Scriptures have not left us to guess as to who the seed of Abraham are. Several New Testament passages clearly define who the true children of Abraham are. In these passages the problems of circumcision and uncircumcision and Jew and Gentile are dealt with in their relationship to the covenant.

Romans 4

a. We do not have the time for a detailed study of this chapter even though it would be very profitable. I therefore propose to deal with the chapter in outline form but concentrating on those verses more directly related to our present subject.

b. Romans 3:23 says, "All have sinned," a conclusion regarding Gentiles and Jews. In chapter 3, verses 22-30, Paul has argued that men are *justified* in God's sight not by the law but by faith. In verse 29 he concludes that it is the same God who is God of both Jews and Gentiles. So in verse 30 he draws the further logical conclusion that because God is only one God, "He will justify the circumcised by *faith* and the uncircumcised through that *same faith*" (NIV).

But Paul knew that the Jews would reject both these conclusions, namely, (1) that men were justified by faith, and (2) that uncircumcised Gentiles had any part in the covenant. With this in mind Paul proceeds in chapter 4 to support his conclusions from the Old Testament.

Romans 4:1-8

a. The whole chapter is a consideration of Abraham. No better example could have been selected from a Jewish standpoint. Surely, they thought, he was justified by his righteous deeds and through circumcision. And did they not consider Abraham to be their father?

   b. In these verses Paul shows that Abraham was *not justified by works* but by faith. Paul quotes Genesis 15:6 to prove his case when he says in verse 3 "Abraham *believed* God, and it was counted unto him for righteousness." In verse 5 he concludes "faith is reckoned for righteousness."

   c. Paul also finds support from David when he quotes Psalm 32:1-2. Blessed is the man whose sin is covered by God and not imputed to the sinner.

Verses 9-12

   a. In verse 9 Paul raises the *specific question* of the relationship of circumcision to blessedness of having sins forgiven. "Is this blessedness only for the circumcised, or also for the uncircumcised?"

   b. He answers that question by relating the historical fact that Abraham was justified by faith as recorded in Genesis 15 and that circumcision was *then added* in Genesis 17 as a sign and confirmation of the fact that his faith was set to his account as righteousness.

   c. From this historical record Paul draws two significant conclusions:

   1. Verse 11: "So then, he is the *father* of *all* who *believe* but have *not* been circumcised, in order that righteousness might be credited to them." (NIV)

   2. Verse 12: "And he is *also* the father of the circumcised who not only are circumcised *but who also walk* in the footsteps of the faith that our father Abraham had *before* he was circumcised."

   From these verses it is clear that Abraham is the *father* of *all* believers whether circumcised *or* uncircumcised, which is another way of saying both Jew and Gentile believers.

   The one prerequisite necessary *for justification* is faith, not ceremony or law. Abraham had the same kind of faith before the rite of circumcision was instituted or before the giving of the law at Sinai. The *true descendants* of Abraham are those that have the *same faith*. So the important relationship to Abraham is the spiritual relationship and not the physical descent as claimed by the Jews.

Verses 13-15

   From these verses we learn that the extent of the promises given to Abraham had universal dimension. Abraham received the promise that he would be *heir of the world*. That promise was received through faith and not through the law.

   Law demands obedience. The want of obedience brings transgression and condemnation. Law and faith are mutually exclusive. In the *realm of justification* there can be no mixture.

Verses 16-17

   a. In verses 1-15 Paul has drawn his argument from the life of Abraham and the words of David to prove that *justification is by faith* in God's promises and not in the works of the law. In verses 16-25 he makes the specific applications of this teaching to the *New Testament believers.*

    b. Verse 16a: "Therefore it is of faith, that it might be by grace: to the end the promise might be sure to *all the seed."*

        1. Since law works wrath in view of transgression, *law knows no grace.* The promised inheritance cannot be secured through the law. God by His grace has appointed faith as the medium of receiving the promised blessings.

        2. It is because of God's grace that the promised blessings are made *"sure to all the seed."* Certainly Paul has in mind the promises made to Abraham in Genesis 15 and 17. He uses the precise word "seed" found in those Old Testament passages. The promises are by grace through faith made "sure to all the seed" of Abraham. The promises could not have been made sure by law.

    c. Verse 16b: ". . . not to that only which is *of the law,* but to that also which is *of the faith of Abraham,* who is the father of us all."

        1. Paul does not leave us in doubt as to who are the "seed" of Abraham. It is the purpose of this portion of verse 16 to clearly designate the "seed."

    The "seed" is identified as being in two categories:

    The seed "which is of the law." "Of the law" here is equivalent in meaning to "of the circumcision" in verse 12. There it was a parallelism between circumcision and uncircumcision, here in verse 16 it is a parallelism between "of the law" and "of the faith." Therefore, "of the law" as well as "of the circumcision" refers to Jews who had the advantage of being under the Mosaic economy.

        2. "Who is the father of us all"

    The reference is to Abraham. Paul draws for us the only possible conclusion: "Abraham is the father of us all." It is clear from what he has written in this chapter and in this verse that by the word "all" he is including the circumcised and the uncircumcised, the Jew and the Gentile. Verse 12 (NIV): All who "walk in the footsteps of the faith that our father Abraham had before he was circumcised."

    Thus as Christian believers, we can claim that Abraham is our father. He is the spiritual father of every believer, Jew or Gentile, who walks in the faith of Abraham.

    d. Verse 17: "As it is written, 'I have made you a father of many nations.' "

    Again Paul appeals to the Old Testament in support of that which he has written. The quotation is from Genesis 17:5. Can you see the tremendous importance of this quotation? What he is saying is that Gentile believers—as well as Jews—are included in the covenant promises of Genesis 17! Not only the Jewish nation was included in the covenant but "many nations."

    If we have the same kind of faith as Abraham then he is our father in God's sight.

Verses 18-25

a. In verses 18-22 Paul recounts the strength of Abraham's faith. He refers back to Genesis 15:5-6. When Abraham received the promise that he would be the father of many nations and God said "So shall they seed be" *he believed God* even though he was 100 years old and Sarah 90. All the natural circumstances were against the promise ever being fulfilled. Yet by faith he held fast to the promise.

It was because of this faith that the Lord "counted it to him for righteousness."

b. In verses 23-25 Paul shows the relevance of Abraham's faith to us as New Testament believers.

1. Verse 23: "The words 'It was reckoned to him' were not written for him alone." These words of Genesis 15:6 were not written for Abraham's benefit alone. They were not merely an enduring testimony to the personal faith of Abraham.

2. Verse 24: "*But for our sake also,* unto whom it shall be reckoned, who believe on Him that raised Jesus our Lord from the dead."

Beloved in Jesus Christ, we ought to read this verse in wonder and amazement.

In these verses Paul demonstrates the *unity* of our faith with that of Abraham and thereby directs our attention to the *continuity* of our faith with his.

There are many in our day who state that New Testament Christians have nothing to do with the Old Testament. But in this verse Paul clearly says that Genesis 15:6 was written for *our* benefit. Abraham was justified by faith. We are justified by faith.

Abraham believed in the God who is able to quicken the dead (vs. 17). We believe in the God who "raised Jesus our Lord from the dead." The nature of our faith is one with that of Abraham. Abraham believed the promise of what God would accomplish. We believe the promise of what God has accomplished. We both rest in the declarations of God. So it is that both are justified by faith and not by works.

3. Verse 25 declares what God accomplished in Jesus Christ. It contains two expressions:

a) Who was delivered up for *our* transgressions.
b) [Who] was raised [up] for *our* justification.

a) So we see the connection between the work of God and our redemption. He put our sins upon Christ. He suffered as our substitute. God provided Him as the One to bear our sins. It was the Lord that delivered Christ up to death.

b) But it was also the Father who raised up His Son from the grave. Again the action on God's part has a relationship to our redemption. It was for our justification. It is in the resurrection that we see Christ's triumph over death, as having completed his propitiatory work and delivered His people from the just

74

deserts of their sins, securing their justification and acceptance with God. His victory was on our behalf.

Conclusions

1. Conclusion to Romans 4

As the whole chapter has shown, the Old Testament Scriptures agree with the New Testament in assuring us that faith alone is the way by which men can be justified in the sight of God.

The true seed of Abraham are those who have the same faith as Abraham. They are justified by faith even as Abraham. As Romans 4 has so clearly demonstrated for us, the seed of Abraham included both Jews and Gentiles.

2. Other Passages

In addition to those passages to which we have already referred there are other passages in the New Testament which teach that the seed of Abraham, God's true children, include both Jews and Gentiles.

Time does not permit a detailed look at these passages, so we will look at some of these references with just a brief comment where needed.

a. John 10:15-16 (NASB): "Even as the Father knows Me and I know the Father: so I lay down My life for the sheep. And I have *other sheep*, which are not of this fold; I must bring them also, and they shall hear My voice; and they shall become *one flock* with *one Shepherd.*"

b. John 11:49-52 (NASB): The prophecy of Caiaphas the high priest, that Jesus would die for the nation (vs. 52), "and not for the nation only, but that He might also gather together into one the *children of God* who are scattered abroad."

c. Acts 3:11-26: Peter at the temple speaks to the people after the healing of the man who had never walked. He points to Jesus as the fulfillment of prophecy, specifically the covenant promises to Abraham. He quotes Genesis 22:18. Note the universal promise now being fulfilled in Christ. "All kindreds of the earth be blessed."

d. Romans 9:1-8: Paul expresses his great sorrow for the Jews. Why? Because all Abraham's natural descendants are not counted as his seed.

Verse 7: Neither are they all children because they are Abraham's seed, but: "In Isaac shall thy seed be called."

Verse 8: That is, "They which are the children of the flesh, these are not the children of God; but the children of the promise are counted for the seed."

e. Romans 9: 9-24: God's sovereignty is displayed in the bestowal of His mercy.

f. Romans 9:25-33: The calling of the Gentiles to faith and the loss by the Jews foretold because they rejected the Messiah.

g. Galatians 3

Notice the relationship of Galatians 3 to Romans 4. Here also Paul deals with Abraham and justification by faith. All is related to the covenant promises made to Abraham.

Verse 28: "For ye are all one in Christ Jesus."

Verse 29: "And if ye be Christ's, then are ye Abraham's seed, and heirs according to the promise."

His conclusion: Jews and Gentiles are Abraham's seed in fulfillment of the covenant promises.

Questions for Discussion

1. Does the language of Genesis 17 support the Jewish idea that they alone are the promised seed?

2. In John 8 why didn't the Jews understand Jesus' invitation to become free by believing in Him?

3. What was their response? What is the response of the Jew today?

4. Did Jesus agree or disagree with their analysis of their position in their covenant relationship?

5. What was Jeremiah's message to the Jews of his day? Why did he relate his message to circumcision?

6. In Romans 4 how does Paul speak of the faith of the Jews and the faith of Gentiles? Was it a different faith?

7. How was Abraham justified before God? How was David justified before God? How are you justified before God?

8. How is Abraham related to Jews and Gentiles?

9. Who are the "seed" of Abraham according to Romans 4:16-17?

10. How does Paul demonstrate the unity of our New Testament faith with Abraham and the continuity of our faith with his?

11. What is the relationship of Christ to our justification?

12. Cite other New Testament passages that show the unity of Gentile believers with Jewish believers. How should this affect our evangelistic outreach?

13

THE UNITY OF THE CHURCH

Acts 7:35-38
Ephesians 2:11-22

Introduction

1. From our studies of Genesis 17:1-14 we discovered that the promises made to Abraham involved promises which were spiritual and eternal.

The covenant finds its highest meaning in the words "to be a God unto thee, and to thy seed after thee" (vs. 7). The covenant finds its fulfillment in union and communion with Jehovah.

From our studies of both Old Testament and New Testament passages we have seen that physical descent alone did not warrant the conclusion that a person was included in the designation "seed" of Abraham. It is evident from our study of Romans 4 and several other New Testament passages that Abraham is the father of all true believers. Justification is by faith, without the works of the law. The justified includes both Jew and Gentile, circumcised and uncircumcised. Those who are justified by faith are included in the covenant promises of Genesis 17 and therefore represent the true "seed" of Abraham.

2. It is therefore concluded that the benefits of the covenant of grace revealed in Genesis 17 are extended to all God's people whether in the Old Testament or in the New Testament period of time.

It is also concluded that the Scriptures teach only one way of salvation, that is—by faith. Abraham is the example. Jews and Gentiles, circumcised and uncircumcised, both before and after the cross are saved by grace, through faith.

3. We believe that our previous studies also warrant the further conclusion that there is a unity and a continuity of the church in all ages. This is true even though there are distinctions to be seen in the administration of the covenant in the Old and New Testaments. Inasmuch as that unity is being denied today we propose to demonstrate that unity from several biblical references.

Acts 7:35-38: The Church

a. This is a part of Stephen's defense before the Jewish Sanhedrin. They accused Stephen of speaking blasphemy, of speaking against Moses, the law and the temple. See Acts 6:14.

b. A portion of his argument is taken up in challenging his judges and showing from the historical evidence that it was they and their fathers that had rejected Moses and the prophets. But it is extremely significant to see that woven into his argument is not only their rejection of Moses and the prophets but also Christ.

1. Verse 35: They rejected Moses even though he had been called by Jehovah Himself at the burning bush.

2. Verse 36: He demonstrates his call by doing wonders and miracles and leading them out of Egypt and during 40 years in the desert.

3. Verse 37: Moses in Deuteronomy 18:15 and 18 promised: "God shall raise up for you a Prophet like me from your brethren." He shall speak God's words.

4. Verse 38: It was the prophet Moses "who was in the *church in the wilderness.*" He received the living word of God. Notice carefully Stephen's words regarding the revelation given to Moses. "He received living words to pass on to us" (NIV).

Moses the prophet was a forerunner of the Messiah. He pointed forward to Christ the greater Prophet. Like the other prophets he pointed forward to "the coming of the Righteous One" (see vs. 52).

It was as a result of the revelation given to Moses that the nation was formed into "the church in the wilderness." Jehovah revealed His holy presence to the congregation at Mt. Sinai. It was there that He gave directions for the building of the tabernacle and its service among the people. The visible representation of God's presence dwelt in the center of the twelve tribes.

The revelation given to Moses was not only for "the Church in the wilderness" but also for all succeeding generations. As Stephen says, "it was given to pass on to us." It is true that the immediate reference by Stephen was the Jewish people of that day and very specifically the Sanhedrin. But I remind you that this was *after the cross.* Christ had already ascended and the New Testament church had been established on the day of Pentecost as recorded in Acts 2.

In verse 39 Stephen refers to the rejection of Moses by the fathers in the wilderness. In verse 51 he charges the Sanhedrin likewise of rejecting Moses and the prophets in the following startling statement: "Ye stiffnecked and uncircumcised in heart, and ears, ye do always resist the Holy Spirit as your fathers did, so do ye." They not only rejected Moses, but they rejected the Holy Spirit who gave the revelation to Moses, and they also rejected Christ. Paul in reference to the wilderness journey in I Corinthians 10:1-4 says that Christ was present and that "they drank of that spiritual Rock that followed them: *and that Rock was Christ.*"

Stephen only knew of *one church.* The church redeemed and fed by Christ. The church where Christ was present. The Sanhedrin was guilty of rejecting Christ even as their forefathers. Stephen believed in the unity and continuity of the church.

Ephesians 2:11-22
    a. Paul in verses 1-10 has set the scene for the remaining verses in this chapter.
        1. Verses 1-3: Describe the spiritual state of the Ephesians before their conversion. They were dead in sins. They served Satan in their evil lives.
        2. Verses 4-6: Describe the spiritual change which God had wrought in them. God in mercy loved them and by His grace gave them new lives in Christ.
        3. Verses 7-10: Describe the purpose of that new life given to us in Christ Jesus. We are to give expression to the new life which God has given us by serving Him.

So, in these verses Paul reminds the Gentiles in the church at Ephesus what their *former* relationship to *God and Christ had been* and *contrasts* that with what it is *now*.
    b. The second half of this chapter deals with another contrast. It deals with the former relationship of Gentile Christians to the church, and that is contrasted with their present relationship to the church.

Verses 11-12: A detailed description of their previous condition.
    1. Verse 11:
        a) ''Remember.'' Paul begins to remind the Gentile Christians of their former status to the people of God. But as he does so Paul himself appears to be reminded of the relationship between Jews and Gentiles.
        b) ''Gentiles in the flesh.'' Refers to the natural birth. To the Jews, ''Gentiles'' was a designation of the heathen. They were the uncircumcised, meaning that they were without the sign of the covenant in their flesh.
        c) Notice how Paul designates the Jews with his play on the word ''flesh.''

    ''Gentiles in the *flesh,* who are called 'uncircumcision' by the so-called 'circumcision,' which is performed in the *flesh* by human hands.''

He points to the Jews as those who were satisfied with the external mark of the covenant. Because they had received the external sign of the covenant they with arrogance exalted themselves over all the uncircumcised nations.
    2. Verse 12: In this verse Paul returns to the original thought which he had when he began to write verse 11. Both the NIV and the NASB begin the verse with the word ''remember.'' Then follows a catalog of privileges from which the Gentiles had been estranged.
        a) ''Without Christ.'' They were ''separate from Christ.'' They were deprived of any union or fellowship with Christ. There was a separation from Christ so that they were far away from Him. They had no part or benefit in Christ.

We must not miss the inference of Paul here, that Christ was with and available to the circumcision in the Old Testament. We have already referred you to I Corinthians 10:4 to establish that point.

b) "Excluded from the commonwealth of Israel." (NIV: "citizenship in Israel.") Gentiles were as aliens to the *theocracy* of Israel. Jehovah is the King of His people and His laws are to govern in all areas of life. To this the Gentiles were strangers for Jehovah was not their King.

This privilege which the Gentiles lacked seems to describe an external relationship. The Gentiles were not only separated from Christ but they were also separated from Israel.

c) "Strangers [foreigners] from the covenants of promise." This thought is close to the previous one but here the thought refers to exclusion from the internal and *spiritual* relationship. Up to this point of time in history Gentiles had generally been strangers to the covenants of promise. "Covenants" designates the repeated renewal of the covenant from Abraham to Moses, and to the prophets. All these repeated agreements to serve the *one* covenant given to Abraham.

d) "Having no hope." Devoid of hope of any kind. They had no promises on which they might set their hopes. Without Christ they could have no hope. They were cut off from anything on which they might set their hopes. The darkness of those without Christ is something that leads to utter despair.

e) "Without God in the world." "Without God," that's the essence of heathenism. They were ignorant of God and were therefore bound by superstition and serving Satan. They were forsaken of God and without His help.

Conclusion to Verses 11-12
1. There was a great gulf between Jews and Gentiles. The vastness of the separation is hard for us today to even imagine. But the catalog of items which separated them should give us some idea of the alienation.
2. It's difficult to see how the picture could have been made any blacker. For the Gentiles it was a picture of gloom without any hope in sight. Being without Christ they are described as being churchless, hopeless, godless and homeless.
3. There was a difference between Jew and Gentile. Verses 11-12 highlight those differences. The picture is one that appears to be without possible reconciliation of those differences.
4. What makes the description so terrible is that it is a description of men who are "without Christ" today.

Verse 13: "But *now in Christ Jesus* you who once were far off have been brought near through the blood of Christ."

a. This verse records that a great change has taken place. Verses 11-12 speak of the past, formerly; once Gentiles were without all those privileges, but "now" that is no longer true. The thought turns from what they once were to contemplate what they are *now*.

   b. The description of the past began with "without Christ," but the present is different because they are now "in Christ." If being "in Christ" makes this difference then we *must conclude* that *now* they are also partakers of the *true commonwealth of the Israel of God,* that they share in the blessings of the covenant of promise, that they rejoice in hope and finally that their life is a walk of fellowship with God.

   c. What made the difference? It was the blood of Christ. We were brought near to God through the instrumentality of another. Jesus interposed His blood. Ephesians 1:7: "In Him we have redemption through His blood." It is through the blood of His cross that we are justified and have access to God.

Verse 14-18: The Reconciliation

   The reconciliation spoken of here has two themes attached to it. It deals with peace with God and peace among men. The prior verses have set forth the negative aspects of these two themes. Separation from God and the marked hostility of Jews me that the emphasis in these five verses is on the human relationship. and Gentiles. Though the two themes of reconciliation are interwoven it seems to Verse 14: "For He Himself is our peace, who made both one."

   a. It is Christ, who through the shedding of His blood has made peace. He has made two groups into one. Christ has brought about reconciliation in human relationships. The "both" refers to the Jews and Gentiles as described in verses 11-13. The two who were previously so widely separated, Christ has joined together as one.

   b. (NASB margin): "And broke down the dividing wall of the barrier." How did Christ make the Jew and the Gentile one? He destroyed the barrier which separated them. A great wall of separation had been erected to keep the Jews from the Gentile and his manner of life. The Lord himself had erected that wall. It was a wall to keep and to protect the Old Testament people of God from paganism.

Verse 15: "By abolishing in His flesh the law with its commandments and regulations."

   a. How did Christ break down that wall? "In His flesh," that is by His life, the shedding of His blood, He abolished the enmity, even the law with its commandments and regulations. Now, the question before us is, What is meant by "the law, with its commandments and regulations"? Does it include the moral and the ceremonial or the ceremonial only?

   I think one's answer depends upon the meaning and the extent of the passage. If you consider the passage as referring to reconciliation with God together with the reconciliation of Jews and Gentiles then the law would refer to both the moral and the ceremonial aspects of the law. No one can be saved by the law. Justification is by grace through faith.

However, if you are convinced, as I am, that the primary reconciliation in view is between Jew and Gentile, then the law refers only to the ceremonial law. It seems to me that it was the ceremonial law that built a wall of separation around Israel. See Exodus 33:16, Deuteronomy 7:2, Leviticus 20:26: "And ye shall be holy unto me: for I the Lord am holy, and have severed you from other people, that ye should be mine." Hebrews 7:18 teaches us that "The former regulation is set aside because it was weak and unprofitable" (NIV). The moral law has not been set aside.

b. "His purpose was to create in Himself one new man out of the two, thus making peace" (NIV).

This sentence states the *purpose* which He had in mind when in His flesh He abolished the law. He by his death destroyed the commandments which *separated* the Jew and the Gentile.

It is those who are "in Himself," in Christ, that are being created into one new man. It is only union with Christ that can bring about such a condition. It is Christ that makes peace and brings about a true reconciliation.

Verse 16:

a. "And might reconcile them both."

This verse is a continuation of the thought expressed in the prior verse. It's a statement of the design and purpose of God. It's a reconciliation which God effects. It's a reconciliation in which He makes "two into one new man, thus establishing peace."

b. "In one body to God through the cross."

The reconciliation just referred to makes two into one new man as in verse 15, or into "one body" as designated in this verse. But now notice carefully the text. The thought is that the "one body" is also reconciled "to God." So there is a double reconciliation of men to men, but then of those so reconciled to a further reconciliation with God. It is this double reconciliation that is accomplished "through the cross."

We are prone to think of the work of Christ on the cross in a very narrow sense, namely the reconciliation of individuals to God. But in this verse we begin to see a much larger work. Paul gives expression to the larger scope of Christ's work in Colossians 1:20: "and, having made peace through the blood of His cross, by Him to reconcile *all things* unto Himself; by Him, I say, whether they be things in earth or things in heaven." The extent of Christ's work is universal. It reaches from heaven to earth and encompasses both.

c. "By it having slain the enmity."

What enmity is referred to here? Some think it is the enmity between God and man. Others believe it is the enmity between Jew and Gentile. But as we have seen the verse refers to a *double reconciliation;* therefore the natural meaning is to include the *double enmity* done away with in the double reconciliation. By the cross God is reconciled to man, and man to man. Christ vanquished the enmity in both cases by His cross. By the cross God's anger against sin is satisfied and the redeemed are constituted one glorious church. See Ephesians 4:1-5.

Verse 17: "And He came and preached peace to you who were afar off and peace to those who were near."

a. By the work on the cross, Christ established peace. Now we are told that He came and preached peace. It is best to see this event after the cross, accordingly His coming is after the resurrection. When the gospel is preached, it is Christ who announces peace to the sinner through his reconciling work at Calvary. II Corinthians 5:20: Paul speaks of himself as an ambassador for Christ. It is Christ speaking when His messengers proclaim the gospel.

b. Two categories are mentioned: those "who were afar off" and "those who were near." The context of this whole passage is referring to Jews and Gentiles. It is therefore evident that those same two classes are referred to here. It is clear that Paul is referring to the Gentiles in verse 13 when he speaks of those "who formerly were afar off were brought near by the blood of Christ." It is then the Jews "who were near," having been the recipients of all the Old Testament benefits and privileges.

Verse 18: "For through Him we both have our access in one Spirit unto the Father."

This verse says it all. The whole argument is brought down to this one simple statement. Both Jew and Gentile have access *through* Christ, *by* the Spirit, *unto* the Father. Because of the peace and reconciliation secured by Christ on the cross, *both* Jews and Gentiles are brought into union and communion with the Father. Christ, the promised Seed of the Abrahamic covenant, is also the "one mediator between God and men" (I Tim. 2:5).

It is the "one new man," the "one body," that the "one Spirit" brings unto the Father. Both parties, Jews and Gentiles, are reconciled to the Father "through" Christ's work. Both are the recipients of the "one Spirit" and both are brought to the same Heavenly Father.

The end of this work of the Trinity is that we might have access to the Father. See Ephesians 3:12; Hebrews 10:19.

Verses 19-22: A description of their present condition.

In these verses Paul sets down for us statements of fact which are conclusions based on that which he has written, especially verses 12-18. These verses are rich in content and meaning. In order to convey something of the tremendous change that has taken place Paul is striving with human language to bring out the character of those changes. Each figure of speech that he uses conveys something of the glorious privileges *now* enjoyed by the Gentile Christians as well as the Jewish Christians.

Verse 19: "Now therefore, ye are no longer strangers and foreigners."
   a. The NIV begins the sentence with the word "consequently," no doubt referring to the reconciling work of Christ about which he has just written. Because of the work of Christ, Gentiles are no longer barred from entrance into the kingdom of God and the relationships which that privilege brings. Gentiles are no longer outside the covenantal relationship: no longer outside the church. Paul continues the description of the new relationship.
   b. "But ye are fellow citizens with the saints, and of the household of God."
   Here again is the twofold effect of the reconciling work of Christ: two figures of speech.
      1. Gentile Christians are with the Jewish Christians *citizens* of the kingdom of God. Both groups together constitute the church of Christ and are therefore called "saints" or literally, "holy ones." The reference is to the saints of all ages who constitute the body of Christ and the commonwealth of the kingdom of God. They are the members of the *new theocracy,* that spiritual community into which both Jew and Gentile Christians have been incorporated. It was this universal theocracy to which the old Jewish theocracy was but a type and a preparatory institution.
      2. Gentiles are now part of God's *household.* That means, they belong to the family whose Head and Father is God. Believers in Christ constitute true children of God. Therefore, the relationship of fellowship extends not only "with the saints" but also to "God" who is the Father of the house. We should see in this figure of speech a reference to the most intimate relationship of a father to his children. The saints constitute one household.

Verse 20: "And ye are built upon the foundation of the apostles and prophets, Jesus Christ Himself being the chief cornerstone."
   a. The household of God is built upon a solid *foundation.* The edifice, or superstructure of the church, is built upon a foundation.
   b. The foundation of the church is the apostles and prophets. There is some difference of opinion as to whom "prophets" refers. It seems to me that the most natural reference in this context is that it refers to the Old Testament prophets. In a setting that has referred to "circumcision," "commonwealth of Israel," "covenants of promise," "commandments," and "ordinances," the reference to prophets would most naturally be to the Old Testament prophets unless otherwise

identified. Professor Allis in his book *Prophecy and the Church* takes the position that ''prophets'' refers to the Old Testament prophets and so sees in this verse that the New Testament church founded at Pentecost is the continuation and successor of the Old Testament church.

c. The foundation of the church is God's revelation to His people through the apostles and prophets. To reject their message was to reject God. Apostles and prophets stood in God's place. They communicated God's message. They were God's spokesmen.

d. In this verse Christ is spoken of as ''the chief cornerstone.'' A cornerstone is placed at the angle where two walls of a building meet. It is laid so as to give strength to the two walls with which it is connected. Christ is the chief cornerstone at the foundation. I Peter 2:7 quotes Psalm 118:22 and refers to Christ as the ''cornerstone.'' The same stone is in view in both texts. So Christ is represented as the chief cornerstone that unites Jews and Gentiles into one holy building.

Verse 21: ''In whom the whole building being fitted together is growing into a *holy temple in the Lord.*''

a. This verse is a continuation of the thought that Jesus Christ is the chief cornerstone uniting Jews and Gentiles together. It is Christ who is the point of union and support. Without Him the building falls.

b. It is *in Christ* that the whole building is being fitted or joined together. The whole church is rising like a great edifice in the process of erection. The text conveys the idea that this process of growing is still going on. Christ is still building His church, which is likened to ''a holy temple in the Lord.''

Verse 22: ''*In whom* you also are being built together into a dwelling of God in the Spirit.''

a. This is a *personal application* directed to the church at Ephesus. They also had a part in that glorious holy temple that Christ is building. *In Christ,* they also had received the benefits of the reconciliation secured by the cross and are therefore being built into God's holy temple. As Peter writes: ''You also, like living stones, are being built into a spiritual house'' (I Peter 2:5).

b. The church is God's place of dwelling. It is the house of God. It is the place of worship. As Peter says in I Peter 2:5, you are ''being built into a spiritual house *to be* a holy priesthood, offering spiritual sacrifices acceptable to God through Jesus Christ.'' See Exodus 19:5-6.

c. God dwells in His church in the person of the Spirit. Where the Spirit is present there is holiness.

Conclusion

It seems to me that Ephesians 2:11-22 firmly establishes the unity and the continuity of God's redeemed people in both the Old Testament and the New Testament periods. I want you to see in quick review the tremendous arguments presented in these few verses.

1. Verses 12 and 19: Gentiles who were once excluded from the commonwealth of Israel and from the covenant promises are now included. The same union and communion extended to the Jews in the Old Testament have now been extended to the Gentiles.

2. Verses 14-15: The divinely established division that existed in the Old Testament has *now* been abolished in Christ.

3. Verse 16: The reconciliation of Jew and Gentile is specifically represented as a part of the work Christ accomplished at Calvary. To deny the fact of this reconciliation is to deny the efficacy of Christ's work.

4. Verse 18: Both Jew and Gentile have *access* to the Father by one Spirit. There is but *one Father* and He has but *one family*.

5. Verse 19: God's people and God's family is not restricted to Old Testament Israel but is inclusive of both Jews and Gentiles.

6. Verse 20: The fact that the prophets and the apostles constitute the foundation of the New Testament church teaches us that the New Testament church is the successor to the Old Testament church. There is both a unity and a continuity. See also Revelation 21:12 and 14.

7. Verses 21-22: Both Jews and Gentiles are living stones being built into God's holy temple.

The same privileges to the Jews now are extended to the Gentiles:

Verse 12: "Without Christ"	Verse 13: "In Christ"
Verse 14: "Christ our peace"	Verse 15: Abolished the enmity
Verse 16: Reconciliation	Verse 17: Same message to Jew and Gentile
Verse 18: Access to the same Father	Verse 19: Citizenship: same family
Verse 20: Same Foundation	Verse 21: Christ the cornerstone of the temple
	Verse 22: Gentiles being built into that same temple

Questions for Discussion

1. How does Stephen use history in his defense before the Jewish Sanhedrin?
2. Who was the prophet of whom Moses spoke?
3. What is the significance of the phrase "the church in the wilderness"? Who was present with the church in the wilderness?
4. Did the Sanhedrin agree with Stephen when he charged them with rejecting Moses?
5. Who else did Stephen charge them with rejecting? What was their response?

6. Show from Stephen's defense that he believed in the unity of the New Testament church with that of the Old Testament.

7. What is the contrast shown in Ephesians 2:1-10?

8. What is the second contrast that Paul deals with in verses 11-22? How does Paul describe the great gulf that separated the Jews from the Gentiles? Discuss the five categories that caused that separation.

9. Discuss the significance of the phrases, ''without Christ'' and ''in Christ.''

10. What effected the reconciliation between the Jews and the Gentiles? Do we as Gentile Christians really think of a reconciliation between Jew and Gentile? What effect should this declaration of Paul's have upon our evangelism to the Jews?

11. How did Christ unite the Jews and Gentiles into one body? What barrier did He break down?

12. According to verse 16 what work of reconciliation did Christ perform? How was reconciliation accomplished?

13. How does Paul set forth the Trinity in verse 18? What is the relationship of the Trinity to the Jew and the Gentile?

14. Contrast the condition of the Gentiles as described in verse 12 with the condition described in verses 19-22. How does each item presented in these verses demonstrate the unity of the New Testament church with that of the Old Testament church?

14

THE SIGN OF THE COVENANT IN THE
NEW TESTAMENT

Matthew 28:18-20

Introduction

1. In our studies of Genesis 17:1-14, we saw the great condescension on God's part in entering into covenant relationship with Abraham. We discovered the essence of the covenant in the words, "I will be a God unto thee, and to thy seed after thee" (vs. 7). That promise was repeated again and again in both the Old and the New Testaments until we find its glorious fulfillment in the new heaven and the new earth where "God Himself shall be with them and be their God" (Rev. 21:3).

2. God's sign and seal of the covenant as given to Abraham was the sacrament of circumcision. In that sign God pledged Himself to honor and fulfill His covenant promises.

3. It is now our purpose to move on into the administration of the covenant in the New Testament era, particularly as it relates to the sign of the covenant and its recipients.

The New Testament Commandment

The Westminster Shorter Catechism, Q. 92, says: "A sacrament is a holy ordinance instituted by Christ." It was the divine commandment given to Abraham in Genesis 17 that instituted circumcision as the sign and pledge under the Old Testament economy. The question now before us is whether there is such a commandment of divine origin in the New Testament. We find such a commandment and the original institution of the New Testament sacrament in Christ's words as recorded in Matthew 28:18-20.

Is this New Testament commandment in any way related to the commandment in Genesis 17?

Matthew 28:18-20

The scene for this text is a mountain in Galilee. At Christ's appointment the apostles and, as Paul relates in I Corinthians 15:6, "above 500 brethren" had gathered to meet the Lord. The event was a prelude to the ascension. The words recorded in these three verses were in anticipation of that event.

Verse 18:

"All authority has been given unto Me in heaven and on earth."

a. Christ declared His kingship. These words are an expression of His glorification and victory. See the Westminster Shorter Catechism nos. 23, 26, and the Confession of Faith, chapter 8, section 1.

b. He claims all power, all authority, both in heaven and on earth. It is universal authority, without limitation. It is indeed significant that He claims supreme authority not only in heaven but also on earth. The events on earth are under His control.

c. These are the words immediately before the announcement of the Great Commission. In the light of the seemingly impossible task the disciples needed these words. They were words of encouragement, strength and assurance.

d. Regardless of what may come, Christ was in control. Nothing could separate them from Christ, for He rules not only in heaven but on earth.

Verse 19-20a:

"Go ye therefore, and disciple all the nations, baptizing them in the name of the Father, and of the Son, and of the Holy Spirit, teaching them to observe all things whatsoever I have commanded you."

a. Here is Christ's announcement of the Great Commission: "Go ye therefore." The command to go is based squarely on Christ's authority and power. It is King Jesus that issues the commandment to the apostles and to the church of all ages. It is the word of our crucified and risen Lord. The work of redemption has been completed. Now it is the time to establish the New Testament church. The types and sacrifices of the Old Mosaic economy have now been fulfilled and it must give way to a glorious, universal church.

b. The Great Commission involves *three* things which the church must do. The words are in the imperative mood; therefore they lay obligations upon the church which are obligatory and can in no way be voided.

1. "Disciple all the nations": Evangelism

Making disciples means bringing people to faith in Christ. It involves the preaching of the gospel so that men are brought to repentance and faith and declare by their confession that they belong to Christ. Also involved is the idea of becoming a follower of Christ and the willingness to learn of Him. "All nations" establishes the universality of the commission.

2. "Baptizing them": Sacrament

The confession of a disciple comes to visible expression in baptism. The rite therefore consists of the initiatory rite expressing entrance into Christ's kingdom. Baptism is the badge and symbol of entrance into the New Testament church.

3. "Teaching them": Teaching

a) The work of teaching is to continue after baptism. It is a continuous process. So important is this work that Paul says, in Ephesians 4:11-12, that Christ gave pastors and teachers for the perfecting of the saints. Teaching is one of the marks of the New Testament church.

    b) Notice that the content of the teaching is defined. It is to be that which Christ committed to the *apostles*. The teaching authority is thereby clearly established. They have the responsibility to give to the church the teaching which *Christ taught them*. The only genuine Christian tradition is that which has been set down in Scripture. Oral traditions always work to make the Word of God of none effect. This statement of Christ's terminates special revelation after the apostolic age.

The Importance of Baptism

The original institution of baptism within the context of the Great Commission certifies to us that baptism is basic to that commission which Christ gave to His disciples as He neared the occasion of His departure to the right hand of the Majesty on High. The construction of the text of Matthew 28:19 indicates that baptism is a necessary part of the process of discipling the nations. But perhaps of greater significance for our present interest is the coordination of baptism with discipling the nations and teaching them to observe all that Jesus had commanded. Erroneous views of baptism must not be allowed to deter us from fully carrying out the commission of our Lord to His church.

The Meaning of Baptism:

    a. What is the meaning of baptism as we find it set forth in the Great Commission? Because the sacrament involves water we too often conclude that the basic idea is that of purification. However, in seeking the meaning of baptism, we should first consider the formula which Jesus used in the institution: "baptizing them into the name of the Father, and of the Son, and of the Holy Spirit."

    b. Consideration must first be given to the phrase "baptizing them into." What is the thought conveyed by this formula? Paul has used this expression several times in I Corinthians.

    I Corinthians 1:13: "Is Christ divided? Was Paul crucified for you? Were you baptized into the name of Paul?"

    I Corinthians 1:15: "So no one can say that you were baptized into my name."

    I Corinthians 10:2: "They were all baptized into Moses in the cloud and in the sea."

    It is apparent that the expression "baptized into" expresses *a relationship* between the one baptized and the one "baptized into." In the first two passages referred to it is obvious that Paul is speaking of a very special relationship when he uses the term "baptized into." To have been baptized in his name was equivalent to saying that they were *joined to* Paul and therefore separated from Christ. Paul is horrified at the thought.

However in 10:2 Paul does speak of our fathers being "baptized into Moses." He states that this occurred when Israel was under the cloud which was the symbol of the divine presence, and when they passed through the Red Sea in their divine deliverance from Egyptian bondage. In this context the words "baptized into Moses" denotes the *intimate* relationship into which they entered with Moses, who as Jehovah's servant and mediator led them from bondage unto the borders of the promised land. It is true that Israel and Moses were inseparably joined together. Israel could not move without Moses and Moses would not move without Israel.

Just a brief comment is necessary on the words "how that all our fathers were under the cloud." The indisputable reference is to Israel. Keep in mind that in this Epistle Paul is writing to a Gentile church. We should therefore see the apostolic view of the relationship subsisting between the people of the Old Testament and those of the New Testament. They were our spiritual fathers and we their spiritual descendants.

c. It is clear therefore that baptism signifies union. If we keep in mind the Great Commission formula where Christ institutes this sacrament we immediately see that the union which Christ declared was more inclusive than that union with Himself.

d. Baptism is into the name of the Father, and of the Son, and of the Holy Spirit. We are therefore forced to the amazing conclusion that *baptism signifies our union* with the one holy Triune God, Father, Son, and Holy Spirit. Jesus had previously referred to this union in John 14. In verses 16-17 He had promised that because of His prayer "the Father" would send them "another Comforter, that He may abide with you forever." Jesus refers to the Comforter, as "the Spirit of Truth." In verse 23 Jesus promised that "If a man love Me, he will keep my words: and My Father will love him, and we will come unto him, and make our abode with him."

e. He who receives the rite of Christian baptism with the prescribed formula of Matthew 28:19 professes to receive God the Father, as his Father; to receive God the Son, as his Savior; and to receive God the Holy Ghost as his teacher and sanctifier. It is a sign and confession that we have entered into a very personal and intimate relationship with the Triune God.

The Relationship of Baptism to Circumcision

a. In Genesis 17:7 the Lord identifies His *covenantal relationship* with Abraham in the words "to be a God unto thee, and to thy seed after thee." The Lord further promised that the covenant would be "for an everlasting covenant." It was at this point that we discussed the threefold promise of Leviticus 26:12:

1. I will walk among you.
2. I will be your God.
3. Ye shall be my people.

We pointed out then that these three items teach us that the covenantal relationship described in these two passages (Gen. 17:7 and Lev. 26:12) involves nothing less than union and communion with Jehovah. The sign and seal of that covenantal relationship was circumcision.

b. Now as we have come to our study of the Great Commission in Matthew 28:19, we find that the baptismal formula signifies our union and communion with Jehovah the Triune God. We should now see that circumcision and baptism have *precisely the same meaning.* The Lord who in Genesis 17 commanded Abraham to perform the rite of circumcision as a sign of the covenant, that same Lord commanded His apostles to perform the rite of baptism as the *new sign* of the covenantal relationship.

Conclusions

1. Our Westminster Standards speak of baptism as the New Testament sacrament—as a sign and seal of the covenant of grace and our ingrafting into Christ. See Confession of Faith, chapter 28, section 1; Larger Catechism no. 165 and Shorter Catechism no. 94.

2. The *objective* end of baptism is the glory of God; the *subjective* end is the happiness and salvation of the persons baptized in that baptism introduces them into the communion with God. The Shorter Catechism no. 1 combines these two thoughts when it answers the question: What is the chief end of man? Answer: Man's chief end is to *glorify* God, and to *enjoy* Him forever.

Questions for Discussion

1. Is there a commandment specifying a New Testament sign?
2. If so, what is its meaning?
3. What is its relationship to the sign of circumcision?
3. What is its relationship to the sign of circumcision?
4. El Shaddai, God Almighty, pronounced the circumcision commmandment. Who pronounced the New Testament commandment? What are the implications?
5. What three things did Christ command in the Great Commission?
6. What is the meaning of the term "baptized into"?
7. What is the place of the apostles in the New Testament church?
8. Does Christ's resurrection have anything to do with the Great Commission?

15

THE MEANING OF BAPTISM

Titus 3:3-7

Introduction

1. Matthew 28:18-20 records the words of Christ setting forth the original institution of Christian baptism. From our study of that text, we discovered that baptism represents our *union* with the Holy Trinity. However, Scripture reveals that baptism has other meanings besides the one indicated in Matthew 28:18-20.

2. Something of the wealth of meaning attached to baptism can be gained from the Westminster Larger Catechism no. 165. Q. "What is baptism?" A. "Baptism is a sacrament of the New Testament wherein Christ hath ordained the washing with water in the name of the Father, and of the Son, and of the Holy Ghost, to be a sign and seal of ingrafting into himself, of remission of sins by his blood, and regeneration by his Spirit, of adoption, and resurrection unto everlasting life: and whereby the parties baptized are solemnly admitted into the visible church, and enter into an open and professed engagement to be wholly and only the Lord's."

3. What is the meaning of "washing of regeneration" in Titus 3:5? What kind of picture does Paul portray of mankind? Does Paul see any hope for mankind?

What We Were

Verse 3:

> **For we also once were foolish ourselves, disobedient, deceived, enslaved to various lusts and pleasures, spending our life in malice and envy, hateful, hating one another (NASB).**

Again we see Paul's familiar way of writing in calling attention to contrasts. It is the same pattern followed in Ephesians, chapter 2. "We also once were foolish." Again, in this text, he begins with what we once were. He reflects on our past. In our former condition we were without understanding so we lived foolishly. He then proceeds to list six manifestations of our foolish lives.

1. "Disobedient." We rejected both divine and human authority, heeding neither divine commandments nor the laws of civil magistrates.

2. "Deceived." The truth escaped us. We were so deluded that we im-

agined that our license was true liberty. Though we thought ourselves to be free, we had become slaves.

3. "Enslaved." Evil passions and pleasures dominated our life and conduct. We were slaves to the evil desires and lusts which controlled us and drove us onward to seek and to serve the evil passions.

4. "Malice and Envy." We lived in malice and envy, which represents the perverse disposition of the mind. Our lives were wholly controlled by malice and envy, which reflected the total corruption to the soul.

5. "Hateful." The original New Testament word used here occurs nowhere else in the New Testament. It means: "detestable, odious, offensive, disgusting, repulsive."

6. "Hating one another." This is the natural result of the catalog of sins which has just been enumerated. Hate prevails in this world. The history of the world is a commentary showing the truthfulness of this statement.

What Made the Change?

Verse 4-5a:

But when the *kindness of God* our Savior and His love toward man appeared, *He saved us*.

a. Paul here begins to introduce the contrast to the picture in verse 3. What was it that caused a change to be made in that horrible picture? Paul says that the change is attributable to God. God's kindness and love toward man appeared. How could God love such sinful creatures? Paul doesn't answer that question but simply states the great fact of God's divine mercy. The change is attributed to divine benevolence and His compassion for mankind.

b. God's activity on our behalf is ascribed entirely to His love. God's saving grace is described as being entirely free and undeserved. As Paul says in Romans 5:8: "But God commendeth His love toward us, in that, while we were yet sinners, Christ died for us." This is nothing less than free and sovereign grace. It was the pleasure of His will, a good pleasure that emanated out of the depths of His own love, that He chose a people to be heirs of God and joint-heirs with Christ. The reason for our salvation resides wholly in Him. It is not in man to plumb the depths of God's love.

c. "He saved us." It was the kindness and the love of God our Savior which came to man's rescue. Paul believed in the knowledge of the assurance of salvation. Paul knew he was saved.

Verse 5a:

He saved us, not because of righteous things we had done, but because of His mercy (NIV).

Paul wants to stress the fact that God did not bestow His kindness and His love upon us because we in any way deserved it. Quite the contrary, we didn't deserve it. There were no works of righteousness. As Paul concludes in Romans 3:9: "Jews and Gentiles alike are all under sin."

We are saved because of God's mercy. The forgiveness of our sins is according to the riches of His grace (Eph. 1:7). The Bible reveals to us something of God's marvelous grace. Paul exalts God's grace and so should we.

d. What made the change? It was God's kindness, God's love, and God's mercy that moved Him to save us.

How Was the Change Accomplished?

Verse 5b:

He saved us through the washing of regeneration and renewing by the Holy Spirit.

Paul is writing here of the *application of redemption. It will help us if we keep in mind that there are two aspects* to the *work of redemption* accomplished in time.

1. The Accomplishment of Redemption. Christ alone accomplished the work of our salvation. Hebrews 9:28: "So Christ was *once* offered to bear the sins of many."

Hebrews 2:17: "Wherefore in all things it behooved Him to be made like unto His brethren, that he might be a merciful and faithful high priest in things pertaining to God, to make *reconciliation* for the sins of the people.

Hebrews 9:26: "But now *once in the end of the world* hath He appeared to put away sin by the sacrifice of Himself.

Christ, and Christ alone, accomplished the work of redemption, reconciling us to God by the sacrifice of Himself. He alone paid the price demanded by our sins.

2. The Application of Redemption. Shorter Catechism, no. 29: "We are made partakers of the redemption purchased by Christ, by the effectual application of it to us by His Holy Spirit."

It is precisely this work of application that is being described in Titus 3:5-7. It refers to a twofold work of the Holy Spirit in the application of redemption even though there is but *one end in view.* Paul refers to this twofold work in Titus 3:5.

"The washing of regeneration."

1. Regeneration is here expressed in terms of washing. Jesus used the same terminology in John 3:5 in speaking to Nicodemus about the necessity of being born again. "Verily, verily, I say unto thee, Except a man be born of water and of the Spirit, he cannot enter into the kingdom of God."

2. What is meant by the word regeneration? The Westminster Confession of Faith, chapter 10, and the Shorter Catechism, no. 31, deal with the work of regeneration under the subject of effectual calling. It is described as (1) the work of

God's Spirit, (2) enlightening our *minds* spiritually and savingly, in the knowledge of Christ, giving understanding in the things of God, (3) taking away the heart of stone, and giving us a *heart* of flesh, (4) renewing the *will* and by His almighty power determining them to that which is good.

3. Regeneration is then an act of God the Holy Spirit implanting in man a new life so that the soul is made holy and is therefore disposed to holy exercises. So it is that the text says: "He saved us." The *whole man* is involved in this work of the Spirit bringing us to the fulness of redemption.

4. In the *accomplishment* of redemption Christ, alone, died in our place but in the *application* of redemption, the Holy Spirit sovereignly works in us, the beginning of which is regeneration and the giving of a new life.

5. It is this dramatic and radical work of God which is required to change us from the sinful creatures which we were by nature to new creatures in Christ.

Purification

a. The text speaks of the *washing* of regeneration. Baptism is washing with water. It is the sacramental use of water which this verse says is an expression of *God's work* of regeneration. However, it is difficult to escape the idea that washing involves the expression of purification.

b. In our study of the Great Commission, which includes the baptismal formula in Matthew 28:19-20, we maintained that the essential meaning of that formula conveyed the idea of *union*. Now we see in Titus 3:5 that baptism also represents the indispensable purification necessary for entrance into the kingdom of God. *Fellowship with God demands holiness* and righteousness. It is said of the heavenly Jerusalem in Revelation 21:27: "And there shall in no wise enter into it anything that defileth, neither whatsoever worketh abomination, or maketh a lie: but they which are written in the Lamb's book of life." Our God has Himself provided for that very demand. There is *cleansing in the atonement.* "The blood of Jesus Christ cleanseth us from all sin" (I John 1:7), and (vs. 9) "from all unrighteousness." Is it not significant that these verses follow the declaration of verse 3 that we have fellowship with the apostles and "with the Father, and with His Son Jesus Christ"?

c. It therefore appears that the words, "He saved us by the washing of regeneration" includes the twofold work in redemption of regeneration and cleansing.

d. Our Lord in John 3:5 taught Nicodemus the same truths. "Verily, verily, I say unto thee, Except a man be born of water and of the Spirit, he cannot enter into the kingdom of God." The two essential elements of *purification and renovation* are inseparably joined together. They represent aspects which constitute a *total change* by which we are called of God and *translated* from death to life and from the kingdom of Satan into God's kingdom. It is a change which provides for all the

96

exigencies of our past condition and the demands of the new life in Christ. It is a change which removed the contradiction of sin and fits us for the fellowship of the Triune God (John Murray: *Redemption, Accomplished and Applied*, p. 100).

Development of the New Life

Verse 5b:

He saved us through the washing of regeneration and *renewing* by the Holy Spirit.

a. Regeneration is followed by renewal. Both are wrought by the Holy Spirit. Regeneration is that definitive, *once for all* work of the Holy Spirit which is never directly perceived by man. Renewing is the continuing work of the Holy Spirit whereby we consciously surrender our whole personality to the will of God.

b. This latter work is commonly called sanctification and is described for us in the Shorter Catechism, no. 35: "Sanctification is the work of God's free grace, whereby we are renewed in the whole man after the image of God, and are enabled more and more to die unto sin, and live unto righteousness."

Sanctification is the daily work of the Holy Spirit cleansing us from the pollution of sin.

c. Again, we see that this is in accordance with our Lord's teaching. At the Last Supper, Jesus was washing the disciples' feet. Peter refused. Jesus responded, "If I do not wash you, you have no part with me," whereupon Peter requested that Jesus wash also his hands and his head. John 13:10 records Jesus' words as follows: "Jesus said to him, He who has bathed needs only to wash his feet, but is completely clean; and you are clean, but not all of you."

1. Jesus is using the situation to teach a spiritual truth which, it is evident, Peter did not understand. The imagery involved is that of a man going to a feast. In the Orient such a one would bathe before leaving home. Upon arrival he needs only his feet washed to sit at the table wholly clean.

2. So the spiritual meaning is that Jesus is speaking of spiritual cleansing.

a) The one who had bathed is the one whose inmost nature has been renovated. He has been cleansed by Jesus' blood. He is justified before God and all his sins have been forgiven. He is altogether clean. The words of Jesus here: "He who has bathed" are equivalent to Paul's words in Titus 3:5, "He saved us through the washing of regeneration."

b) But the bathed person's feet get dusty in the walk to the banquet hall. His feet only are in need of washing. So it is that the regenerated person needs daily cleansing because of his contact with a sinful world. There is the daily need "to die unto sin, and live unto righteousness." We need the daily cleansing from the pollution of sin. So we see that Jesus' words "needs only to wash his feet" pertain to the same topic as the "renewing by the Holy Spirit" of Titus 3:5.

Verse 6:

Whom He poured out upon us richly through Jesus Christ our Savior.

a. Notice how beautifully the saving work of the Holy Trinity is represented for us in this verse.

The *Father* pours out the *Holy Spirit* upon us, through *Jesus the Son.* In Joel 2:28 God promised to pour out His Spirit upon all flesh. That prophecy is quoted in Acts 2:17 by Peter. It was the day of Pentecost (50th day after the Passover) when the church was gathered together and the Holy Spirit was poured out upon the church. Peter said that this was the fulfillment of the prophecy in Joel.

In Acts 2:33 we have a passage similar to our verse 6. Again it concerns the Trinity and the giving of the Spirit. With reference to the risen Christ, Peter says: "Therefore having been exalted to the right hand of God, and having received from the Father the promise of the Holy Spirit, He has poured forth this which you both see and hear" (NASB).

b. It is the sovereign Holy Spirit that has been poured out upon the church. On Pentecost He made the church His dwelling place and ever abides with the redeemed. He dwells with us richly and abundantly. Christ by His atoning sacrifice secured for His people the gift of the Spirit thereby assuring the application of redemption.

Verse 7:

So that, having been justified by His grace, we might become heirs having the hope of eternal life.

a. It is important to see that Paul is *continuing* to deal with the *application* of the redemption purchased by Christ. He first deals with justification.

b. "Having been justified." Notice the past tense. It is a transaction already completed.

Shorter Catechism, no. 33: "What is Justification?" "Justification is an act of God's free grace, wherein he pardoneth all our sins, and accepteth us as righteous in His sight, only for the righteousness of Christ imputed to us, and received by faith alone."

c. Justification, like every other part of redemption, is "by His grace." It is the *declaration* of God that we are counted righteous before Him. How can it be that such guilty sinners as we could be declared righteous? As II Corinthians 5:21 tells us that the Father laid our sins on Jesus so that His righteousness was put to our account. Or as Romans 3:24 says: "Being justified freely by His grace through the redemption that is in Christ Jesus." Romans 1:16-17: The gospel applies to us "the righteousness of God."

d. Christ paid the price of our justification. Therefore, we have been *acquitted* from all the guilt and punishment of our sins, and so found favor in God's sight.

That has *consequences* for the everyday existence. Paul says in Romans 5:1 that because we are justified by faith, we have peace with God through our Lord Jesus Christ. The knowledge and the assurance of justification by faith fills the soul with peace. It sets the heart to rejoicing and thanksgiving. It should lead us to be ever faithful in praising God for His marvelous grace and to walk in obedience to His Word. This is calculated to teach us that doctrine is not and cannot be divorced from life.

e. Paul concludes that because we are justified therefore we have "become heirs having the *hope of eternal life*."

The assurance of justification brings with it the assurance that we have become heirs of the hope of eternal life. Paul knew that he already possessed "eternal life" even as Jesus said in John 3:36: "He that believeth on the son *hath* everlasting life." It is evident that as he speaks of "heirs having the hope of eternal life," he is *speaking of something yet to come*.

What is that something yet to come? It is *glorification*. What is glorification? It is the *final phase of the application of redemption*. It is that which brings to completion the whole redemptive process which began with God's effectual call. Paul refers to this final step in Romans 8:17: "And if children, then heirs; heirs of God, and joint-heirs with Christ; if so be that we suffer with Him, that we may be also glorified together." Glorification of the saints takes place when Christ Himself returns in glory. It is for that reason that Paul in Titus 2:13 has exhorted us to be "Looking for that blessed hope, and the glorious appearing of the great God and our Savior, Jesus Christ."

Because of the love and kindness of God, we who were once destitute are now heirs of all the riches of God's redemption. As children of God we are already justified and we should therefore be glorifying and abundantly enjoying the goodness and mercy of our covenant God.

We are *now* the beneficiaries of Christ's Will. Christ died for us to seal His covenant promises and purchased our inheritance. The will was opened at Christ's death. Now we have the revelation of the inheritance through the apostles. Now we are heirs with the title to all the benefits of Christ's redemption already put in our name. None can rob us of that inheritance. Hebrews 9:16-17 has the idea of inheritance. The inheritance comes through a will or testament. When the testator dies the will becomes effectual. Christ has died; therefore the legacy of His will is now made available to the redeemed.

Conclusion

From our study of this passage we should now see that baptism, the covenant sign of union and communion with God, is also a sign of God's work of regeneration and purification.

Questions for Discussion

1. Are men really wise? Do they know the truth?
2. Are men truly free today? How does Paul say that men are set free?
3. Do men really show brotherly love in the world today?
4. Why does God love us? What difference does it mean to us that God loved us?
5. What has Christ done for us that we could not do for ourselves?
6. What has the Holy Spirit done for us that we could not do for ourselves?
7. What is required if we are to have fellowship with God?
8. Does the Christian have any need for cleansing after the initial cleansing of the Holy Spirit?
9. What activity is ascribed to the Trinity on the day of Pentecost?
10. Does doctrine have any effect on the way we live each day?
11. What aspect of redemption is pictured for us in baptism according to Titus 3:5?

16

REPENT AND BE BAPTIZED

Acts 2:37-42

Introduction

1. Based on our study of Matthew 28:19, we believe that baptism replaced circumcision as the sign of the covenant in the New Testament church. If this is true, the New Testament church history should confirm that conclusion beyond a shadow of any doubt.

2. How did the apostles understand the command to baptize in the Great Commission? Did they draw the conclusion that baptism was now the covenant sign and therefore replaced circumcision as the sacramental sign?

3. What did Peter have in mind when he referred in verse 39 to "the promise"? Are there any indications in Peter's message that point to the meaning of "the promise"? What about those who heard? What did they think of when he referred to "the promise"?

4. These and similar questions lead us to give serious consideration to Acts 2:37-42.

The Setting of Acts 2:37-42

a. Acts, chapter two records the establishment of the New Testament church.

b. It is the Day of Pentecost which fell on the 50th day after the Sabbath of Passover week. It was also called the Day of First Fruits for it was a harvest festival, and its observance included the presenting to the Lord two loaves made from the ripened wheat. Therefore throughout the centuries it had pointed forward to the events of Acts 2, when the first great gathering of converts were brought into the Christian church.

c. The events of Acts 2 occurred within a very few days after the giving of the Great Commission in Matthew 28:19.

d. Verses 1-13 record the outpouring of the Holy Spirit upon the apostles and the other disciples. Through the gift to speak with other tongues, Jews from many nations, who had gathered at Jerusalem, heard the gospel message in their own languages.

Verses 14-36 record Peter's sermon in response to their question as to "What meaneth this?" (vs. 12). He expounded the Old Testament Scriptures and preached Christ.

1. Verses 14-21: In answer to the question, "What meaneth this?," Peter reminds them of the prophecy of Joel as recorded in Joel 2:28-32. The events which they had just witnessed were in fulfillment of that prophecy. The Holy Spirit had been poured out upon the church. The New Testament church was born when the Holy Spirit was poured out on the Day of Pentecost. It ushered in the age of the Spirit. It was the glorious fulfillment of God's promise "I will pour out of my Spirit upon all flesh." This was a once-for-all event. Pentecost itself is not repeated.

The events of Pentecost marked a turning point in history. Peter in Acts 2:17 refers to the events of Pentecost as constituting "the last days." It was on that day that the Spirit was poured out upon the church, endowing it with the power to fulfill its glorious place and mission in this world. It was the Spirit that set the church on fire. That fire has now encompassed the world.

Peter closes his quotation from Joel with the divine promise: "And it shall come to pass, that whosoever shall call on the name of the Lord shall be saved."

2. Verses 22-36 present a threefold argument:

a) Verse 22: Jesus had been approved of God by mighty works and wonders and signs. They had been witnesses of those miracles. His works had been available for all to see.

b) Verses 23-32: In accordance with God's plan and purposes they had crucified Jesus. God, in accordance with His mighty power, raised Him from the dead. This was in accordance with the prophecy of David in Psalm 16:8-11.

c) Verses 33-35: God exalted Christ to the place of authority at His own right hand. This also was in accordance with the prophecy of David in Psalm 110:1. It was then that Christ "received from the Father the promised Holy Spirit." What they had witnessed was the Holy Spirit being poured out upon the church by the exalted Christ.

Conclusion: In verse 36 Peter presses home the conclusion. Jesus is both the Lord and Christ. The One who had so recently walked in their midst was the long-promised Messiah. Many in Peter's audience were now convinced of that, but—they had consented to His crucifixion. Their concern is expressed in their searching question: "Brethren, what shall we do?"

Verse 38:

Then Peter said unto them, Repent, and be baptized everyone of you in the name of Jesus Christ for the remission of sins, and ye shall receive the gift of the Holy Spirit.

The magnitude of their sin now beats upon their consciences. What hope of salvation was left for them now—they who had crucified the Messiah? That was

102

their deep concern. It is to that concern that Peter is responding. It is a response that brings hope. Note his threefold answer involving two commands followed by a promise.

1. Repent
2. Be baptized
3. The promised Holy Spirit

Repent

Peter, under the influence of the Holy Spirit, had proclaimed the gospel of Jesus Christ in fullness, clarity and power. Now the Spirit was working in the hearts of his hearers. They were convinced that they had crucified the One who was "both Lord and Christ."

"What is repentance unto life?" That is question no. 87 of the Westminster Shorter Catechism. The answer is: "Repentance unto life is a saving grace, whereby a sinner, out of a true sense of his sin, and apprehension of the mercy of God in Christ, doth, with grief and hatred of his sin, turn from it unto God, with full purpose of, and endeavor after, new obedience."

"Then hath God also to the Gentiles granted repentance unto life" (Acts 11:18). Repentance, like faith, is a gift freely given to us by God for Christ's sake, as well as a duty required of us. Calvin writes on the subject of repentance in his *Institutes,* book 3, chapter 3. He defines repentance as "a true conversion of our life to God, proceeding from a sincere and serious fear of God, and consisting in the mortification of our flesh and of the old man, and in the vivification of the Spirit." In the context of Acts, chapters 10 and 11, it cannot be doubted that the phrase "repentance unto life" includes more than sorrow for sin. It includes what Calvin calls a "true conversion of our life to God." Acts 10 declares that God had poured out His grace and blessings upon the Gentiles. He gave them new hearts and new minds. They were gloriously converted.

The essence of repentance includes a true hatred and sorrow for our sin. Repentance includes an actual turning away from our sins, turning unto God with the purpose of walking in His commandments. Something of the extent of repentance can be seen from Paul's words in II Corinthians 7:10-11: "Godly sorrow brings repentance that leads to salvation and leaves no regret, but worldly sorrow brings death. See what this godly sorrow has produced in you: what earnestness, what eagerness to clear yourselves, what indignation, what alarm, what affection, what concern, what readiness to see justice done" (NIV).

It is the ground of repentance that gives us hope. Despair is turned to hope when in the consciousness of our own unrighteousness and guilt before God we turn in faith to apprehend God's grace and mercy revealed to us in Jesus Christ. We have an example of true repentance when David cries out to God in Psalm 51:

Have mercy upon me, O God, according to thy lovingkindness: according to the multitude of thy tender mercies blot out my transgressions. Wash me thoroughly from mine iniquity, and cleanse me from my sin (Ps. 51:1, 2).

The fruits of repentance bring forth the spirit of holiness towards God, a sense of compassion towards men and a great desire for truth and righteousness in the heart. The call to repentance was an essential element in the proclamation of the Christian message in the New Testament church. No fewer than five times is the call to repentance recorded in the Book of Acts. The command to repent is the forgotten element in the preaching of the gospel today. There will be no great revival in the church until we call the church to repentance.

Be Baptized

In our consideration of baptism in the prior two chapters we concluded that baptism signifies our union with Jehovah the Triune God and that it is a sign of God's work of regeneration and purification. The Book of Acts shows us how the apostles and the early New Testament church received baptism as the substitute for circumcision as the sign of the covenant and as a sign of purification.

The substance of the gospel is given to us in Christ's words recorded in Luke 24:47: "and that repentance and remission of sins should be preached in his name among all nations, beginning at Jerusalem."

In Acts 2:38 Peter is giving the substance of the gospel after the manner of Christ's commandment in Luke 24:47. He does the same in Acts 3:19 when he said, "Repent ye therefore and be converted, that your sins may be blotted out when the times of refreshing shall come from the presence of the Lord." Therefore, in Acts 2:38 the command to be baptized is to be connected to the words, "Repent—for the remission of sins."

Both Mark 1:4 and Luke 3:3 record that John the Baptist preached "the baptism of repentance for the remission of sins." Like John, Peter was proclaiming the baptism of repentance for the remission of sins. However, now it is to be administered "in the name of Jesus Christ" and it is associated with "the gift of the Holy Spirit."

We must not forget that Peter was responding to the question: "What shall we do?" Inherent in that question is the question: "How can we escape the consequences of our sin?" His answer was "Repent of your sins and receive the cleansing of your sins through Jesus Christ whom you have crucified." It was Jesus Christ whom they had rejected as the Messiah. It is that same Jesus whom they must now acknowledge as the Redeemer. Baptism was the visible sign of their inward repentance and the washing away of their sins and the acknowledgement that Jesus was both Lord and Christ.

The record of the Book of Acts establishes the consistent practice of baptism in the New Testament church. Acts 8:12 tells us that when the Samaritans believed, "they were baptized, both men and women." Acts 8:37-38 records the baptism of the Ethiopian eunuch after his confession: "I believe that Jesus Christ is the Son of God." Acts 10:47-48: Cornelius and the Gentiles gathered at his home were baptized with water after they had received the Holy Spirit. See also Acts 16:30-33 for the record regarding the Philippian jailor and Acts 19:4-6 regarding the disciples at Ephesus. It appears that the assumption is made that upon evidence of faith in Christ baptism was to be administered.

The Promised Spirit

And ye shall receive the gift of the Holy Spirit.

a. It is not within the scope of this book to consider and try to resolve all the difficulties inherent in this text. In chapter seven of his comprehensive work, *The Work of the Holy Spirit*, Abraham Kuyper refers to the problems encountered in Acts 2 as "very intricate and hard to explain; and he who earnestly tries to understand and explain the event will meet more and more serious difficulties as he penetrates more deeply into the inward connection of the Holy Scripture." Dr. N. B. Stonehouse has given consideration to Acts 2:38 in an article appearing in the *Westminster Theological Journal* XIII (November 1950):1. In that article he wrote: "Acts 2:38 assuredly confronts the interpreter with weighty problems." The following comments on this text have been greatly influenced by this article.

b. What did Peter have in view when he stated, "and ye shall receive the gift of the Holy Spirit"? Was he referring to special gifts bestowed by the Holy Spirit or did his reference include the whole work of the Holy Spirit?

c. In response to the events which had accompanied the outpouring of the Holy Spirit upon the church, especially that the Cretes and Arabians heard the apostles "speak in our own tongues the wonderful works of God," they were moved by curiosity to ask: "What meaneth this?" That question may well have been in Peter's mind as he spoke the words of Acts 2:38. However, the chief concern of his hearers now was how they could get rid of their sins. It was precisely to that question that he was concerned to respond.

Peter's basic and primary demand is to call the hearers to repentance. The giving of the Holy Spirit is a gift and Peter's thought seems to be that the promise of the Spirit is assured upon the basis of conversion. We may not insist that Peter is setting forth the chronology of events in salvation as repentance, baptism and the gift of the Holy Spirit.

d. The evidence contained in Acts 2:37 shows that they had already received the gift of the Holy Spirit.

1. "Now when they heard this they were pricked in their hearts." That is the work of the Spirit. He convinces us of our sins and enlightens our minds. Ezekiel 36:26-27: "A new heart also will I give you, and a new spirit will I put within you: and I will take away the stony heart out of your flesh and I will give you a heart of

flesh. And I will put my spirit within you, and cause you to walk in my statutes, and ye shall keep my judgments, and do them.'' Their enlightened consciences had heard the gospel and now they were responding. Their hearts were smitten with the weight of their sin.

2. "What shall we do?" How can we get rid of the consequences of our sin? Is there any hope left for us now? This is the burden of their cry. Such a cry only comes forth from a new heart given by the Holy Spirit. They were sinners and now they knew it so they cried out for relief.

e. What is the extent of the meaning of the phrase, "ye shall receive the gift of the Holy Spirit"? Is it limited in its scope to the gift of salvation only, or does it include the gifts conferred by the Holy Spirit? Certainly there is a difference of opinion among Reformed theologians. However we answer that question we do well to keep in mind that it is the Spirit who distributes to us various gifts for service in the church. I Corinthians 12:4: "Now there are diversities of gifts, but the same Spirit.'' In this regard the whole chapter of I Corinthians 12 must receive consideration.

The following two paragraphs are quoted from Dr. Stonehouse's article already referred to. These two paragraphs constitute a portion of his conclusions after a study of various passages in the book of Acts.

> The question remains, however, whether possibly on certain occasions, and particularly in Acts 2:38, the designation "the gift of the Spirit" may not be employed somewhat more comprehensively than is suggested by the above. May it not include the gifts of a more distinctively religious and ethical character in addition to the miraculous charismata? Though Acts gives great prominence to the miraculous activity of the Spirit, and on occasion seems to refer to the Spirit as if there were no other kind of activity for which he was responsible, it is equally clear that the fruits of Pentecost are not restricted to miraculous activities. All of Christ's work is viewed as accomplished through the Spirit, and this would quite well allow that all of the gifts bestowed upon the church and upon individual Christians would be regarded as the gift of the Holy Spirit.

> It would be particularly appropriate to regard the qualifications of wisdom and faith mentioned in connection with the appointment of the seven as fruits of the Spirit (cf. Acts 6:3,5). But it may be that salvation itself, considered comprehensively as the total saving work of God, is understood as the work of the Spirit. The quotation from Joel concludes with the intimation that the age of the Spirit is to be a time of salvation (cf. 2:21). The "seasons of refreshing" in Acts 3:19 also appropriately describe the joyous benefits of salvation experienced by those who turn to the Lord.

f. Therefore, in the light of the immediate consideration of Acts 2:37 and its cry for help, together with Peter's response in verse 38, it appears that we are on solid ground when we conclude that the words "the gift of the Holy Spirit" include the saving benefits of Christ's redemption as applied to the believer by the Spirit. If, however, Peter was also answering their question in verse 12: "What meaneth this?" then "the gift of the Holy Spirit" has to be extended to include all the spiritual gifts which are bestowed by the Spirit upon God's redeemed people for the benefit of the church.

Verse 39:

For the promise is for you and your children, and for all who are far off, as many as the Lord our God shall call to Himself.''

"The Promise"

a. The question which we must face is: "What promise?" It would be strange indeed if the context of Peter's message did not answer that question. What did his audience understand by the words "The promise"?

b. "For the promise" must have some reference to his preceding words found in verse 38. There he had invited men to come to Christ for the remission of sins. Peter is saying: "This is the promised day of salvation. Christ is the promised Redeemer. Come and put your faith in Him and be washed clean." That is the central promise; but like a huge diamond, it has many facets. Let's look at some of Peter's remarks that refer to and give some explanation of the promise.

c. Verse 21: "And it shall come to pass, that whosoever shall call on the name of the Lord shall be saved." Those words conclude Peter's quotation from Joel chapter 2. Certainly those words *contain a promise*. It is the same promise, in its content, which Peter made in verse 38. It is an invitation to come to Christ.

d. Verse 28: "Thou hast made known to me the ways of life; Thou shalt make me full of joy with Thy countenance." With these words Peter concludes his quotation from Psalm 16. The rendering of these words in Psalms 16:11 is as follows:

Thou wilt show me the path of life: In Thy presence is fulness of joy.

Those words give expression to the *central theme of the covenant with Abraham:* namely, to enjoy union and fellowship with God. It is the echo of Genesis 17:7 where God promises to be a "God unto thee."

Peter sees the fulfillment of these words in Christ's resurrection and exaltation. Nevertheless, David certainly expressed *his own* personal hope of life and fellowship with God. In those same words every believer in Christ can express his faith of union and communion with God.

e. In verse 33 Peter points out that it was the *Holy Spirit* that had been promised through the prophet Joel that had been poured out that day upon the church. Joel's prophecy is a description of the *messianic age*. Peter is saying in verse 33 this is the New Age prophesied by Joel. The proof is that it is the exalted Christ who has poured out the promised Holy Spirit to dwell in the midst of His people.

Peter began his quotation from Joel chapter 2 at verse 28, but for our discussion at this moment, I believe that verse 27 is very significant.

And ye shall know that I am *in the midst* of Israel, and that I am the Lord *your God*, and none else: and *My people* shall never be ashamed.

Here God expresses His covenant relationship in three different ways: (1) "I am in the midst of Israel," (2) "I am the Lord your God," and (3) "My people shall never be ashamed." It is these covenant promises that find their *fulfillment* in the outpouring of God's Spirit upon all flesh.

Isaiah 59:20-21 sets clearly before us the close relationship existing between the covenant, the Redeemer and the giving of the Holy Spirit.

And the Redeemer shall come to Zion, and unto them that turn from transgression in Jacob, saith the Lord. As for Me, this is *My covenant* with them, saith the Lord: *My Spirit* that is upon thee, and *My words* which I have put in thy mouth, shall not depart out of thy mouth, *nor* out of the mouth of *thy seed, nor* out of the mouth of thy *seed's seed*, saith the Lord, from henceforth and *forever*.

It is with the redeemed that the Lord establishes His covenant. The language which the Lord uses is strikingly similar to that found in Genesis 17:7. It is the Lord's covenant which He establishes. It is an everlasting covenant. Its provisions extend to "thy mouth," "the mouth of thy seed," and "the mouth of thy seed's seed." The significant addition of the words "My Spirit" would indicate that it was through the spirit that the Lord would *accomplish* His covenant. Do not the events of Acts 2 and the words of verse 39 abundantly indicate the fulfillment and the continuity of this promise?

f. On the Day of Pentecost, Peter spoke to pious Jews that had gathered from many nations. They had traveled great distances to be in Jerusalem because they believed that they were the children of Abraham. They counted themselves to be children of the covenant promise found in Genesis 17. I remind you of the conversation between Jesus and the Jews recorded in John 8. In verse 33 they said: "We be Abraham's seed."

Is there any question in your mind as to what Peter's words, "for the promise," would mean to them? Peter, as a Jew, and speaking to Jews, knew very well that those words, understood in their Old Testament context, referred to God's promise made to Abraham and subsequently confirmed to Isaac and to Jacob.

g. From these various arguments, we conclude that "the promise" of which Peter is speaking is the original covenant promise of Genesis 17:7 which is now seen in the light of the New Testament revelation. This understanding of "the promise" is confirmed by the words that follow.

"For the promise is for you and your children."

a. There is no question that the parents *and their children* are included in the promise. There is nothing in the text to restrict the age of the children referred to.

There is nothing in the teaching of Jesus which would give credence to a distinction being made between the children of the covenant in the Old Testament and the children of believers in the New Testament. *Peter sees no distinction in this text*. Rather, we see Peter placing the children in the same category as their parents in reference to the promise. This means that the promise is to the children as well as to the parents. The children have an interest in the promise.

Peter's reference to "the promise" and the relationship of children to that promise can be appreciated and something of its meaning grasped only in the light of the Old Testament promise of Genesis 17:7. That *was* God's promise and it was "an *everlasting* covenant, to be a God unto thee and to thy seed after thee." It does not appear that Peter's words can have any other reference or meaning.

In his book, *Christian Baptism*, John Murray writes on page 71: "Now, what does this imply? It demonstrates that Peter, in the illumination and power of the Spirit of Pentecost, recognized that there was *no suspension or abrogation* of that divine administration whereby children are embraced with their parents in God's covenant promise. It is simply this and nothing less that Acts 2:39 evinces."

Now it is certainly true that *believing Jews* receiving baptism in the New Testament church would be concerned about the relationship of their children in this new dispensation. For nigh unto 2000 years every male child had received circumcision as the sign of the covenant. It was a natural and legitimate question: "What must I *now* do with my children?" Peter answers that question on the inauguration day of the new dispensation. Children, along with their parents are the possessors of God's covenant promise. The covenant provisions are operative in the New Testament as well as the Old Testament. Peter simply repeats the original covenant promise and *states that it is applicable in the new administration of the covenant.*

b. David Kingdon, in his book, *Children of Abraham,* presents his arguments against children being included in the covenant promises in the New Testament administration. On page 34 he writes the following conclusion:

> I would argue then that the principle of believers and their seed no longer has covenantal significance, precisely because the age of fulfilment has arrived. The age of preparation has passed and the dispensational elements that were found in the covenant of promise in Genesis 17 are no longer operative, and it is to these dispensational elements that the principle of "thee and thy seed" is tied.

We have tried to show that the covenant promises do continue and still are in force in the New Testament administration. That is the force of Acts 2:39.

It appears to me that Kingdon's position simply does not do justice to an understanding of Acts 2:39. Kingdon devotes but one paragraph to this vitally important text. It appears in his book on pages 88-89. A correct understanding of that text announces the continuation of the principle of "thee and thy seed."

To take Kingdon's position is to do violence to the *words* of the covenant promise of Genesis 17:7. His argument fails to take into consideration that God declared it to be "an *everlasting covenant.*" Twice within the confines of this one verse, God includes the provision that "thy seed" is included in this everlasting covenant.

"And for all who are far off."

a. These words designate a third group to whom the promise is applicable. Here the gospel promises are extended beyond the borders of Israel "unto the uttermost part of the earth." The gospel invitation now reaches out to the Gentiles of every tongue and tribe and nation.

b. We see the beginning of the preaching of the gospel to Gentiles when Peter under divine constraint brings the gospel to Cornelius, a centurion stationed at Cesarea, recorded in Acts 10 and 11. In chapter 11, verse 14, it is reported that the angel commanded Cornelius to send for Peter, "Who shall tell thee words, whereby thou and *all thy house* shall be saved." So now the covenant promises are extended to Gentiles as Paul so clearly states in Galatians 3:14, "That the blessing of Abraham might come on the Gentiles through Jesus Christ." And verse 29: "And if ye be Christ's then are ye Abraham's seed, and heirs according to the promise."

As the Lord reaches out to the Gentiles, new covenant homes are established and in Christ the promises made to Abraham and his seed are claimed anew. So it is that the church is perpetuated throughout the ages.

"As many as the Lord our God shall call to Himself"

a. Peter is referring to what we refer to as effectual calling as opposed to a general invitation of the gospel. Paul has such a call in mind when I Corinthians 1:9 he writes: "God is faithful, by whom ye were called into the fellowship of His Son."

b. The Shorter Catechism no. 31 describes effectual calling as follows: "Effectual calling is the work of God's Spirit, whereby, convincing us of our sin and misery, enlightening our minds in the knowledge of Christ, and renewing our wills. He doth persuade and enable us to embrace Jesus Christ, freely offered to us in the gospel."

c. It appears to me that the words "as many as the Lord our God shall call to Himself" refers to the whole company of the redeemed. There does not appear to be any grammatical construction in the text to limit God's calling to any one of the three groups mentioned. Furthermore, the biblical teaching appears to refer the call of God to those who were near and to those who were far off. There is good reason to believe that Peter had Isaiah 57:19 in mind:

110

I create the fruit of the lips; Peace, peace to him that is far off, and to him that is near, Saith the Lord; and I will heal him (also quoted by Paul in Eph. 2:17).

It is the Lord who creates the praise that flows from the lips of men. It is the Lord who gives peace to both Jew and Gentile. It is the Lord who brings healing to the soul. In the light of Acts 2:39, it would appear that this healing *includes God's effectual calling.*

d. As we see from I Corinthians 1:9 it is the call of God that unites men to Christ. It is the purpose of God's call to *effect our fellowship* with God and with His Son. Was not that the essence of the covenant *promise to Abraham* in Genesis 17:7? God is faithful. He will perform His covenant promises in the effectual calling of His people.

Genesis 17:7 tells us *what* God will do. He promised fellowship with Himself. It remained for further revelation to tell us *how* this would be accomplished.

Verse 40:

With many other words he warned them; and he pleaded with with them, "Save yourselves from this corrupt generation" (NIV).

a. Peter reasoned with them out of the Scriptures and witnessed to them of the facts of the gospel. But he also exhorted them to repent, believe the gospel, and to separate themselves from the world.

b. Peter saw no problem in ascribing salvation to God's calling and also ascribing responsibility to men for rejecting the gospel.

Verse 41:

So then, those who had received his word were baptized; and there were added that day about three thousand souls (NASB).

a. God honors and uses the preaching of the Word. Three thousand souls who heard the gospel that day embraced the Savior. It was through the faithful preaching of the Word that God called these souls into His kingdom and to embrace the promise.

b. Those who believed the message were baptized as a sign of their repentance and their remission of sins through Christ. They heeded the apostolic exhortation not only to believe but to be baptized.

c. Those three thousand souls were formed into a distinct community based on the apostolic authority and teaching. Baptism constituted the initiatory rite for entrance into the community. So the New Testament church was born that day with three thousand souls as the first fruits. Baptism was clearly established as the sign of the covenant in the New Testament church. The old had now formally given way to the new and, at Christ's commandment, circumcision had given way to baptism in the name of the Father, and the Son, and the Holy Spirit.

111

d. In this verse those who believed and were baptized are referred to as "*three thousand souls.*" Notice the different language in Acts 4:4 where it refers to those who believed the message as "and the number of the *men* came to about five thousand."

From Genesis 46:25-27 we find that the designation "souls" represents men, women, and children. The end of verse 27 reads: "All the souls of the house of Jacob, which came into Egypt, were threescore and ten." Also in Romans 13:1, "soul" is used to designate persons: "Let every soul be subject unto the higher powers."

1. Acts 2:41 then is not speaking about three thousand men but three thousand people. It was those souls that were that day baptized and added to the church. We must grant that the text does not specifically state that women and children were included, but it would certainly be strange if no women or children were added to the church on that Pentecostal Sunday when the New Testament church was brought into being. Did Peter's reference that "the promise is unto you, and to your children" indicate that there were children present? Probably so. It certainly would be strange—if not unbelievable—if no women were present and included in the "three thousand."

Verse 42:

And they were continually devoting themselves to the apostles' teaching and to fellowship, to the breaking of bread and to prayer.

a. This verse describes the activity of the primitive New Testament church. Their close association shows the unity created by faith. It was a true communion of the saints. Truth bound them together in Jesus Christ.

b. They devoted themselves to the apostles' teaching. It is here that we find the obedience of the apostles and the church to the Great Commission of Matthew 28:19-20. They had been discipled and then baptized and now, they were being taught. But we also see the place of authority in the church given to the apostles. It was "the apostles' doctrine" that was taught. It is that doctrine to which the New Testament church is committed by Jesus Christ Himself in Matthew 28:20. The New Testament church is devoted to hearing the preaching of the Word. The proclamation of the Word is a central element in the New Testament church.

c. The *fellowship.* The citizens of the new community continued in fellowship. Fellowship with Christ binds together those who are united to Christ. There was separation from the world but a joining together of those who confessed Christ. There was a mutual concern for each other. *They bore one another's burdens.*

d. *"The breaking of bread."* The phrase "breaking of bread" does not always refer to the celebration of the Lord's Supper. Only the context can show if such celebrating is in view and in some cases we cannot be certain. However, it does appear that in this verse it does refer to the observance of the Lord's Supper. "The breaking of bread'' is stated as a separate item from the fellowship of the saints, thereby indicating something different from the fellowship.

e. *Prayer.* The New Testament church was given much to prayer. Some believe that the text should read ''the prayers.'' Possibly this refers to their own appointed seasons of prayer. However, at this time they also continued to meet in the temple and keep the times of prayer there. See Acts 2:46; 3:1.

f. So we have set before the church the *means of grace* by which Christ establishes and nourishes the church: the preaching of the Word, the two appointed sacraments (baptism and the Lord's Supper), and finally prayer. It also seems quite appropriate to think of fellowship in the New Testament sense as a means of grace. God's people need one another to exhort and to encourage each other in the daily stresses and strains of life.

Questions for Discussion:

1. What significant events occurred on the New Testament Pentecost?
2. What answer did Peter give to the question: ''What meaneth this?''
3. What is the significance of Peter's reference to Jesus as ''both Lord and Christ?''
4. Why did Peter's hearers cry out ''What shall we do?'' Do we need the same response?
5. Is it important to be baptized? Why?
6. How can dead men repent and exercise faith?
7. What was the promise made to ''you and your children''?
8. What time-limit did God place upon the promise in Genesis 17:7? Does this have any implications for us in the New Testament church?
9. Does Acts 2:39 have any hope for Gentiles?
10. Who were included in the ''three thousand souls'' who were baptized and added to the church? Were no women or children included?
11. How is the life of the New Testament church described? Is this a good example for us to follow?

17

JOHN'S BAPTISM

John 1:19-34

Introduction

1. Many heard and responded to the preaching of John the Baptist.

2. His message called men to prepare for the coming of the the Lord. His message was that men should repent of their sins and be baptized. "Repent ye for the kingdom of heaven is at hand" (Matt. 3:2).

By what authority did John baptize? Was it by divine or human authority?

Verse 19: The success of John's preaching caused quite a stir in Jerusalem, so much so that verse 19 seems to indicate that the Sanhedrin sent out an official delegation to find out what was going on. Their task was to find out who he was. "Who art thou?"

Verse 20: "I am not the Christ." Did the delegation ask John if he was the Christ? The question is not reported in Scripture but it seems clear that John knew that such a delegation was present and also its purpose. His answer was quite clear, "I am not the Christ."

Verse 21: "Art thou Elijah?" "Art thou the Prophet?"

a. Are you Elijah? Again his answer was, No. These men knew of the closing words of the Old Testament. Malachi 4:5: "Behold I will send you Elijah the prophet before the coming of the great and dreadful day of the Lord."

However, Matthew 17:10-13 records that Jesus refers to the prophecy of Malachi 4:5 and says that "Elijah is come already." He had suffered at the hands of the leaders even as Jesus Himself would also suffer at their hands. The disciples then understood that He spoke of John.

Because Elijah left the earth in a chariot of fire without passing through death, the Jews expected the person of Elijah to return in fulfillment of Malachi 4:5. However, Luke 1:15-17 resolves the problem. The angel's words make it clear that John was the answer to the prophecy in that he came "in the spirit and power of

Elijah, to turn the hearts of the fathers to the children and the disobedient to the wisdom of the just; to make ready a people prepared for the Lord.'' It is John the Baptist that Malachi 3:1 refers to as the forerunner of "the messenger of the covenant.''

   b. "Art thou the Prophet?" Again he clearly answered, No. The reference to a prophet leads us back to Deuteronomy 18:15-18. The prophecy seems to refer to a very special Prophet. "Unto Him ye shall hearken" (vs. 15). Though prophets had been sent to Israel in the past, there appears to be an understanding that "The Prophet" had not yet appeared before this time. Now the question was: Was John the prophet? He answers, No. Significantly, Peter in Acts 3:12-26 refers to the promised Prophet of Deuteronomy 18:15-18 and identifies Him as Christ, the Prophet whom the Jews had rejected and slain and whom Peter now declares to be the promised Savior.

Verse 22: "Who art thou?" Until this point they had only received negative answers. They have run out of suggestions as to who he is. They can't report negatives to the Sanhedrin so their last question is "What have you to say about yourself—who are you?''

Verse 23: This time he gives them an answer by quoting and applying to himself the words of Isaiah 40:3. "I am the voice of one crying in the wilderness, Make straight the way of the Lord.'' That identified him, his work, and his significant place in history. He was the forerunner of the Lord Himself. His answer should have moved them to give great consideration to his place and message. Certainly, it was a call to repentance. It was a call to make preparations to meet the Lord who must be close behind.

Verse 25: "Why then do you baptize if you are not the Christ, nor Elijah, nor the Prophet?''
   Doesn't this strike you as a strange question? They were perplexed. John denied being the Christ, Elijah, or the Prophet yet a significant part of his work was baptizing.
   By this statement they indicate that they expected Christ to come baptizing and that such activity would identify Him. Such expectation could only have been based on the Old Testament Scriptures. This should tell us two things: (1) That baptism was not something new but was known in the Old Testament. (2) There must be some reference in the Old Testament to someone coming who would baptize and that this activity would be a distinguishing factor.
   What Old Testament passages did the Jews have in mind when they looked for the Messiah to perform the work of baptism? We do not really know the answer to that question, but we can confidently point to Isaiah 52:13-15 and Ezekiel 36:25-28 as passages which must have been given some consideration. Because of the importance of these two passages, we shall very briefly consider their message.

Isaiah 52:13-15

These verses give the theme and summarize the contents of chapter 53.

Verse 13: Jehovah introduces "my servant." The servant acts wisely. He shall be exalted.

Verse 14: Here is the first part of a deep contrast. Many were astonished at Him because of terrible disfigurement in His appearance.

Verse 15: His disfigurement was for others. "He shall *sprinkle* many nations." He would cleanse nations. This refers to a rite of cleansing. See Leviticus 4:6; 8:11; 14:7. The servant was a Priest. Here is the second part of the contrast. Kings are speechless. Gentile kings bow before Him.

Ezekiel 36:25-28

Verse 25: "Then will I *sprinkle* clean water upon you, and ye shall be clean."

Again the rite of purification is in view. The sprinkling with clean water is to signify an act of consecration which the Lord declares that He will perform.

Verse 26: "A new heart also will I give you, and a new Spirit will I put within you. . . ."

Verse 27: "And I will put My Spirit within you, and cause you to walk in my statutes. . . ."

Verse 28: "And ye shall dwell in the land that I gave to your fathers; and ye shall be My people, and I will be your God."

There are obvious differences in these two passages yet they are both represented by the rite of "sprinkle"-ing. How can we reconcile the fact that sprinkling is applied to both?

We are back again to the *twofold work of redemption* which we pointed to in our study of Titus 3:3-7. Christ *accomplished* the work of salvation. In the Isaiah passage Christ cleansed the nations through his work of *expiation*. It is precisely that thought which the Hebrew word translated "sprinkle" conveys (NÂZÂH = naw-saw'). The price and penalty of sin is atoned for and therefore the cleansing is performed.

However, in the Ezekiel passage there is cleansing through *purification*. The Lord puts His Spirit within us and gives us new hearts. Here is the second part of the work of redemption; by the work of His Spirit within us He *applies* the redemption purchased by Christ. He sanctifies us unto Himself. That act of sanctification is represented in the Hebrew as being "sprinkle"-d. (ZÂRAQ = zaw-rak').

Hence, we find that the *atonement* purchased by Christ *and* the work of *regeneration*, or the new birth, are both represented by the ceremonial act designated as "sprinkling."

Why did the Jews expect Christ to come baptizing? Simply because of the work described in these two prophetical passages and referred to as "sprinkling."

It is through the work of Christ and the Holy Spirit that the covenant promise made to Abraham in Genesis 17 is to be fulfilled, i.e., "And ye shall be My people, and I will be your God" (Ezek. 36:28).

But now are we not in great difficulty? John 4:2 says, "Though Jesus Himself baptized not, but His disciples." Keep the problem in mind as we continue the passage.

Verse 26: "John answered them saying, I baptize with water; but there standeth one among you, whom ye know not."

a. Here is John's answer to the question: Why did he baptize if he wasn't the Christ, or Elijah, or the Prophet?

b. John's answer is recorded in verses 26-27. "I baptize with water." The thought seems to be, "I only baptize with water" or "All I do is to baptize with water." The unspoken question behind his statement is, "Is this all you expected the Christ, or Elijah, or the Prophet to do? Would simply baptizing with water fulfill those prophecies which you expect to see fulfilled?"

It was the *baptizing* rather than the preaching which caused the priests to question his activities. It was the priests who knew about the rites and ceremonies. It was not just anybody that could perform the rites of purification.

At this point in his response, it would be natural to expect some reference to another kind of baptism. If he only baptized with water then what was involved in the baptism of the Messiah? However, rather than continuing to discuss baptism, he points to the greatness of Christ. Even though Christ stood in their midst, they did not know Him.

Verse 27: Here he continues to point to Christ even as he had done in verse 15. He speaks of Christ's preeminence and at the same time refers to his own personal unworthiness. He was not worthy to even unloose the sandal-straps and remove the sandals from his feet. Humility could scarcely take a lower place.

Verse 28: These events took place at "Bethany beyond the Jordan, where John was baptizing."

Verses 29-34 record the events which transpired the next day.

Verse 29: As John saw Jesus approaching he pointed to Him declaring: "Behold, the Lamb of God that taketh away the sin of the world." In Christ the type of the sacrificial lamb was fulfilled. Christ was the actual sin offering. The offering required by Isaiah 52:13-15 and Isaiah 53.

Verse 30: Here he refers back to his statement of the previous day, recorded in verse 27; i.e., that the greatness of Christ far exceeded the person of John the Baptist.

Verse 31: It was John's duty to prepare Israel for His coming. Repent, the Messiah is coming.

Verse 32: At the baptism of Jesus, John witnessed the descent of the Holy Spirit upon Jesus. See also Mark 1:10.

Verse 33:

a. It appears that until the day of the baptism, John did not know that Jesus was the Messiah. However, by revelation he had been given the knowledge that the one on whom the Spirit would descend was the Messiah.

To this John adds, that *the one* who gave him this message also sent him to baptize with water. On the previous day the Jewish leaders wanted to know by what authority he performed the rite of baptism. Here is their answer. He did so by *divine commission*. His authority came from heaven. I seriously doubt that they would have accepted that explanation.

b. But there was another part to the revelation; a most significant part. The one on whom he saw the Spirit come down and remain *"He it is who baptizes with the Holy Spirit."*

Again, on the previous day John had stated that he baptized with water only but left unspoken anything about the baptism that Christ would baptize with. But now he discloses the content of the revelation that the Christ would baptize with the Holy Spirit.

Think of the great *significance* of that statement. First, it is Christ that would fulfill the hopes and expectations of those Old Testament prophecies which pointed to some great person to come. It is obvious that the Jews were looking for some such person.

Second, He would fulfill the expiation and the purification rite described in Isaiah 52:15 and Ezekiel 36:25 as "sprinkle"-ing. But now we clearly see that His sprinkling meant the *baptism of the Holy Spirit*. It meant the cleansing performed by the Holy Spirit at regeneration. It is that activity described in Titus 3:5: ". . . according to His mercy He saved us, by the washing of regeneration, and renewing of the Holy Ghost." The work of Christ in the atonement and the giving of "the promise of the Holy Ghost, He hath shed forth" (Act 2:33).

The sacrament is a visible representation designed to represent Christ and the benefits which He bestows upon His people.

Verse 34: With this verse the testimony of John is brought to its conclusion but also to its climax. His testimony was that this is the Son of God. He had been given the revelation concerning Christ. He had seen the Holy Spirit descend upon Him. He had heard the voice from heaven declare, "Thou art My beloved Son" (Luke 3:22). That terminology in the Gospel of John can mean nothing less than the second person of the Godhead, the divine Creator and the divine Redeemer. Matthew describes Him as Emmanuel, God with us (1:23).

Conclusions

We submit the following conclusions from this study of John 1:19-34.

1. Because of his work of baptism, the Jews concluded that John could be the promised Christ.

2. This event shows the importance of baptism to the Jews of Jesus' day. We can only wonder why such is missing in Judaism today.

3. The sprinkling of Isaiah 52:13-15 and Ezekiel 36:25-28 is in fulfillment of the covenant of grace and secures the provisions of the covenant.

4. Jesus is the offering of expiation promised in Isaiah 52 and 53.

5. Jesus' baptism is the baptism of the Holy Spirit. He it is that cleanses His redeemed people and brings them into covenant fellowship with the Holy Trinity.

Questions for Discussion

1. Why did the Jews want to know who John was?

2. By what authority did John baptize? Was it by divine or human authority?

3. What are the implications of the question posed to John: ''Why then do you baptize if you are not the Christ, nor Elijah, nor the Prophet?''

4. What is the difference between Isaiah 52:15 and Ezekiel 36:25? How can both activities be represented by sprinkling?

5. What connection do these two Old Testament passages have to the covenant of grace?

6. What significant position did John the Baptist hold?

7. What is the difference between the baptism of John and the baptism of Jesus?

8. How do we resolve the problem raised by John 4:2?

18

VARIOUS BAPTISMS

Hebrews 9:10

Introduction

1. In this lesson we want to look at the question of baptism in the Old Testament in the light of Hebrews, chapter 9, especially verses 10, 13, 19, and 21.
2. From this passage we want to consider two things:
   a. Purification baptism in the Mosaic law, and
   b. The mode of those baptisms.

Hebrews 9:10

They are only a matter of food and drink and various ceremonial washings— external regulations applying until the time of the new order (NIV).

a. The prior verses indicate that the author is dealing with the Mosaic law, its temple, and its regulation. Those Old Testament regulations and sacrifices were shadows of what was yet to come. They were only external things which could not cleanse the conscience of the worshiper.

The bloody sacrifices of bulls and goats were ineffectual to cleanse the conscience, otherwise they would have continued to be offered. See Hebrews 10:1-2.

It was the applications of the blood of Christ that set the guilty conscience free. That alone was effectual in making a free access to God (vs. 14).

b. "Washings." As we look at verse 10 let us first resolve the meaning of the original word which is translated "washings."

1. The original word is *baptismos*. It denotes ceremonial washing, ablution, with special reference to purification.

"Bap-tis-mos" is used in the following passages:
   a) Mark 7:4—translated "washing."
   b) Hebrews 6:2—translated "baptisms."

2. The word in all three passages has reference to ceremonial washings or as Hebrews 6:2 renders it "baptisms." It would then appear that in all three instances it could well be translated "baptism." The important thing to remember is that *baptismos* is a ceremonial rite representing purification.

c. Our text of Hebrews 9:10 refers to "various baptisms." The baptisms

120

referred to are the ceremonial baptisms under the Mosaic law.

It is significant that the purification baptisms are expressly referred to in the succeeding verses of this same chapter. Three times the writer illustrates what Old Testament ceremonial baptisms he had in mind. For the New Testament Christian those Old Testament illustrations are very informative. Let us look at them briefly:

Verse 13: "The blood of goats and bulls and the ashes of a heifer sprinkled on those who are ceremonially unclean sanctify them so that they are outwardly clean" (NIV).

The Old Testament reference is Numbers 19;11-22. We shall refer only to verses 16-19. The person who has touched the dead is unclean for seven days. These verses describe how the uncleanness is removed. Ashes from the sin offering are mixed with water. "A clean person shall take hyssop and dip it in the water, and sprinkle it on the tent and on all the furnishings and on the persons who were there, and on the one who touched the bone or the one slain or the one dying naturally or the grave" (vs. 18). The sprinkling was to be performed on the third and the seventh days.

But in Hebrews 9:14, we see that rite contrasted with the sacrifice of Christ's blood. It was the efficacious sacrifice. The Old Testament ceremony pointed to the work of Christ. It is significant that the type was performed by sprinkling. That being so, why should sprinkling not also represent the efficacious cleansing which is performed by baptism in the New Testament?

See verse 14 in NIV: "cleanse our consciences from acts that lead to death, so that we may serve the living God." Notice the sharp contrast between death and living.

In the Old Testament law death flows from sin. It is sin that leads to death. Before we can serve the living God, we need cleansing. We are desperately in need of purification. The dead cannot wash away the stains of sin. It is only the blood of Christ, the spotless Lamb, who can purge the guilty conscience from works that lead to death. It was His death for our death, His blood for our cleansing.

Verse 19: "When Moses had proclaimed every commandment of the law to all the people, he took the blood of calves, together with water, scarlet wool and branches of hyssop, and sprinkled the scroll and all the people" (NIV).

a. The Old Testament reference is Exodus 24:6-8. Israel was encamped at Mt. Sinai. The scene describes the ratification of the covenant. Moses read God's ordinances to all the people. They responded, "All the words which the Lord has spoken we will do." It appears that half of the blood of the sacrificial bulls was sprinkled on the altar. The other half he sprinkled upon the people declaring: "Behold the blood of the covenant, which the Lord has made with you in accordance with all these words." Hence the covenant was ratified and sealed by the sprinkling of the blood first upon the altar of sacrifice and then upon the people.

121

All the people took part in this ratification ceremony and Hebrews 10:19 says that Moses sprinkled "all the people." The text says it was done by hyssop. Did "all the people" include women and children?

    b. Again we have a ceremony of purification also performed by sprinkling. It is another illustration of the various baptisms spoken of in verse 10.

Verse 21: "In the same way, he sprinkled with the blood both the tabernacle and everything used in its ceremonies" (NIV).

    a. After its completion the tabernacle and all the vessels of divine service were purified and consecrated to God by the sprinkling of blood.

    b. The Old Testament reference is Leviticus chapter 8. In this second chapter we find the consecration of the tabernacle, the vessels and Aaron with his sons to the priesthood. All accomplished by sprinkling.

Verse 10: Refers to the anointing of the tabernacle and the vessels.

Verse 11: Says they were sprinkled 7 times.

Verse 19: Says that blood was sprinkled upon the altar and "around on the altar" (NASB).

Verse 30: Anointing oil and the blood were sprinkled upon Aaron and his sons; so they were sanctified. This consecration took 7 days.

    c. We have here the third example of Old Testament baptisms and again for the third time it was accomplished by sprinkling.

Verse 23: "Therefore it was necessary for the copies of the things in the heavens to be cleansed with these, but the heavenly things themselves with better sacrifices than these.

    a. Here it is expressly stated that these ordinances already referred to were rites of purification. The "various baptisms" referred to in verse 10 were various rites of purification.

Those Old Testament cleansings were real and effective only so far as they went but they did not remove the inward and spiritual defilement. The Old Testament tabernacle, sacrifices and purifications were but copies of the true spiritual realities. That which was foreshadowed required a superior sacrifice and a more efficacious cleansing. The following verse (vs. 11) tells us that the real sacrifice which really put away sin was the sacrifice of Christ.

    b. The purpose of the Old Testament rites of purification was to make them ritually clean so that they could serve and worship God. It therefore follows that the spiritual cleansing accomplished by the blood of Christ is to cleanse the people of God that they might serve Him. From verses 11 and 24, we discover that the sanctuary in which He ministers is the true heavenly tabernacle of which the Mosaic tabernacle was but a material copy. He entered the sanctuary made without hands.

It is the people of God who require that spiritual inward cleansing if they are to be truly God's people and He our God. We need the cleansing that only Jesus' blood can supply if we are to be free from defilement that He may dwell in us and we are to be consecrated to His worship and service. It is the church of God that is "being built together into a dwelling of God in the Spirit" (Eph. 2:22). It is the people of God who, "like living stones, are being built into a spiritual house to be a holy priesthood, offering spiritual sacrifices acceptable to God through Jesus Christ" (I Pet. 2:5).

It is significant that Peter represents this whole work of purification in the following words, "Elect according to the foreknowledge of God the Father, through sanctification of the Spirit, unto obedience and sprinkling of the blood of Jesus Christ (I Pet. 1:2).

Conclusions

Let us draw some conclusions from our study of the words "various baptisms" in Hebrews 9:10.

1. Baptism was not new in the New Testament but was established in the Mosaic law.

2. Baptism can be performed by sprinkling. The three examples in Hebrews 9:13, 19, and 21 were all baptisms by sprinkling. This denies the position that baptism must always mean immersion.

3. In the Old Testament there were "various baptisms." They are described as sprinklings of water alone, sprinklings of water and ashes, sprinklings of oil, and sprinklings of blood.

4. The biblical evidence points to baptism in its origin as performed by sprinkling and not by immersion. We do not find any New Testament evidence to the effect that a change in mode was made in the New Testament church. Baptism by sprinkling was in the Old Testament by divine commandment, therefore failing any clear evidence of change; biblical consistency demands that baptism by sprinkling be continued in the New Testament. This conclusion is certainly supported by I Peter 1:2.

Questions for Discussion

1. What is the meaning of baptism in the New Testament? See Westminster Shorter Catechism no. 94.

2. Was baptism known in the Old Testament? What was baptism called in the Old Testament?

3. What New Testament passages prove that baptism was known and practiced in the Old Testament?

4. What symbolic meaning did baptism have in the Old Testament?

5. What was used in the performance of the Old Testament baptisms?

6. What was the mode of baptism used in both the Old and New Testaments referred to in this chapter? How many times is the mode of baptism referred to in these passages?

7. What relationship did Christ have to those Old Testament baptisms?

8. Do we have any New Testament warrant for changing the mode of baptism?

19

BAPTIZED INTO JESUS CHRIST

Romans 6:1-14

Introduction

1. What is the significance of being baptized into Jesus Christ? Does Romans 6:3-4 teach us the mode of baptism?

2. For immersionists, Romans 6:3-4 is a very important passage. They conclude two things from this passage:

    a. The significance of baptism is in its commemoration of the burial and resurrection of Jesus Christ.

    b. From that naturally flows the mode of baptism which they believe to be represented in Romans 6:3-4. G. B. Wilson, a Reformed Baptist, writes in his commentary on Romans 6:3: "The believer's union with Christ is illustrated by the rite of baptism in the mode of immersion. The three actions therein are symbolic: into the water—death; under the water—burial; and out of the water—resurrection."

3. Though it might appear that Romans 6:3-4 indicates such symbolism, the question is: Is that really the meaning of the passage, and is the reference dealing with the mode of baptism?

Verse 1:

What shall we say then? Shall we continue in sin, that grace may abound?

    a. The question introduces us to the problem to be discussed in these verses. The problem arises out of the comment in the last verse of chapter 5: "But where sin abounded, grace did much more abound." Paul is dealing with the charge that salvation bestowed by the free and sovereign grace of God leads to unrighteousness. Shall we still live in sin, on the ground that thereby we may give an opportunity for the grace of God to be more abundantly exercised?

    b. This verse introduces us to the discussion involved in the next three chapters. The subject is the believer's relationship to sin, and his sanctification which flows out of his union with Christ.

Verse 2:

God forbid. How shall we who died to sin live any longer therein?

    a. Paul having raised the problem by means of a question strongly repudiates such a thought and then proceeds to give his reason, not in the form of an argument but in the form of another question. The form of the question *demands the answer* that a believer in Christ *cannot* continue in sin. But as Christians we must not miss the reasoning of Paul in this verse.

    b. "We who died to sin"

    1. That statement has far-reaching consequences for our daily Christian living. And we must not miss the point that he made this statement precisely with our daily living in view.

    2. We *must* not, as Christians we *cannot,* daily live in sin! The question persists: Why not? Paul simply answers, "we died to sin." But—you ask—what does that mean?

    What happens at physical death? The bond which united that person to this life and activity in this world has been severed. He is no longer active in this sphere of life. He is dead to all the relationships of this life. It is this analogy that Paul is applying to the realm of sin. We died to sin. The text is insisting on a *once-for-all* definitive separation with sin. It is precisely this event that identifies the *true Christian* believer. We no longer live in the realm or the sphere of sin. The believer has died to the kingdom of Satan and his sphere of sin, and darkness and death, and the kingdom of iniquity. The rule of that dominion has been broken because the believer has died to it. He no longer lives in that kingdom. It is no more the realm of his thought, affection, will, life, and action. Paul puts this thought rather vividly when he states in Colossians 1:13. Speaking of the activity of our Heavenly Father in our behalf he writes: "Who hath delivered us from the power of darkness, and hath translated us into the kingdom of His dear Son."

    The believer has died to sin once and he has been translated into another kingdom. So it is that the believer is dead to sin, and that means that he has been freed from its dominion and to the gratification which it may promise. To continue in sin would be utterly inconsistent with our death to sin and life to God.

    It is absurd for a person who has died to sin still to set his *affections* upon sinful desires and to be *governed* by sinful principles. If we live in sin, we have not died to it. If we are in Christ, we have been set free from bondage to Satan. We have been emancipated from the dominion of sin.

    3. Unless we appreciate Paul's argument in this verse and the radical meaning set forth we shall miss the full meaning of the following verses. What follows is the expansion of the thought conveyed in this verse. It is the death referred to in this verse that is the theme of verses 2-14. Twelve times the term *death* or *died* is used and the term *crucified* is used once.

Verse 3:

Or, do you not know that all of us who have been baptized into Christ Jesus have been baptized into His death? (NASB).

126

a. In this and succeeding verses, Paul gives us the explanation of the phrase, "We who died to sin." The idea is so revolutionary that it needs validating and explaining. When did we die to sin? What are the implications of that death?

b. He begins the explanation by an appeal to their knowledge of the *spiritual meaning* of baptism. The recipient of baptism professes to belong to Christ and avows a participation in the death of Christ.

c. His appeal to their knowledge of baptism indicates that they were aware of its place in the church and also the importance of baptism in the Christian profession. Their baptism was the sign and seal of membership in the church of Christ.

d. In this verse Paul affirms two things regarding baptism:

1. "Baptized into Christ Jesus." "All of us," every believer has been baptized into Christ. That statement simply means baptism into *union with Christ*. To get "into Christ" must mean to get into union with Him. Therefore, baptism signifies union with Christ and participation of all the benefits which He secured for His people.

2. "Baptized into His death." "If baptism signifies union with Christ, it must mean union with Him in all that He is and in all phases of His work as the Mediator. Christ cannot be contemplated apart from His work nor His work apart from Him. Neither can one phase of His redemptive accomplishment be separated from another. Therefore union with Christ, which baptism signifies, means union with Him in His death" (John Murray, *The Epistle to the Romans,* vol. 1, p. 214).

Keep in mind that Paul is explaining his statement, "We who died to sin," in verse 2. In beginning his explanation in verse 3, he first makes a statement of fact and then draws out an implication of that statement.

Everyone who has been baptized into Christ has been united to Him in an inseparable union. That's a statement of fact.

Union with Christ also means union with Him in His death. If baptism means union with Christ in His death, then believers died with Christ in His death. That's the implication. Here Paul is setting forth first the death of Christ and then the death of every believer.

Christ as our Saviour must be seen as our Substitute. He died for us. His death was a representative death. He died representing us. As we look to the cross, whom do we see dying there? We see God's people in the person of Jesus, their representative. The cross means our death. By means of union with Christ, His death became our death. We died to sin. Christ died on account of our sin, but we died to sin.

e. In this verse Paul is using the term "baptized" to represent the actual event of which water baptism is the sign and seal. It should therefore be evident that he is not speaking about water baptism but of the *true baptism* accomplished by the work of the Holy Spirit as set forth in Titus 3:5 as "the washing of regeneration, and renewing of the Holy Spirit."

Verse 4:

Therefore we have been buried with Him through baptism into death, in order that as Christ was raised from the dead through the glory of the Father, so we too might walk in the newness of life.

a. "Therefore," the first word in this verse, clearly links what he has just said with what he is going to say. He is going to draw a conclusion from his previous statement. Because we have been joined to Christ in His death, therefore we also were joined with Him in His burial. We were buried together with Him.

b. The verse is simply stressing the complete identification or union between Christ and His people. We were joined together in His death and we were joined together in His burial. Christ's death was our death, so His burial was our burial.

c. How were we buried with Him? Was it by our baptism? Not at all. The text says: "buried with Him through *baptism into death.*" In verse 3, we concluded that the phrase "baptized into His death" means that we were so united to Him that His death became our death, so here we have the same thought carried forward another step. We are buried with Him because we were united to Him in His death. Burial is the confirmation of death. Burial is the definitive expression of death. "Baptism into death" in this verse is the parallel expression found in verse 3, "baptized into His death," and has the same meaning.

d. "In order that as Christ was raised from the dead . . . so we too might walk in newness of life." Paul does not stop with Christ's death and burial but he extends the analogy between Christ and the believer, so as to include the resurrection. That's very significant in clarifying the question of baptism but even more so for our Christian living. In fact it would appear from the words of the text that Paul had contemplated our union with Christ in His death and burial in order that he may prepare the way for introducing the idea of a resurrection.

e. The whole purpose of Paul's discussion in this chapter is the life of the believer and God's requirement for righteousness and holiness in daily living. Where is the source of power to break the power of sin and daily walk with God? Paul says it is in *our union with Christ.* It is in our relationship to the death and resurrection of Christ.

f. When Paul reaches the subject of Christ's resurrection, he reaches the source of the power in the believer to live in holiness. It is Jesus' resurrection that guarantees for the believer the power of that resurrection to walk in a manner befitting the children of God.

g. In verse 2, Paul asserts that "we died to sin." In these verses he is answering the question: "How did we die to sin?" His answer is in verse 3 that we were "baptized into Jesus Christ." That means union with Christ. But now we see three parts of that union.

1. Verse 3: "baptized into His death." We were joined together with Him in death.

2. Verse 4: "buried with Him." We were buried together with Him.

3. Verse 4: "as Christ was raised . . . so we also." We were raised from death together with Him.

h. "So we too might walk in newness of life." We must not miss in our discussion the purpose of this whole passage. It is Paul's concern for holy living in the life of every believer. It is his concern that we no longer walk in sin but that we "walk in newness of life." It is that subject that drives him to a prolonged discussion of our union with Christ and the consequences of that union.

It is because Paul is dealing with our newness of life that what is thrust into the foreground in this passage is not the fact that Christ died and rose again for believers, but rather the fact that *believers died and rose again with Christ.*

i. The same power exemplified in Christ's resurrection is operative in the life of the believer. That is precisely Paul's teaching in Ephesians 1:19-20. The NIV renders it, "and his incomparably great power for us who believe. That power is like the working of His mighty strength which He exerted in Christ when He raised Him from the dead, and seated Him at His right hand in the heavenly realms." Christ lives as the resurrected Lord with efficacy, virtue, grace, and power accruing from His death and resurrection. And since believers have been raised with Him, they live in the abiding virtue, grace, and power of Jesus' resurrection life so that Paul can say "we walk in newness of life."

Verse 5:

For if we have been planted together in the likeness of His death, we shall be also in the likeness of His resurrection."

a. Verses 5 and 6 confirm the teaching in verse 4. They carry on the same thought in different terms. Believers shall walk in a new life because of their identification with Christ in His death and resurrection.

b. Again the theme of the verse is the inseparable union of believers with Christ. If we were united with Him in His death, we must also be united with Him in His resurrection. The word translated "planted" is found only here in the New Testament. It means: planted together, grown together, grown along with, united with. The term conveys the intimacy of the union which is here spoken of.

c. When Paul refers to the "*likeness* of His death" and "the *likeness* of His resurrection" he shows us that he is not speaking of our physical death and resurrection; he is dealing with our death to sin and our resurrection to the spiritual life; a new life. To die with Christ is, therefore, to die to sin, and to rise with Him is to rise to a life of new obedience. It is to live not to ourselves but to Him who died for us and rose again. Christ's resurrection is the pledge that we shall be partakers of the new life that is found in Christ.

d. Believers died and rose again with Christ. It is the burden of these verses to show that our relationship to Christ in these events constitutes the power, the dynamic, to live the life of death to sin and of the newness of obedience. The power and virtue emanating from the death and resurrection of Christ, viewed also as the believer's death and resurrection is to be a constant force in the daily sanctification of believers. The Westminster Confession of Faith, chapter 13, section 1, says: "They, who are once effectually called, and regenerated, having a new heart, and a new spirit created in them, are further sanctified, really and personally, through the virtue of Christ's death and resurrection, by His Word and Spirit dwelling in them: the dominion of the whole body of sin is destroyed, and the several lusts thereof are more and more weakened and mortified." Christ's resurrection life is an abiding fact, and it is in that resurrection life that believers share.

e. Too often we associate our union with Christ in His death and resurrection in the accomplishment of our redemption and forget completely this area of biblical teaching that also associates our union with Christ in the realm of our sanctification. We should give heed to Paul's determination to count all things but loss that he might know Christ and "the power of His resurrection and the fellowship of His sufferings, being made conformable to His death" (Phil. 3:10).

Our union with Christ makes impossible the inference that we may continue in sin that grace may abound. Grace reigns only through the mediation of Christ, and this mediation is operative for us through union with Him in the efficacy of His death and the virtue of His resurrection. See John Murray's commentary, vol. 1, p. 219.

f. Is it not significant that in verse 5 and the succeeding verses that the word "buried," or the thought of burial is found wanting in the text? If, as the immersionist claims, to be buried is the important item in the baptismal sequence, then it would surely have been retained throughout the passage.

Again, if immersion is a prerequisite to the sacrament of baptism, is it not strange that it is not so directed in Matthew 28:19 where Christ institutes the sacrament? Neither Christ nor the apostles gave any commandment to immerse. The commandment is to baptize.

Verse 6:

Knowing this, that our old man was crucified with Him, that our body of sin might be done away with, that we should no longer be in bondage to sin.

In this verse Paul states that as Christians we are to *know* three things which affect our daily walk:

1. We have been crucified with Christ.
2. Our old body of sin is destroyed.
3. We should no longer live in bondage to sin.

1. "That our old man was crucified with Him"

a. It is "our old man" who has been crucified. It is the corrupt and polluted nature which we had because of our *union with Adam*. The "old man" is the old sinful self. It is the unregenerate man in his total being. It is the "old man" that

130

Paul sees as the antithesis of the regenerated man, who is a new man in the totality of his being. The Christian is crucified with Christ that the power of sin might be broken.

b. It is that "old man," the unregenerate man, that "was crucified with Him." The tense speaks in the past tense. It is something already accomplished. The old, unregenerate man has died (vs. 2). He was crucified with Christ. The old man and the new man do not co-exist in the believer. The "old man" is not in the process of being crucified. We were crucified with Christ. Therefore it states that our old man has been put to death just as decisively as Christ died upon the accursed tree. When He died we died with Him. To suppose that the old man has been crucified and yet still lives is to contradict the meaning of crucifixion represented in the text. See Galatians 5:24.

c. I am only too conscious of the problem this passage raises. The question is: What about our daily life and experience? What about my sin?

The believer is a new man, a new creation, but he is a new man not yet made perfect. Sin dwells in him still, and he commits sin. He is the subject of progressive renewal. As Paul says in II Corinthians 3:18: "And we, who with unveiled faces all reflect the Lord's glory, are *being transformed* into His likeness with ever-increasing glory, which comes from the Lord, who is the Spirit." It is the grace of God working in us to renew us in His own image. But that work of renewal involves the activity of the regenerated man as Paul wrote in Romans 12:2: "Be not conformed to this world, but *be ye transformed* by the renewing of your mind, so that ye may prove what is the good and acceptable and perfect will of God." This is the progressive renewal of the new man. John Murray deals with this problem on pp. 217-219 in his book, *Principles of Conduct.*

d. In Romans 6:2 and the succeeding verses, Paul is dealing with the thought that believers died once to sin, and yet in Romans 7:14-25, he acknowledges that sin still lives in the believer. In the first case he is dealing with the definitive breach with sin. In the second case he is dealing with the fact that the believer is not yet perfect. Though it may be a problem to us, it is evident that Paul saw no incongruity in these two lines of thought.

2. "That our body of sin might be done away with"

a. The term "body of sin" should not give us any trouble. It is evident that Paul is referring to the "mortal body" as he puts it in Romans 8:11. Paul is simply recognizing that sin and sanctification are associated with the body. The body is conditioned and controlled by sin. It is the body that is employed and is the means for the gratification for sinful practices. The body is the instrument of a sinful soul.

b. The body is an integral part of our personality. It is the body that brings to expression the sinful thoughts and imaginations. Therefore Paul is concerned to point out that it is necessary that the body of sin be destroyed. Dying to sin

131

demands the destruction of the body of sin and a radical transformation to take place in the entire personality.

c. We must not miss what Paul is saying here in this part of the verse. The old man is crucified with Christ, in order that the body of sin might be destroyed. The purpose of the crucifixion of the old man is the destruction of the body of sin. "We died to sin."

3. "That we should no longer be in bondage to sin"

a. Again, we have another purpose clause. Here is another benefit flowing from our crucifixion with Christ. We were crucified with Christ in order that we should no longer serve sin. Our bondservice to sin is to be terminated.

b. Unbelievers are the slaves of sin. Notice that this slavery is voluntary. It serves the desire of the unregenerate nature, that "old man." But the "new man," the regenerate man, is released from bondage to sin. If we are still living in bondage to sin then we cannot be counted as having been crucified with Christ.

The Symbolism of Immersion

a. We have previously pointed out that for the immersionist the three actions of the baptismal ceremony are symbolic:
1. Into the water—death.
2. Under the water—burial.
3. Out of the water—resurrection.

We want to look at that symbolism for a few minutes.

b. It is unquestionable that what Paul is writing about in Romans 6:1-14 is the believer's union with Christ. How did Paul illustrate that union in these verses?
1. Verse 3: "baptized into His death."
2. Verse 4: "baptism into death."
3. Verse 4: "buried with Him."
4. Verse 4: "as Christ was raised up—even so we."
5. Verse 5: "we have been planted together."
6. Verse 5: "we shall be also in the likeness of His resurrection."
7. Verse 6: "crucified with Him."

It is easy just to look at verse 4 and then insist that only immersion provides any analogy to burial. But are we justified in isolating this one verse from the context? Paul illustrates our union with Christ by our being planted together and being crucified together. Surely, they will not bear the analogy to immersion so immersionists isolate verse 4 to maintain their position.

c. Crucifixion

Christ died on a cross. It is dangerous to forget that fact. But crucifixion cannot be symbolized by immersion. Therefore because baptism has to fit into his threefold meaning, the immersionist actually forgets that Christ died by crucifixion when he performs the rite of baptism.

d. Burial

Christ's body was laid in a sepulchre. His dead body was laid in a room and the door was closed. The body at burial was *not* put down into the earth. That form of burial is found chiefly in Western culture and also where Western culture has had its influence. Therefore, the burial of Jesus has no resemblance to our manner of burial. Immersion in no respect symbolizes the burial of Jesus.

e. Resurrection

We are not told how Christ arose but it is certain that He did *not come up* out of the earth because He was never put down into the earth. Luke 24:12 says: "Then arose Peter, and ran unto the sepulcre; and stooping down, he beheld the linen clothes laid by themselves. . . ."

It is apparent that baptism does not symbolize the resurrection of Christ.

f. When we see all of Paul's expressions and their meaning, we see that burial with Christ cannot be appealed to as providing an index to the mode of baptism. There are many aspects to our union with Christ. It is arbitrary and unwarranted to select one aspect as setting forth the mode of baptism. See John Murray's work, "Christian Baptism," pages 29-33.

Verse 7:

For he that hath died is justified from sin.

a. This is a continuation of the thought introduced in the latter part of verse 6. This verse gives us the ground or basis for the prior statement. The believer cannot continue in bondage to sin, because he that has died with Christ is justified, and therefore free from sin and its dominion.

b. "Justified from sin" means to be delivered from sin by justification. Deliverance from sin is twofold. First, there is the judicial deliverance by God's declarative act releasing us from the penalty of sin. But in the context of verse 7, Paul is dealing with the power of sin; therefore to be justified is also to be delivered from the power of sin. Sin has no further claim upon the person who has been justified. To be justified is to be freed from the dominion of sin. See Westminster Shorter Catechism, Q. 33.

c. We have failed to appreciate that justification is also the basis for the deliverance from the power of sin. The judicial declaration of God is the basis of our justification, but it also lies at the basis of sanctification.

Verse 8:

Now if we died with Christ, we believe that we will also live with Him.

a. The emphasis in the previous verses has been on our union with Christ in His

133

death but now the emphasis changes to the thought of our union with Christ in His resurrection.

b. "We believe"—this is the language of faith, but that faith is grounded in the certain consequence of our union with Christ. It is an article of faith, not of conjecture, that we also shall live with Him even as we died with Him.

c. Paul's thought is that we participate in the resurrection life now. This idea comes to clear expression in Colossians 3:1: "If ye then be risen with Christ, seek those things which are above, where Christ sitteth on the right hand of God."

Because of our union with Christ we have already participated in a spiritual resurrection and we shall no doubt take part in the bodily resurrection.

d. If we have been raised with Christ to a new life then it follows that we can no longer live a life that is devoted to sin. We should be devoted to a new life of righteousness. We can no longer live in the dominion of sin. It is Jesus' resurrection that guarantees to the believer the power to live the new life.

Verse 9:

Knowing that Christ being raised from the dead dieth no more; death no more hath dominion over Him.

a. Here is the ground of our assurance. It is in Christ. The resurrected Christ is no more liable to death. Death has no power over Him.

b. Death hath no more dominion over Him. This implies that death did at one time rule over Him. That was because He was vicariously identified with sin. Christ died once to bear the sins of His people. See Hebrews 10:26-28. His resurrection is the guarantee that He has forever vanquished the power of death. He is henceforth free from its domain.

Verse 10:

For the death that He died, He died to sin, once for all; but the life He lives, He lives to God (NIV).

a. Paul never wearies of his considerations of the work of Christ. It is a theme that is ever before him.

b. There was purpose in Christ's death and there was efficacy in Christ's death. "He died to sin." He died to destroy the dominion of sin. He submitted Himself to the dominion of death in order to free His people from the dominion of sin. "God made Him who had no sin to be sin for us, so that in Him we might become the righteousness of God" (II Cor. 5:21, NIV). It was by His own death that He destroyed the power of sin.

c. The once-for-all sacrifice demonstrates the efficacy of the sacrifice. "By His own blood He entered in once into the holy place, having obtained eternal redemption for us" (Heb. 9:12). He submitted to the power of death once in order that He might destroy its power.

d. Having died to sin once He now lives unto God. Having accomplished the work of redemption, He ever lives unto God. His relationship to sin was but temporary but His relationship to God is eternal.

Verse 11:

Even so reckon ye also yourselves to be dead unto sin, but alive unto God in Christ Jesus.

a. Having clearly set forth the *union* with Christ by every believer, not only in redemption but also in sanctification, Paul now dwells upon its application to daily living.

b. The words of the exhortation are in the imperative mood. It is not just a suggestion; it is a divine command. It is God's word to His people.

c. "Even so" or "likewise" or "in the same way" introduces us to the parallelism begun in verse 10 and concluded in verse 11. (vs. 10) *Christ* died to sin but now He ever lives unto God, *even so we* (vs. 11) must reckon ourselves dead to sin and alive unto God.

d. "In Christ Jesus": Even in the exhortation Paul emphasizes our union with Christ. The exhortation is based on what has been presented as fact. Because of our union with Christ, we died and rose again with Him. That is fact. Now we are exhorted to live according to those facts. What is true in itself, should be true in our convictions. This truth has to be *part of our consciousness* so that we live by it. We are to see things as they really are. Sin blinds men to the truth. We are to look upon ourselves as dead to sin, but alive unto God. We have been freed from the dominion of sin so that we might walk in true holiness. Believers are alive unto God in Jesus Christ and receive from Him the virtue whereby their spiritual life is begun, maintained and perfected.

e. Paul is exhorting us to come to grips with things as they really are. That which occurs in the life of every believer is analogous to that which occurred when Jesus died and rose again. Jesus died once and he rose again once. Even so, the soul that has been joined to Christ in faith has also died to sin once and risen again to a new life in Christ Jesus. As true believers in Jesus Christ, we have no trouble in believing in His death and resurrection. Why is it that we have trouble in exercising our faith to see also our *own death and resurrection?* The death and resurrection of the believer are just as decisive and definitive as those events in the life of Jesus. We must let nothing obscure this parallelism.

Verse 12:

Therefore let not sin reign in your mortal body, that ye should obey it in the lusts thereof.

a. Verses 12-14 contain the gospel imperatives for every believer. These verses contain what should be every Christian's response to the fact that we "died to sin."

b. Again we have the language of exhortation based on the fact that we are "alive unto God."

But the exhortation is also based on his statement of fact in verse 14: "For sin shall not have dominion over you." "For sin shall not be your master" (NIV). It is because sin is not our lord and master that Paul can write, "Therefore let not sin reign in your mortal body." We have been emancipated from the slavery of sin. Sin does not have dominion over us, therefore we must not allow it to reign in us.

c. "Let not sin reign." Sin is not to be on the throne of our hearts. It is not to have dominion. It is not to be the master of our lives. But in this passage Paul does not teach us that we can attain a life of sinless perfection. It is because he recognizes the presence of sin that he exhorts "let not sin reign." In the process of sanctification it is our responsibility to see that sin does not reign in us.

d. The "mortal body." It is the body that is the instrument by which the sins of the heart find expression. In the reign of sin the lusts of the body demand obedience. Matthew Henry: "It was sin that made our bodies mortal, and therefore do not yield obedience to such an enemy." Christ demands holiness in our physical bodies. The meditations of the heart come to expression in the acts of the body—whether good or evil.

Verse 13:

Do not go on presenting the members of your body to sin as instruments of unrighteousness; but present yourselves to God as those alive from the dead, and your members as instruments of righteousness to God.

a. This verse is substantially what was presented in verse 12 but in an expanded form. It presents the subject under the analogy of two masters. Which one are we serving?

b. The first master presented is sin. We are not to dedicate our bodies as weapons in the service of unrighteousness. Our bodies are not to be used to advance the cause of sin. We have died to sin "that the body of sin might be done away" (vs. 6).

c. The second master presented is God. Here we are exhorted to dedicate ourselves unto God in a once-for-all act of self-surrender. The total faculties of the believer, his heart and mind and body are to be consecrated to God's service without any reservation. Committed to the service of righteousness.

Again the exhortation is based upon the fact that we have died to sin but are now alive unto God.

Verse 14:

For sin shall not have dominion over you: for ye are not under law, but under grace.

a. "For sin shall not have dominion over you" is a statement of assured fact.

We cannot "continue sin" nor "Yield the members of our bodies as instruments of unrighteousness unto sin." "For sin shall not have dominion over you." To those who are united to Christ the dominion of sin has been broken. This is the great argument which Paul has been stating from verse 2 on, that those who are in union with Christ "died to sin."

b. "For ye are not under law, but under grace." Why could Paul be so sure that the Christian was no longer under the dominion of sin? His answer: Because we are no longer under law, but under grace. It is precisely because we are not under law, but under grace that sin shall not have dominion over us.

What does the designation "law" refer to here? The correct translation is "not under law" not as the King James translation "not under the law." "Law" in this context is not a specific reference to the Mosaic economy but to law in general.

God deals with all men covenantally. We have been dealing at length with the covenant of grace, but there is another covenant in Scripture, that is, the covenant of works, or as it is also called, the covenant of life, because life was promised on condition of obedience. As Paul so clearly teaches us in Romans 5:12, all men are under the curse and penalty of that covenant of which Adam was our representative. "Therefore, just as sin entered the world through one man, and death through sin, and in this way death came to all men, because all sinned" (NIV). The demand for perfect obedience still is binding upon all men. Like Adam all men sin. "Like Adam, they have broken my covenant" (Hos. 7:4, NIV).

The "law" to which Paul refers in Romans 6:14 is the moral law as a covenant of works. It is that law to which all men are subject. And as the covenant of works it demands perfect obedience.

The following is quoted from John Murray's commentary, p. 229:

> In order to understand the force of the clause in question it is necessary to state what law can do and what it cannot do, and it is in the light of what it cannot do that the meaning of "under grace" will become apparent.
> 1. What Law Does:
> a) Law commands and demands.
> b) Law pronounces approval and blessing upon conformity to its demands (Rom. 7:10; Gal. 3:12).
> c) Law pronounces condemnation upon every infraction of its demand (Gal. 3:10).
> d) Law exposes and convicts of sin (Rom. 7:7, 14; Heb. 4:12).
> e) Law excites and incites sin to more aggravated transgression (Rom. 7:8, 9, 11, 13).
> 2. What Law Cannot Do:
> a) Law can do nothing to justify the person who has violated it.
> b) Law can do nothing to relieve the bondage of sin; it accentuates and confirms that bondage.

Therefore, if "law" has reference to the covenant of works, so also does "grace" have reference to the covenant of grace. By grace we are God's covenant people. We now see how God fulfills His great promise of Genesis 17:7. "I will be a God unto thee." He joined us together covenantally "into Christ." Isn't that what Paul is stressing throughout these first 14 verses of Romans 6? We died in our covenantal union with Christ, we were buried in our covenantal union with Christ, and we rose again in our covenantal union with Christ. So it is that we died to sin, its curse, and its dominion. By grace we are God's covenant people; therefore "sin shall not have dominion over you: for ye are not under law, but under grace." "Shall we continue in sin, that grace may abound? God forbid. How shall we, that are dead to sin, live any longer therein?" It is the covenantal relationship that settles the question of life and death, sin and righteousness.

Conclusions

1. Paul's concern in this passage is the everyday life of the Christian. He wants to show that Christians are not free to continue in sin.

2. We cannot continue in sin because we have been "baptized into Jesus Christ" with the full meaning that Paul pours into those four words.

3. We cannot continue in sin because we were joined to Christ in His death, burial, and resurrection. We were crucified with Him. When He died, we died. We died to sin.

4. It is through the true spiritual baptism that we "were baptized into His death."

5. We therefore conclude that this passage does not speak to the question regarding the mode of baptism but to our union with Christ and the daily consequences of that union.

It is possible that you have wondered why this long discussion on Romans 6:1-14. Why didn't the study finish at verse 4 or 5? The answer is as follows:

a. To be "baptized into Jesus Christ" is to be brought into covenant relationship with Him. It is to be in union and communion with God our Creator and Redeemer. This is the glorious teaching of Scripture which has been lost to the church of today.

b. It is my belief that verses 4-14 represent the divine commentary and application on the words "baptized into Jesus Christ." Therefore they cannot be divorced from verses 1-3.

c. To be in covenant relationship with Christ brings a corresponding responsibility to live as covenant people. That is Paul's concern in this passage. The teaching of these verses is extremely relevant to the daily walk of every Christian. The covenant relationship demands a covenant response in both faith and life.

Questions for Discussion

1. If I have been "saved," am I then free to sin? How does Paul answer that question?

2. What is the Christian's relationship to sin? Is this true of every Christian?
3. Are you a citizen of a kingdom? If so, which kingdom? Who is the king?
4. Is it possible to have been baptized without having been baptized with water? How can that be?
5. What is the meaning of the phrase "baptized into Jesus Christ"?
6. Why is Paul dealing with the question of being baptized into Christ?
7. From what bondage have we been freed?
8. If we are living in bondage to sin what is the inference that we must draw?
9. Does immersion performed in the rite of baptism symbolize all the figures of speech showing our union with Christ as given in this passage? Does immersion clearly represent the burial of Christ?
10. Have you been crucified with Christ? If so, when?
11. Why do we know that we can overcome sin in our daily walk?
12. How is the covenant promise of Genesis 17:7 brought to realization?

20

THE BAPTISM OF JESUS

Mark 1:9-11
Matthew 3:13-17

Introduction

1. In our previous studies we have concluded that the rite of baptism is the New Testament sign of the covenant of grace and that it replaces the Old Testament rite of circumcision.

2. It is now time first to discuss the mode of baptism and then to give some consideration to the question of infant baptism. I believe that this is the correct order because if we should conclude that immersion is the correct mode of baptism then the question of infant baptism would be resolved.

3. This is the first of two studies dealing with actual baptisms in the New Testament. The purpose in these studies is to look at the record of these baptisms to discover if we can, the mode of baptism from the facts and circumstances given in each case.

4. In this study we want to consider the baptism of Jesus by reference to Mark 1:9-11 and then Matthew 3:13-17.

Was it imperative that Jesus be baptized? Why? Was Jesus' baptism by immersion? When we discover that all four Gospel writers make some reference to the baptism, or the events related to it, then we conclude that this was an important event in Jesus' life.

Mark 1:9-11

And it came to pass in those days, that Jesus came from Nazareth of Galilee, and was baptized of John in Jordan. And straightway coming up out of the water, he saw the heavens opened, and the Spirit like a dove descending upon him: and there came a voice from heaven, saying, Thou art my beloved Son, in whom I am well pleased.

a. This is Mark's record of Jesus' baptism by John the Baptist.
Verse 9 tells us that He "was baptized of John *in* Jordan."
Verse 10 tells us that as He was "coming *up out* of the water"—the Spirit

140

descended upon Him. It is on the basis of the language used in these two verses that immersionists have concluded that Jesus was immersed.

b. However the text is significantly silent as to the mode of baptism. The record does not describe an act of immersion. There is no record of John putting Jesus down into or under the water. But the immersionist points out that Jesus was baptized "in Jordan" and that it is recorded that he came "up out of the water." But does that language require immersion? The language can be understood as simply saying that Jesus walked into the Jordan, that the baptism took place, and that as He walked out of the Jordan the Spirit descended upon Him. The text does not state that an immersion took place. It does not appear that Mark was addressing himself to the question of the mode of baptism. The question was probably of no concern to him. Jesus' baptism was an Old Testament rite and in the Old Testament symbolism baptism by immersion was unknown. See chapter 18 for a discussion of Old Testament baptisms.

c. Actually Mark in his characteristically cryptic style records the baptism event in verse 9 by simply stating Jesus came "and was baptized of John in Jordan." It was Mark's concern to record the witness of the Spirit and of the Father on this occasion. Verse 10 is given over to the witness of the Spirit by stating that after the baptism the heavens opened and the Spirit descended upon Jesus. Verse 11 records the witness of the Father. After the descent of the Spirit, the Father's voice is heard to declare that Jesus was His beloved Son in whom He was well pleased.

d. It is recorded in verse 8 that John baptized by water but that Jesus would baptize with the Holy Spirit. Verse 10 records that the Spirit descended upon Jesus. For the believer, baptism represents washing by the Holy Spirit, but the Spirit descends upon us. The immersionists symbolism of going down into the water and coming up out of the water representing death and resurrection is certainly wanting in Jesus' baptism.

Matthew 3:13-17

a. Matthew's account of Jesus' baptism is recorded in Matthew 3:13-17. He gives us much more detail than Mark. Matthew's account records significant details not recorded in any other Gospel.

b. The Nature of John's Baptism

Matthew's Gospel records something of the nature of John's baptism. Here we discover that his message and his baptism were inseparable.

Verse 6: Those coming to John "were baptized of him in Jordan, confessing their sins."

Verse 8: His message was: "Bring forth therefore fruits meet for repentance."

Verse 11: It was a baptism of repentance: "I indeed baptize you with water unto repentance."

John's baptism was for sinners. It was a repentance and a baptism in preparation for receiving the coming King. See verses 2-3.

 c. John Resists Jesus' Request

Verse 14 presents us with a great surprise. It is here that we discover that John resisted Jesus' request for baptism. Why should that be? What caused John's refusal?

Verse 14 (KJV): "But John forbade Him saying, I have need to be baptized of thee, and comest thou to me?"

(NIV): "But John tried to deter Him."

(NASB): "But John tried to prevent Him."

John recognizes that the character of Jesus puts Him beyond the need of his baptism. John's baptism was for repentant sinners, but it is evident that John did not consider Jesus a sinner, and he certainly did not call Him to repentance. John's response, "I have need to be baptized of thee," shows that he was convinced that Jesus was the Messiah and that He would baptize with the Holy Spirit. John's baptism was in preparation for the coming of the King. The King is here!

John considered it totally improper that he should baptize Jesus. What justification did he have, a sinner, who only baptized with water, to baptize the holy Jesus who would baptize with the Holy Spirit?

 d. What Changed John's Mind?

What compelling argument did Jesus present to John that changed his mind?

Verse 15 (NASB): "Permit it at this time; for in this way it is fitting, for us to fulfill all righteousness."

(NIV): "Let it be so now; it is proper for us to do this to fulfill all righteousness."

(Phillips): "It is right for us to meet all the Law's demands."

 1. When Jesus stated, "Permit it at this time," he agreed with John. He was not a repentant sinner in need of baptism. Yet, Jesus persists. There was a necessity why He should be baptized. He states the reason in the words, "for in this way it is fitting for us to fulfill all righteousness." It is that statement that changed John's mind. But what does it mean?

 The problem is the word "righteousness." Though the word "law" does not appear in the original, as translated by Phillips, nevertheless, it does appear that "righteousness" here does have reference to the Old Testament law. That was the righteousness of God. "Righteousness" in this context was what Jehovah required. "And it shall be our righteousness if we observe to do all these commandments before the Lord our God, as He hath commanded us" (Deut. 6:25).

Righteousness involves obedience to the law of God. "It is proper for us to do this to fulfill all righteousness." With these words Jesus laid upon John the divine necessity to perform the baptism. John must have so understood it for he presents no further objections. It was that statement that changed his mind. But notice carefully that Jesus included Himself when He referred to "us." It was a divine necessity that He submit to baptism by John. It was a duty imposed upon Him.

We learn from other passages of Scripture that Jesus was subject to the law. It is therefore significant that Paul writes in Galatians 4:4: "God sent forth His son, made of a woman, made under the law." Jesus as our Redeemer kept both the moral and ceremonial law. Luke 2:21 records the circumcision of Jesus in accordance with Leviticus 12:3. Luke 2:22-23 records Jesus' presentation in the temple in accordance with Exodus 13:2, 12, 15. In Luke 22:8 we have the record of Jesus keeping the passover feast. These examples show His subjection to the Old Testament law.

2. Now the logical question which presents itself is: What Old Testament law did Jesus obey at His baptism? If Jesus was not a repentant sinner, then what was the meaning of His baptism?

The text does not state the Old Testament reference but there is one Old Testament rite that fits the occasion. It is described in Numbers 8:6-7: "Take the Levites from among the children of Israel, and cleanse them. And thus shalt thou do unto them, to cleanse them: Sprinkle water of purifying upon them."

Verse 5 informs us that this is a divine commandment for these words were spoken by Jehovah to Moses. The text describes the consecration of the Levites to priestly service. It presents us with the formal ceremony in which this setting apart to God's service was performed. They were sprinkled with the water of purification.

It is beyond question that Jesus became and continues to be our great High Priest. See Hebrews 3:1; 4:14 and 9:11. But at this point it is important that we give some consideration to Hebrews 5:5.

"So also Christ did not glorify Himself so as to become a high priest, but He who said to Him: 'Thou art my Son, Today I have begotten Thee' " (NASB).

The prior verse reminds us that no man takes the office of a high priest unto himself. That's God's decision and not within the ability of any man to choose. So, the text informs us, Christ did not assume to Himself the glory associated with the office of high priest. He did not assume the priestly office of His own initiative. The One who called Him to this high office was His heavenly Father. The writer of the Hebrews quotes Psalms 2:7 as identifying Jesus as being called to the office of high priest. It was the Father who called Him that referred to Him as "My Son."

Matthew 3:17 tells us that after the baptism and after the Holy Spirit had descended upon Him, the Father declared, "This is My beloved Son, in whom I am well pleased.'' These words were pronounced only after some significant event had taken place. The important event on this occasion was Jesus' baptism.

3. The baptism of Jesus was the ceremonial act of His consecration to His high priestly office in accordance with the Old Testament law. Surely that was a significant event. But in Hebrews 7:11-14, we are reminded that Jesus came from the tribe of Judah and not from the Levitical line. Though, not of the priestly line, He had been divinely appointed; therefore He must needs fulfill all righteousness; therefore He insisted on the baptism by John. He submitted to the divine ordinance of consecration as set down in Numbers 8:6-7. That text states that the rite of consecration was performed by *sprinkling*. There is no reason to believe that the divine commandment was not followed on this occasion. It therefore follows that Christ was not immersed by John the Baptist—but sprinkled.

e. The Language of Verse 16

It is now appropriate that we give some consideration to the language of Matthew 3:16:

"And Jesus, when He was baptized, went up straightway out of the water" (KJV).

"And after being baptized, Jesus went up immediately from the water" (NASB).

"As soon as Jesus was baptized, He went up out of the water" (NIV).

"Then John agreed to his baptism. Jesus came straight out of the water afterward" (Phillips).

The language in each of the above versions describes two distinct events and not one as the immersionist would have us believe. First, Jesus received the rite of baptism, secondly Jesus went up immediately out of the water. The language is a chronological description of two events. One event following upon the completion of the other. The description of Jesus coming "out of the water" is not a part of the narrative describing the baptism. Matthew is moving on to record another event which occurred immediately following the baptism. The "out of the water" statement relates to the time sequence of the second event. It was as Jesus left the water that the Spirit descended upon Him, followed by the Father's voice saying, "This is My beloved Son, in whom I am well pleased."

It is therefore concluded that the statement "out of the water" is not a description of a part of the baptismal ceremony but a statement of fact which joined the narrative of two events.

Questions for Discusssion

1. Why was the baptism of Jesus an important event? Did Jesus consider it so?
2. Does Mark 1:9-11 say that Jesus was immersed? Does the text deal with the mode of baptism?
3. How did the Holy Spirit come upon Jesus? How does the Holy Spirit come

upon believers? Does the symbolism of immersion represent this activity of the Spirit?

4. What was the relationship of John the Baptist's message to his baptism?

5. What connection did John's baptism have to Jesus?

6. Why did John refuse to baptize Jesus?

7. What is the difference between the baptism of John and the baptism of Jesus?

8. What argument did Jesus present to John that changed his mind?

9. What is the meaning of the statement "to fulfill all righteousness"?

10. Where did Jesus place the authority for His baptism?

11. Do we have other instances where Jesus submitted Himself to the Old Testament law?

12. What was the meaning of Jesus' baptism?

13. What was the mode of consecration used in the Old Testament commandment?

14. Discuss the meaning of Matthew 3:16. Is Mark 1:9-10 in agreement?

15. Is there any record of immersion in either of the above two references?

21

CASES OF BAPTISM

Acts 8:26-39 and 9:17-19

Introduction

We propose in this lesson to look at the record of two cases of baptism which are recorded for us in the book of Acts. This book is the history of the establishment of the New Testament church and as such it ought to have something to say on the manner of baptism in the church.

We will look particularly at the baptism of the Ethiopian and then Paul's baptism. How were these baptisms performed?

Philip and the Ethiopian (Acts 8: 26-39)

a. Verse 26: Philip is directed by divine commandment to go south to a road that travels between Jerusalem and Gaza "which is desert."

Verse 27: On that road he met an Ethiopian who had been to Jerusalem to worship and was now returning home.

Verse 28: He was sitting in his chariot reading the book of Isaiah.

Verse 30-31: Philip asked him if he understood what he was reading. He confessed that he did not and asked Philip to explain the passage.

Verse 32-33: He was reading from Isaiah 53:7-8.

Verse 35: "And beginning from this Scripture he preached Jesus unto him."

Verse 36: "Look here is water. What prevents me from being baptized?"

Verse 38: "And they *both* went down into the water. Philip as well as the eunuch; and he baptized him" (NASB).

Verse 39: "When *they* came up out of the water."

b. The question to resolve is: Which mode of baptism best fits all the circumstances described in this passage—immersion or sprinkling?

The passage simply states that he was "baptized." We maintain that all the circumstantial evidence is against immersion. Let us look at the passage under three headings.

First: The Area

Verse 26 is careful to describe the scene where this event took place as "which is desert."

In verse 36 the Ethiopian simply said: "Look! Water!" The quantity of water is in no way referred to unless, as one writer says, the original is "a little water." It is an established fact, that no river or stream is to be found in that region now. Furthermore, there is no geographical note of there ever having been any. The only water to be found is an occasional little spring trickling from a bluff or hillside.

Second: The Language

Verses 38-39 describe the baptism and the activity in relation to the water.

Verse 38: "They *both* went down into water"

"Philip as well as the eunuch"

"and he baptized him."

Verse 39: "*they* came up out of the water."

If the language of these two verses describes immersion, then the text says that *both* Philip and the Ethiopian "went down into the water," and both "came up out of the water." Luke records but one baptism in verse 38 "and he baptized him." It is quite obvious from the narrative that only one baptism took place.

It should be quite clear to immersionists that the language "down into the water" and "up out of the water" cannot be used to establish immersion. These expressions are satisfied only by the thought that they both went down to the water, stood on the brink or stepped into the edge, and that Philip baptized the eunuch by scooping up the water and pouring it or sprinkling it on him.

Third: Philip's Text

a. Acts 8:32-33 records the words being read by the Ethiopian. He was reading Isaiah 53:7-8.

b. As he traveled homeward he was reading the book of Isaiah. When interrupted by Philip he was reading one of the prophecies concerning the Servant of Jehovah. His scroll was not divided into chapters and verses like our Bibles. The prophecy which Philip expounded began at chapter 52:13 with the words: "Behold, My Servant."

c. In his exposition Philip must have covered the words of 52:15 which begins: "So shall He sprinkle many nations." Philip had to point to Christ as the suffering Servant who would purify many nations by shedding His own blood and the application of that purification by the baptism of the Holy Spirit. The outward sign of these inward and spiritual things is the *outward sign* of purification by water baptism. Isaiah says that the cleansing rite was by sprinkling.

d. It was the Ethiopian who, upon seeing water, requested baptism. What gave him such an idea? Was it not Philip's exposition of Isaiah 52:15? Note how appropriate is the clause "So shall he sprinkle many nations." Isaiah with prophetic vision is looking forward to the priestly work of Christ and His cleansing of the nations. He saw the establishment of the New Testament church with its inclusion of both Jews and Gentiles. The purification required for entrance into the church of Jesus Christ is symbolized by sprinkling.

Surely in this context it seems reasonable to assume that Philip in his explanation of Isaiah 52:15 pointed first to the cleansing work of Christ and then to baptism as the symbol of that work. If that were not the case, why did the Ethiopian express himself, "Look! Water! What prevents me from being baptized?"

Is it not also reasonable to conclude that Philip had conveyed the idea that the New Testament baptism also carried forward the Old Testament symbolism of sprinkling? If that were not the case why should he expect to receive the rite of baptism in such a small amount of water; a quantity that could not possibly accommodate an immersion?

Paul's Baptism (Acts 9:17-19)

a. Verse 3: Paul was traveling to Damascus to persecute the Christians. The glorified Christ appeared unto him as he traveled.

b. Verse 8: When Paul arose from the earth and opened his eyes, he was unable to see. They led him by the hand and brought him into Damascus.

c. Verse 9: "He was three days without sight, and neither did he eat nor drink."

d. Verse 17: Ananias, at the Lord's direction, goes to Paul. His message was that he would receive his sight and be filled with the Holy Spirit.

e. Verse 18: He received his sight and was baptized.

f. Verse 19: He took some food and was strengthened. Do those events indicate that an immersion took place? Let us look at what those events tell us.

First: Paul's Physical Condition

Three days had passed since the dramatic events on the road to Damascus. The text is careful to record Paul's physical condition. "He could see nothing." What a terrible physical and mental reaction that must have caused. That reaction is stated for us in verse 9: "And he was three days without sight, and neither ate nor drank." There is conveyed to us in that text something of Paul's agony in body and soul.

The events of those three days must have had a tremendous physical and emotional drain upon Paul. Three days of total fasting—neither eating nor drinking—most certainly would have left his body in a weakened condition. This is supported by verse 19, where we are informed that "he received meat and was strengthened."

When was Paul baptized? Note the chronology of events:

Verse 17: Ananias laid his hands on him.

Verse 18: He receives his sight.

Verse 18: He is baptized.

Verse 19: He ate and was strengthened.

He was baptized after receiving his sight and before he ate. Would Paul in this weakened physical condition have been taken through the city streets in search of a suitable place to perform an immersion? It is doubtful that such a place was near at hand. It is certain that the record contains no such search. Also, it is questionable that in such a weakened physical condition he would have been subjected to such a physical ordeal as required by immersion.

Second: The Language of Verse 18

(KJV) "and he received sight forthwith, and *arose,* and was baptized."
(NASB) "and he regained his sight, and he *arose* and was baptized."
(NIV) "and he could see again. He *got up* and was baptized."
(Phillips) "and he could see again. He *got to his feet* and was baptized."

In the consideration of the question dealing with the mode of baptism, the language of verse 18 is significant.

The original word translated arose is *an-is'tay-mee.* It means to "stand up," "arise," "lift up," or "raise up." So the text literally means that standing up he was baptized. The narrative does not allow for a time interval or even for a moving, not even several steps. He stood up and was baptized. It was after the baptism that he ate meat and was strengthened.

Verse 11 tells us that Ananias was to go to a street named Straight and that there he would find Saul.

Verse 17 records Ananias' entrance into the house. Certainly the narrative conveys the impression that the events which transpire in verses 17 and 18 together with the words in verse 19 "and when he had received meat, he was strengthened," all take place in the house on a street named Straight. If there had indeed been a change of location for the baptism it hardly seems likely that such a significant movement would not have been recorded.

Conclusion

The consideration of all the facts and circumstances in the two baptisms which we have just reviewed brings us to the logical conclusion that in neither case did an immersion take place. In the case of the Ethiopian the geographical area did not supply sufficient water. In Paul's case, his physical condition forbade such an experience. In the recorded narratives neither makes specific reference to an immersion. Finally, as we have studied the language in each case there does not appear evidence to support an immersion, rather the evidence is in favor of either sprinkling or pouring.

Questions for Discussion

1. Where did Philip find the Ethiopian? Describe the area.

2. What was the Ethiopian doing when approached by Philip?
3. Discuss the Old Testament text which the Ethiopian was reading.
4. Discuss Philip's explanation and application of the text.
5. What in the Old Testament text would have raised the question of baptism?
6. Does the language of Acts 8:38-39 refer to immersion? Who went down into the water? Who came up out of the water? What is the meaning of these two verses?
7. Why was Paul going to Damascus? What happened on the road to Damascus that changed Paul's life?
8. What does Paul's experience teach us about the sovereignty of God? What lessons for evangelism does that experience teach us?
9. What effect did Paul's experience have on his physical condition? How many days was he without food or drink?
10. Can we conclude from the narrative the place of the baptism?
11. Discuss the language of Acts 9:18.
12. From the evidence presented in the text which mode of baptism is most likely?

22

INFANT BAPTISM

Genesis 17:1-14

Introduction

We have now come in our studies of the covenant of grace to the consideration of infant baptism. It is with great sorrow that we must recognize that a sacrament of divine appointment has been a cause for division in the church of Jesus Christ.

Can we establish from Scripture our position that infants are to be baptized? We believe that this is indeed the teaching of the whole of Scripture. But the immersionists demand that we produce a positive command in Scripture to support our position on infant baptism. How do we respond to such a demand?

First, we freely acknowledge that there is no express command in the New Testament.

Second, we believe that we can demonstrate their inconsistency in making such a demand.

Third, we believe that Scripture does provide a positive command to extend to children the covenant sign and seal.

Let us give further consideration to these three responses.

First: No New Testament Command

There is no command in the New Testament expressly stating that infants are to be baptized. If there were such a command, it would be so recognized by the church and there would be no need for the controversy. That would end the matter for Bible-believing Christians.

Does the fact that we cannot point to an express command defeat our case for infant baptism? Certainly not. It is our position that none is necessary. We hope to demonstrate that position.

Can those opposed to infant baptism point to a positive command in that New Testament stating that infants are not to be baptized? No such command exists.

However, it is our position that infant baptism has the sanction of Scripture. It is only those who practice infant baptism that are fully in accord with the provisions of the covenant of grace.

Second: The Immersionists' Inconsistency

Those opposed to infant baptism state that they require a positive command to support our practice and that inference is not sufficient. We propose to show that they also use inference regarding the ordinances and institutions of the church.

The Christian Sabbath

The sabbath day was first commanded and appointed to be kept in Exodus 20:8-11. The day appointed to be kept holy was the seventh day of the week, which is Saturday.

Most Christians in the world keep Sunday, which is the first day of the week, as the sabbath day or Lord's Day. Why does the New Testament church keep the first day of the week? What New Testament commandment established this new day? There is none. The day has been changed by inference. The inference has logically been deduced from such passages as John 20:19, 26, Acts 20:7, and I Corinthians 16:2.

The Old Testament sabbath was to commemorate the completion of creation, and from Deuteronomy 5:15 we learn that it was also a memorial of the deliverance from Egyptian bondage. But the New Testament sabbath is a reminder of Christ's resurrection from the dead. The work of redemption has been completed and deliverance from the bondage of sin has been accomplished. Such momentous events call for a change. A change which we conclude from Scriptures by inference.

All immersionists, except Seventh Day Baptists, have agreed with us in drawing this inference.

The Lord's Supper

The Passover feast was first established in Exodus 12. The lamb was to be killed and its blood sprinkled upon the side posts of the door and the upper door post. The Lord passed through the land of Egypt that night. When He saw the blood, He passed over them and they were saved from the plague. The annual feast was a memorial of that event.

Jesus established the Lord's Supper on the evening just prior to His crucifixion. He had just eaten the Passover feast with His disciples. He commanded them to observe the Lord's Supper with the words, "This do in remembrance of me" (Luke 22:19).

But where is the command to cease keeping the Passover? It is by inference. Christ the real passover Lamb has now been slain. That sacrifice calls for a change in the memorial and so with the estabishment of the Lord's Supper, we infer that the Old Testament supper is discontinued. Every immersionist agrees with us in that inference.

Third: The Positive Commandment

a. It is the Reformed position that there is a positive commandment in Scripture directing us to extend to children the sign and seal of the covenant of grace. That commandment is found in Genesis 17:10: "This is my covenant, which ye shall keep, between me and you and thy seed after thee; Every man child among you shall be circumcised."

That command requires that every covenant child bear the sign and seal of the covenant. We do not find any New Testament command repealing the principle established in Genesis 17:10.

A commandment of Scripture is binding until its obligation ceases, or it is repealed, or is modified. It is the teaching of the book of Hebrews that the Mosaic ceremonial laws have been fulfilled in Christ. Therefore, such laws are no longer binding. They have been repealed. Christ's own sacrifice rent the veil of the temple which had kept Israel from entering into the Holy of Holies. What the veil typified, Christ fulfilled. Through Christ we can now enter into the true Holy of Holies. The temple veil has therefore ceased to exist. See Hebrews 10:2 and 20.

However, we fail to find a revocation of the command to administer the sign and seal of the covenant to infants. That law has never been repealed. It is true that as the Old Testament sabbath law has been changed, even so the Old Testament law of circumcision has been changed. Baptism is now the sign and seal. That change was by Christ's appointment as recorded in Matthew 28:19.

b. The Immersionists' Assumptions

Immersionists reject infant baptism on the basis of following two assumptions:

1. That the command to extend to children the sign and seal of the covenant was peculiar to the Mosaic dispensation and has therefore ceased.

2. That there are two different churches: one in the Old Testament and another in the New Testament.

Let us look briefly at these two assumptions.

I. That the command applied only to the Mosaic dispensation.

We were addressing ourselves to this problem when we earlier dealt with the provisions of the covenant in Genesis 17. In chapter 3, "The Everlasting Covenant," we gave serious consideration to the time element. Genesis 17:7 states that the covenant is "an everlasting covenant." Dealing with the sign of the covenant, verse 13 says, "and my covenant shall be in your flesh for an everlasting covenant." The provisions of the covenant are eternal. If the covenant is eternal then the commandment to extend to infants the covenant sign, without a time limitation or a future abrogation, then the law must stand.

Again we were looking forward to this point in our studies when in chapter 12 we dealt with the question, "Promised To Whom?" Genesis 17:9 says that the covenant is with Abraham "and thy seed after thee in their generations." Paul is making the New Testament application of this verse when he writes in Galatians 3:29, ''And if ye be Christ's, then are ye Abraham's seed, and *heirs* according to *the promise.''*

Here is the extension of the covenant promises given to Abraham, now extended to New Testament believers. Also by implication the extension of the covenant commandment to extend to infants the sign of the covenant. Paul did not extend God's obligations of the covenant and abrogate Abraham's covenant obligations.

Reformed Baptists limit the application of Galatians 3:7 and 29 by holding that only actual believers are in view in these verses and therefore deny its application to the children of believers. This interpretation cuts the heart out of the covenant of grace. It fails to do justice to the everlasting provisions of the covenant and the response of faith commanded in Genesis 17:9-14. Nor does the Reformed Baptist's understanding of Galatians 3:7 and 29 stand up in the light of Peter's statement in Acts 2:39: ''For the promise is unto you, and to your children.'' The everlasting promise was to Abraham and his seed, and in these New Testament passages we see that promise renewed.

The sign and seal of the covenant instituted in Genesis 17 was not a Mosaic law. It preceded the Mosaic period by over 400 years.

This was not a law typical of Christ, nor His work, and it was therefore not fulfilled by Christ as were the ceremonial laws of Moses. The law still stands because it has neither been fulfilled nor has it been repealed. Is it not significant that Genesis 17:11 states that circumcision ''shall be a token of the covenant betwixt me, and you''? The token of the covenant has changed and every immersionist agrees with us when we make that statement.

The covenant promises are still in effect. Therefore the divine commandment to extend to infants the sign of the covenant is still as binding today as when first given to Abraham.

II. That there are two different churches.

a. It is teaching of all Reformed churches that the church from the time of its formal organization under Abraham to the end of the world is and continues to be but one church. The Old and the New Testament churches are essentially one church. The Old Testament church as well as the New Testament church are founded upon the covenant of grace made with Abraham. The New Testament church is but the extension and the further development of the Abrahamic covenant.

Paul deals with this problem when writing about the covenant promise made to Abraham. He wrote in Galatians 3:17: ''What I mean is this: The law, introduced 430 years later, does not set aside the covenant previously established by God and thus do away with the promise'' (NIV).

Paul believed in the unity and the continuity of the church. It is that teaching which we have consistently established throughout this series of studies. We specifically dealt with this problem in chapter 13, "The Unity of the Church." In that chapter we referred to Acts 7:35-38 and in some detail dealt with Ephesians 2:11-22 which in this regard is one of the most significant passages in the New Testament. We also pointed out the unity of the church in chapter 7, "The Covenant's Final Fulfillment" in the exposition of Revelations 21.

b. The covenant promises of Genesis 17 are made to Abraham "and to thy seed after thee." In these words God in His gracious providence established His covenantal relationship with covenant families. That provision of the covenant was and continues to be an essential element of the covenant. It is with utter amazement that we read in Kingdon's book, *Children of Abraham,* page 34, the following paragraph:

> I would argue then that the principle of believers and their seed no longer has covenantal significance, precisely because the age of fulfillment has arrived. The age of preparation has passed and the dispensational elements that were found in the covenant of promise in Genesis 17 are no longer operative, and it is to these dispensational elements that the principle of "thee and thy seed" is tied.

It is obvious that Kingdon has failed to take into consideration such passages as Psalm 102:28. In the light of the above quotation, it appears that he must of necessity relegate it to the Old Testament church with no relevance to the New Testament church. But is this so?

Psalm 102:28: "The children of thy servants shall continue, and their seed shall be established before thee."

The psalmist is in great affliction. Having poured out his soul in anguish he consoles himself in the eternity of God (vs. 12). From that he draws the further comfort that God will in His mercy deliver him. The time of that deliverance is sure because God has set it. It is the sovereign Lord and Creator in whom the psalmist puts his trust. His final comfort is in the continuance and the perpetuity of the church. The generation of God's servants will not perish, but will ever have a seed. It is the seed of successive generations that is established before the Lord and in which the psalmist takes comfort.

But the question which we must face is this: "Does this psalm have any New Testament application? Can Christians draw any consolation from this passage?"

Hebrews 1:10-12 is a quotation of Psalm 102:25-27. The passage is there applied to Christ. The psalm therefore is a messianic psalm and has its ultimate fulfillment in Christ and His New Testament church. We must be careful in our explanation of Scripture that we do not rob God's people of this glorious promise and the great comfort it affords to Christian parents. Psalm 102:28 is a promise given to the New Testament church which finds its source in the promises given to Abraham.

We therefore are driven to the conclusion that the covenant principle of "unto thee and to thy seed after thee" ' is still very much a part of the covenant in the New Testament era.

c. It is obvious that there are divisions within the Christian church. People who stress the dispensational aspects of the Bible find two churches; one in the Old Testament and another in the New Testament. It is that same dispensationalism that cuts off some or all of the provisions of the covenant made with Abraham and then concludes that immersion is the only form of baptism and that infants no longer participate in the covenant blessings and therefore they are not to be baptized.

On the other hand, the Reformed churches maintain that the church in the Old Testament and the church in the New Testament are generically one. We hold that the New Testament church is built upon the covenantal promise "I will . . . be a God unto thee and to thy seed after thee."

Romans, chapter 11, is a classic New Testament passage teaching the unity and the continuity of the church. The olive tree representing the church is one tree. Some of the branches were broken off and a "wild olive tree was grafted in among them, and with them partakest of the root and fatness of the olive tree" (vs. 17). The Gentiles were grafted into the true church. The New Testament church and the Old Testament church are both part of the one tree.

Because of the importance of this subject, we propose to further demonstrate the unity of the Old Testament church with the New Testament church by showing that the following essential characteristics are applicable to both:

1. Faith in Christ
   - a. N.T. Acts 16:31: "Believe on the Lord Jesus Christ, and those shalt be saved" (cf. John 1:12; Phil. 3:9).
   - b. O.T. Hebrews 11: Especially clear is that Moses' faith was in Christ (vvs. 24-28).

        II Timothy 3:15: The Holy Scriptures referred to here is the Old Testament. They were "able to make thee wise unto salvation."

        John 8:56: "Abraham rejoiced to see My day."

        Romans 4:11: "father of *all* them that believe."

2. Justification by Faith
   - a. N.T. Romans 3:24: "Being justified freely by His grace through the redemption that is in Christ Jesus" (Gal. 2:16).
   - b. O.T. Romans 4.

        Verse 3: "Abraham believed God, and it was counted unto him for righteousness."

Verse 13: Not through law but righteousness of faith (cf. Gal. 3:8-9; Rom. 4:23-24; 3:25-30).

3. Heavenly Inheritance
   a. N.T.—Hebrews 12:22: "the city of the living God, the heavenly Jerusalem." See also Revelation 21:1-4.
   b. O.T.—Hebrews 11:10-16: City builded by God.
      Revelation 21:12-14: OT Israel and NT Israel united.
4. Citizens in the Kingdom of God
   a) N.T.—II Thessalonians 1:5: ". . . that ye may be counted worthy of the kingdom of God for which ye also suffer."
   b) O.T.—Luke 13:28-29: Abraham, Isaac, Jacob, and all the prophets in the kingdom of God.

Conclusions

We therefore conclude that there is one covenant of grace applicable to both the Old Testament church and the New Testament church; that there is only one way of salvation; that the saints of every age are justified by grace through faith; and that there is but one church. We further conclude that the covenant of grace with its seals remains unimpaired by either the giving or the removing of the Mosaic law.

We believe that our studies have established the unity and the continuity of the church and of the covenant. In the light of these findings, it would appear that if infants are no longer to receive the sign of the covenant, then the New Testament should record a revocation of the covenant commandment. It is therefore fitting that we demand the immersionists produce that specific commandment reversing the commandment to Abraham.

Questions for Discussion

1. Where in the New Testament is there a command to baptize infants?
2. Can immersionists always point to a New Testament command to support their practice and worship?
3. If we cannot produce a New Testament command to support infant baptism can we be sure that we are right in this practice?
4. When was circumcision instituted? Relate circumcision to the Mosaic law.
5. What New Testament passages indicate that the covenant of grace is carried forward to the New Testament church?
6. What is the relationship of the Old Testament church to the New Testament church? Support your conclusion with New Testament passages.
7. What is the meaning and importance of Psalm 102:28?
8. What four essential characteristics of the New Testament church are also true of the Old Testament church? Relate to Scripture.

9. What do these characteristics tell us about the covenant of grace and the unity of the church?

10. What is the positive commandment in Scripture to support infant baptism?

11. Is there any commandment in Scripture which abrogates the positive commandment?

23

WHY DO WE BAPTIZE COVENANT CHILDREN?

Genesis 17:10-14

Introduction

The basic premise of the argument for infant baptism is that the New Testament economy is the unfolding and fulfillment of the covenant made with Abraham and that the necessary implication is the unity and continuity of the church. We believe that our past studies have demonstrated this unity of the church and therefore the extension of the covenant made with Abraham to the New Testament church.

The Divine Command

a. Why do we baptize covenant children? Answer: Because infants received the sign of circumcision. That sign was administered to them by the divine command contained in Genesis 17:10-12. It is a fact beyond dispute that the covenant made with Abraham included the infant offspring of Abraham.

b. We learn from Genesis 17:14 that the penalty to one not receiving the sign was that he "shall be cut off from among his people: he hath broken my covenant." We studied Exodus 4:24-26 which shows God's displeasure with Moses when he neglected to abide by God's commandment.

c. If infants are now excluded from the covenant and therefore denied the sign of the covenant, then this is a complete reversal of the divine commandment of Genesis 17:10-14. Are we to believe that there is less blessing for infants in the New Testament than in the Old Testament? I do not think that this is the teaching of Scripture.

d. We believe that we have demonstrated from Scripture that:

1. The new covenant is based upon and is the unfolding of the Abrahamic covenant.

2. There is the same basic identity of meaning attaching to circumcision and baptism.

3. There is a unity and continuity of the covenant of grace administered in both dispensations.

In the light of these three biblical propositions, we believe it is the burden of the immersionists to provide us a positive commandment showing the revocation or repeal of the commandment to Abraham to set the sign and seal of the covenant upon covenant infants.

Covenant Administration

a. God, who in His infinite grace and mercy has established the covenant of grace with Abraham and his seed, also in divine grace and wisdom established the administration of the covenant. The sacraments are divine institutions designed to carry out the administration of the covenant.

b. Genesis 17:1-14 teaches us that God has ordained that the infant seed of believers be included in the covenant relationship, therefore they are to receive the sign and seal of the covenant. It is in Genesis 17 that Jehovah not only formally establishes the covenant of grace but also the administration of the sign and seal of the covenant.

c. When we ask the question, Why do we baptize infants?, it is sufficient for us to know and to answer that it is a divine institution. God has ordained it as one of the provisions whereby He administers His grace in the world. It is a means of grace.

To require any further information than the divine commandment would go beyond the warrant of Scripture. We should need no further reason than that God says so!

d. In the administering and the receiving of this ordinance we plead the promises of God which He has attached to faith and obedience, and we rest our faith and hope upon God's faithfulness. However, faith is not the ground of infant baptism. The ground is that which God has established and revealed in His word. The ground is that *God has said* that the infant seed of believers are to receive that sign and seal of the covenant of grace. We strongly believe that to do otherwise is to disobey God's word.

Luke 18:15-17

a. Again we ask the question: Why do we baptize covenant children? Answer: Because according to Scripture, covenant children are citizens of the kingdom of God.

b. It is the position of the immersionist that children in the New Testament must have faith before they can be baptized. It is therefore fitting that we now turn our attention to a New Testament passage to demonstrate that children are members of the kingdom of God and should therefore receive God's sign of ownership.

c. David Kingdon discusses this subject on pages 82-88 of his book. He arrives at the following three conclusions:

1. "Children belong to the kingdom of God only if in simple trust, they come to Christ."

2. "If utter dependence and open-hearted receptivity are pleasing to God, we cannot say that children are incapable of such."

3. "The child he placed in the midst of his disciples is a symbol as a child,

not as a child of believing parents."

Kingdon arrives at these conclusions after a discussion of Matthew 18:1-6 and Matthew 19:13-15. He makes reference to the parallel passages found in Mark and Luke. Can these conclusions be sustained in the light of Scripture?

d. Luke 18:15-17

Verse 15: "And they brought unto him also infants, that he would touch them: but when his disciples saw it, they rebuked him."

Verse 16: "But Jesus called them unto him, and said, Suffer the little children to come unto me, and forbid them not: for of such is the kingdom of God."

Verse 17: "Verily I say unto you, Whosoever shall not receive the kingdom of God as a little child shall in no wise enter therein."

The parallel passages are found in Matthew 19:13-15 and Mark 10:13-16.

Jesus was used to being thronged about by crowds. Demands were constantly placed on Jesus' time and energy. On this occasion a group of children were brought into His presence. The request was made that He would put His hands on them and pray. It was a request for His benediction.

Children Brought to Jesus

Matthew and Mark tell us that the children brought to Jesus were young children or little children. They both use the Greek word *paidion* which signifies a little or young child, an infant, or a more advanced child. However, Luke designates the children as *brephos*. Vine's Expository Dictionary lists eight New Testament references to this word. Five of these references are found in Luke's Gospel as follows:

1. Luke 1:41: "the babe leaped in her womb."
2. Luke 1:44: "the babe leaped in my womb for joy."
3. Luke 2:12: "Ye shall find the babe wrapped in swaddling clothes."
4. Luke 2:16: "and the babe lying in a manger."
5. Luke 18:15: "And they brought unto him also infants."

The remaining three references are as follows:

1. Acts 7:19: "to throw out their newborn babies so that they would die" (NIV).
2. II Timothy 3:15: "and how from infancy you have known the holy Scriptures" (NIV).
3. I Peter 2:2: "As newborn babes."

There can be no doubt that Luke's reference is to children which we readily refer to as little children, infants, or babes. It is significant that David Kingdon grants this conclusion when he states on page 85: "Luke employs *brephos* instead of *paidia,* making it clear that the children were babes in arms. The Greek can therefore mean that the kingdom of heaven belongs to children such as those brought to Jesus, or more unlikely, that it consists of such children."

Children in the Kingdom

The children were brought to Jesus but the disciples' reaction was consternation. Surely, they thought, Jesus could have no time for little children. Consequently, they "rebuked those that brought them." Mark records that Jesus "was much displeased." Then we have that glorious invitation, "Suffer the little children to come unto me, and forbid them not: for of such is the kingdom of God."

Those in the center of this scene are "the little children." It was with the little children that Jesus was concerned. Jesus does not repel those that brought the children; rather he issues a strong invitation. "Let the little children come to me. Do not hinder them from coming." To his invitation Jesus appends his reason, "For of such is the kingdom of God." Clearly, Jesus' words can only mean that these little children are citizens in the kingdom of God.

Opponents to infant baptism have tried to evade the implications of Jesus' statement by concluding that Jesus was speaking not of the children but those who had a child-like faith. However, this conclusion cannot stand. It is clear from both accounts in Mark and Luke, that Jesus, having made his first point that "of such is the kingdom of God," then uses the occasion to teach a second lesson. Luke 18:17 is the message to those capable of repentance and faith. It is the message that we must come in child-like faith otherwise we shall not enter into the kingdom of God.

However, we must not loose sight of the first and primary pronouncement by Jesus that little children, including babes, are citizens in the kingdom. Kingdon makes a significant admission when on page 86 he writes: "In the light of these examples our Lord must mean that the kingdom belongs to these children and all others like them."

The Blessing

Luke states that the infants were brought to Jesus "that he would touch them." Mark states that they brought young children to him, that he should "touch them." Matthew 19:13 gives us additional information when it states: "Then were there brought unto him little children, that he might lay his hands on them and pray." The parents desired that Jesus should give the children his benediction. They coveted for their children the spiritual blessing which this great teacher and healer could provide for their children.

Jesus responded to the parents' plea. What a touching scene Mark portrayed for us when he wrote, "And he took them up in his arms, and put his hands upon them, and blessed them." How many artists have tried to paint that dramatic event? Contemplating this scene Edersheim wrote: "What power and holiness must these mothers have believed to be in His touch and prayer; what life to be in, and to come from Him; and what gentleness and tenderness must His have been, when they dared so to bring these little ones!"

A Covenant Situation

David Kingdon dismisses the strong arguments in favor of infant baptism found in this passage with the following comment on page 86: "Before our Paedobaptist friends rejoice with great glee in what appears to be a capitulation to their position, it must be pointed out that there is not a word in the passage which would oblige us to restrict our Lord's statement to 'covenant' children. He does not say that to covenant children belongs the kingdom of God, but to children without distinction."

Kingdon wrote that statement even though he had before him John Murray's book on Christian baptism with his comment on page 66 as follows: "The statements of our Lord with reference to the membership of infants in the kingdom of God can be applied only to such little children as come within the compass of a covenant situation analogous to that in which our Lord's words were spoken. Any universalizing of the assertion would violate the most elementary canons of proper interpretation." Kingdon offers us no proof that Jesus was speaking outside the covenant relationship.

Was this a covenant situation? It appears incredible that anyone claiming adherence to any system of covenant theology could infer that Jesus' declaration "of such is the kingdom of God" was to children outside the covenant relationship.

From Matthew 19 and Mark 10 we learn that the blessing of the children took place during the Perean ministry. Three events are recorded. Lange in his commentary on Matthew 19:1-26 writes the following introductory statement:

> Contents: This section sets before us, in their remarkable connection, the three principal features of the Christian household as it should exist in the Church of Christ: viz., the marriage-relationship in the Church, Ch. 19:1-12; children in the Church, Vers. 13-15; and property in the Church, Vers. 16-26.

Edersheim aptly writes:

> We can understand how, when One Who so spake and wrought, rested in the house, Jewish mothers should have brought their "little children," and some their "infants," to Him, that He might "touch," "put His Hands on them, and pray."

These were Jewish mothers, daughters of the covenant, who were bringing their covenant children seeking the benedictory blessing of Jesus. This was practiced long in their history when the patriarchs gave their blessings to their sons.

Truly this was a covenant situation, and when these mothers brought their little children to Jesus for His blessing they demonstrated their covenant faith.

Conclusions

From this short study of Luke 18:15-17, we believe that the following conclusions are justified:

1. Jesus announces the relationship of little children and infants to the kingdom of God. He declares that they are members of the kingdom. Luke puts the question beyond any doubt when he uses the word *brephos*—infants, newborn babes. It is clear that children of this age are incapable of even simple trust in Christ, and yet it is equally clear that Jesus considered them citizens of the kingdom.

2. The children brought to Jesus received His benediction. We must take great precaution at this point that we do not infer that blessing was a hollow, non-meaningful act. Though they were incapable of faith, nevertheless He gave them His blessing. He did so only because they were members of the kingdom. Shall we not then give the children of the covenant, and therefore members of His kingdom, the Lord's blessing by the sign and seal of the covenant?

3. The children receiving the blessing in this passage were covenant children. When these daughters of Abraham brought their children for His blessing, Jesus invited them and received the children even though the disciples had tried to discourage them.

4. There is no evidence in Luke 18:15-17 that Jesus uses the children, or refers to them, as a symbol. The children were themselves the center of His attention. On this occasion He did not place a child "in the midst of his disciples as a symbol of a child." It is true that Jesus took the opportunity to remind His disciples that in order to enter the kingdom they must receive it as a little child in faith, receptiveness, meekness, and humility. However, it is significant that the account in Matthew 19:13-15 omits any reference to this application.

Questions for Discussion

1. Where do we find the divine commandment extending to children the sign and seal of the covenant?
2. Where does Scripture repeal this commandment?
3. Discuss the question of covenant administration. What is the meaning of "covenant administration"? Are we free to administer the sacraments in any manner pleasing to ourselves?
4. What is the ground of infant baptism?
5. Was faith required before children received the sacrament of circumcision?
6. Which passage of the New Testament proves that infants are members of the kingdom of God? Does this apply to all children without exception?
7. What was Jesus' response when His disciples tried to turn back the mothers who were bringing their children to Him?
8. Why were the children being brought to Jesus?
9. Discuss any conclusions which can be drawn from Luke 18:15-17 and its parallel passages in Matthew and Mark.
10. Why do we baptize covenant children?

24

THE SIGNIFICANCE OF INFANT BAPTISM

Genesis 17:7, 9-12, 14

Introduction

If you are going to insist on infant baptism, what is the meaning of the sacrament to the child? Are you going to maintain that adult baptism and infant baptism are the same? Is there not a great difference inasmuch as the adult knows and understands the meaning of the sacrament but obviously the infant does not? It is the purpose of this chapter to give some consideration to such questions.

Genesis 17:7, 9-12, 14

It is not our purpose to deal at length with these verses at this point. We have done that in the earlier parts of this study. We propose only to make some comments which are relevant to the present subject.

Verse 7 contains the heart of the covenant promise, when God promises "to be a God unto thee." But the covenant promise did not stop with Abraham the adult. No, the promise continues, "and to thy seed after thee." Verses 9-12 make it perfectly clear that God includes in the covenant relationship infants, for they are commanded to receive the sign of the covenant on the eighth day.

By the sign of the circumcision, God claimed His covenant people. By receiving the sign of circumcision God's people declared that they were covenant people. Each succeeding generation was to claim the covenant promise through the sacrament. In chapter 11 we dealt with the terrible announcement of verse 14 regarding the uncircumcised: "that soul shall be cut off from his people; he hath broken my covenant."

The covenant institution in Genesis 17 does not put adults into one category of covenant relationship and children into another category. There is but one covenant, but one covenant sign, and but one covenant people, which includes parents and their children.

By the right of birth, children were born into covenant families and by that very birth they became members in covenant relationship. The sacrament sealed that relationship. If the child did not have that covenant relationship by birth then the Lord could not have said in verse 14, "he hath broken my covenant." One must be in the covenant before he can become a covenant-breaker.

Infant Baptism

Drawing our conclusion from infant circumcision we believe it is proper to administer baptism to infants. Again drawing our conclusion from the Old Testament sacrament we believe the meaning of baptism must be the same for infants as for adults. It cannot have one meaning for infants and another for adults. Baptism is the sign and seal of the covenantal relationship to God. It is God's sign that we are His and that we are members in His church.

We baptize children of believing parents not because they are in a state of innocency but rather on the basis of the promises and commandments of the covenant of grace. We demonstrate our faith in God's covenant promises when in obedience to God's commandment we bring our children for baptism. By faith we claim those promises for our covenant children.

Children need the benefits of Christ's redeeming work. Paul in Romans, chapter 5, sets forth the universal effects of Adam's fall. After declaring in verse 5 that sin entered the world by one man, he goes on to state, "and so death passed upon all men, for that all have sinned." It is clear that in this chapter Paul is dealing with the transgression of Adam as our representative. In Adam all die. There are no exceptions.

We also conclude from Genesis 17 that children are capable of receiving the benefits of Christ's redemption. If this were not so, God would not have commanded that infants were to receive the sign of the covenant blessings. The Holy Spirit's work of regeneration is not limited to adults. He calls whom and when He pleases. Luke 1:44 teaches us that John the Baptist was regenerated from his mother's womb.

Children dying in infancy who are saved, are saved not because of their goodness or innocence but because of the application of the covenant blessings secured by Christ's saving merits.

In his book *Christian Baptism,* on page 88, in his extensive footnote, John Murray wrote: "That which is signified by baptism, namely, union with Christ, regeneration, and justification, is not in the case of infants mediated by intelligent faith. Yet infants may possess these graces to the fullest extent. Infants may have full possession of that which baptism signifies, and it is the possession that baptism signifies and seals."

Two Problems

It is at this point that we acknowledge two problems. It does not follow that everyone who bears the sign of baptism is an actual partaker of the grace signified. The problem is applicable to two classes of people and therefore requires two different considerations.

a. The first class are those who receive the sign of baptism but never partake of the actual spiritual blessings represented by the sacrament. It must be admitted that this presents us with great difficulty.

Those opposed to infant baptism endeavor to resolve the problem by insisting on "believer's baptism." However, we should realize at this point that the problem under consideration concerns not only infant baptism. The question carries over to adult baptism as well. Is every one who has received "believer's baptism" truly a believer in Jesus Christ as Saviour? I know of no church that makes such a claim to be able infallibly to read men's hearts. I fear that many receiving baptism on the basis of confessing Christ have never experienced, and may never experience the saving work of the Holy Spirit. "Believer's baptism" does not resolve the problem.

Does this problem appear in Scripture? It is quite clear from the biblical accounts that we have infants in the Old Testament receiving the sign of circumcision who were never partakers of the covenant of grace.

Genesis 17:23 records the circumcision of Ishmael. Abraham circumcised Ishmael even though in verses 18-21 it is revealed that the covenant promises are to be established with Isaac, the son of Sarah, who was yet to be born. Isaac was the child of promise. It was through him that the covenant promises and the promised seed was to flow.

Genesis 25:20-26 records the birth of twins to Isaac and Rebekah. The Lord revealed to Rebekah that she was about to give birth to "two nations" "and two manner of people" and "the elder shall serve the younger." So Rebekah bore two sons, Jacob and Esau. Though there is no record of the actual circumcision of Jacob and Esau, there can be no question that both received the rite.

It is obvious that here we face a problem. How could it be that both Ishmael and Esau received the sign of the covenant when the covenant was established with neither? Did Abraham and Isaac make a mistake when they circumcised these two sons?

When Abraham circumcised Ishmael he did so with the understanding that it was the sign of the covenant. When Isaac circumcised Esau he did it with the understanding that it was the sign of the covenant. Isaac did not attribute one meaning of the sacrament to Jacob and another meaning to Esau. The biblical rite only carried one meaning. Is it not significant that neither Abraham nor Isaac were told to withhold the sign of the covenant from either Ishmael or Esau?

There appears to be but one satisfactory explanation. The divine commandment in Genesis 17:9-14 specifically states that all males should be circumcised, including those born in the house or bought with money of any stranger. It provided for no exceptions. It therefore becomes quite clear that for Abraham not to circumcise Ishmael and for Isaac not to circumcise Esau would have been a violation of the divine commandment.

It is that same commandment that lays upon us as covenant people in the

167

New Testament era the obligation to baptize our children and thereby extend to them the sign of the covenant of grace.

It is God's revealed will that is to be our guide. We are never to rest on God's secret will as a guide for our actions. In this instance we administer the rite of baptism in accordance with God's word in setting up the institution. We do not try to discover His secret purposes.

The divine method of administering the covenant in the world is that God has committed to fallible men the ordinances of administration. We apply the requirements which God has set down. When certain conditions given by divine prescription are met, then we administer the rite. Those conditions are such that fallible men are capable of judging from visible means.

We are not given a divine assurance that every time we administer baptism that the operations of God's saving grace are also present. This is true among adults as well as infants. We rightly administer baptism to an adult upon confession of faith supported by a godly life, and yet the saving work of God's Spirit may be absent! Yet the discrepancy does not preclude the administration of the ordinance. The divine conditions have been fulfilled which man can judge. We do not resort to God's secret will. All this is true of infants as well. When the divine prescription is fulfilled, we baptize without seeking God's secret will.

b. The second class of people which we must consider are those who receive the sign of the covenant in baptism but who at that moment of time had not received the inward working of the Holy Spirit.

The framers of the Westminster Confession of Faith were conscious of this problem and addressed the subject in chapter 28, section 6, which is as follows:

> The efficacy of Baptism is not tied to that moment of time wherein it is administered; yet, notwithstanding, by the right use of this ordinance, the grace promised is not only offered, but really exhibited, and conferred, by the Holy Ghost, to such (whether of age or infants) as that grace belongeth unto, according to the counsel of God's own will, in His appointed time.

We believe that in accordance with the principles of administration given in Genesis 17 that covenant children are to receive the sign of the covenant. However, it is granted that most children have not received the spiritual realities displayed by baptism at the time of receiving the sacrament. Though this may cause us problems we are convinced that this is in accordance with the divine commandment and therefore in accordance with "the right use of this ordinance."

The biblical record is in support of this statement. Jacob appears to be a good example of this class of people. It was as he returned to the promised land that he met the Lord at the brook Jabbok. It was here that his name was changed from Jacob, the supplanter, to Israel, the one who wrestled with God. The Lord conquered. It was here that Jacob cast himself upon the Lord. It was here that he became the possessor of the spiritual blessings of the covenant. So, though he had been circumcised as a covenant child in infancy, it was not until much later in life that the efficacy of the sacrament came to fruition. See Genesis 32:24-28. The Lord has not promised, nor has He tied the efficacy of baptism to that moment of time wherein it is administered. In His discussion with Nicodemus, recorded in John chapter 3, He taught us that the Spirit works when and where He pleases. Is not Nicodemus also a classic example of the class of people whom we are discussing? No doubt he had been circumcised on the eighth day. However, at this point of time, even though he had become a ruler in Israel yet he did not understand the working of God's Spirit. He had not yet been born again. However, his appearance at the cross and his part in the embalming of Jesus' body and then placing it in the sepulchre gives evidence that he had become a true disciple of Jesus sometime subsequent to the conversation of John chapter 3. Though circumcised in infancy he became the possessor of its spiritual realities many years later.

It seems fitting to close this chapter with two quotations from commentaries written on the Westminster Confession of Faith. Both quotations are comments on chapter 28, sec. 6, which is quoted above.

The first quotation is taken from the work of A. A. Hodge:

(c) The efficacy of the sacrament is not due to any spiritual or magical quality communicated to the water.
(d) But this efficacy does result (1) from the moral power of the Truth which the rite symbolizes. (2) From the fact that it is a seal of the covenant of grace, and a legal form of investing those embraced in the covenant with the graces promised therein. (3) From the personal presence and sovereignly gracious operation of the Holy Spirit, who uses the sacrament as his instrument and medium.

The second quotation is taken from G. I. Williamson.

Baptism never causes union with Christ. It never has that effect. That is not the purpose of baptism. The purpose of baptism is not to effect union with Christ but rather to confirm and testify such. And this is precisely why baptism is of increased efficacy not being tied to the moment of administration only. In this way baptism testifies that God gives union with Christ to whom he will, as he will, and when he will. The effect of baptism is not that it causes union with Christ, but that it testifies of this union. Baptism, like circumcision, may have no such effect upon some people. But infant baptism, like infant circumcision, does have a profound effect upon some who are converted long after they are baptized.

Questions for Discussion

1. Can we prove from Genesis 17:7-14 that infants are included in the covenant of grace?
2. What is the meaning of the sign of the covenant? What is the meaning for adults? Does it have another meaning for children?

3. What is involved for parents when they bring their children for baptism?
4. Do children need the benefits of Christ's redeeming work? Why?
5. What various classes of people, adults and children, receive baptism? What problems does this raise? Does ''believer's baptism'' resolve these problems?
6. Discuss some biblical examples of the various classes.
7. Did Abraham and Isaac err in circumcising Ishmael and Esau?
8. What does the Westminster Confession of Faith say about the time of baptism and its efficacy? Is this according to Scripture?

25

OBJECTIONS TO INFANT BAPTISM

Introduction

This seems an appropriate time to consider several objections which have been made to the practice of infant baptism. It is not my purpose to deal with these objections at length but simply to state the objection and then give a short answer.

1st Objection: There is no record in the New Testament of a clear case of infant baptism.

Answer: The case of infant baptism rests on evidence drawn from Scripture of good and necessary inference. We have already demonstrated that immersionists also use inference in regard to the Sabbath day.

We have set before you the covenant of grace. We have demonstrated the unity and the continuity of this gracious covenant in both the Old Testament and the New Testament. Children were included in the covenant in the Old Testament and we believe by good and necessary inference that they are also included in the covenant in the New Testament.

We want now to refer you to three passages of Scripture that have a bearing on this objection.

Acts 16:14-15

a. These verses record Paul's first convert in Macedonia. Lydia had settled in Philippi. The Lord opened her heart and she acknowledged Jesus Christ as her Lord and Savior.

b. Verse 15 begins, "And when she was baptized, and her household."

Acts 16:33-34

a. This is the record of the conversion of the Philippian jailer.

b. Verse 33: "And he took them the same hour of the night and washed their stripes; and was baptized, he and all his, straightway."

I Corinthians 1:16

"I baptized also the household of Stephanas: besides, I know not whether I baptized any other."

These passages record household baptisms. By putting together Acts 11:14 with Acts 10:47-48, we can infer another household baptism.

Is it not significant that Scripture itself uses the term and designation of "household" baptisms? It must mean that the New Testament church believed in the unity of the family. That principle of unity comes to us through the Old Testament teaching of the covenant of grace.

As a question of probability, are we not to conclude that there were infants in some of those households? It would be practically impossible to believe that in none of these households were there any infants. Infants are certainly members of the household and would therefore be baptized.

In these passages presumption stands in our favor that at least one child was involved in these "household" baptisms. This being so, we believe that Scripture does record in the New Testament instances of infant baptism.

2nd Objection: Baptism presumes a confession of faith, but infants are incapable of making such a confession.

Answer: Peter in Acts 2:38 exhorted his hearers to "repent, and be baptized every one of you in the name of Jesus Christ for the remission of sins."

Paul and Silas in Acts 16:31 exhorted the Philippian jailer to "believe on the Lord Jesus Christ, and thou shalt be saved, and thy house."

Such preaching and the response of faith before baptism is directed to adults. In the case of adults we also require repentance, faith, and a credible confession before baptism. However, it does not follow that infants who are incapable of making such a response are thereby ineligible for baptism. Repentance and faith are not the conditions of salvation in the case of infants.

Mark 16:16: "He that believeth and is baptized shall be saved; but he that believeth not shall be damned."

Those opposed to infant baptism reason this way: We are commanded to repent and believe, and then be baptized. Infants cannot repent and believe, therefore they cannot be baptized.

Let's extend that logic: Faith is essential to salvation. He that believeth not shall be damned. Infants cannot believe, therefore they cannot be saved!

I'm sure that they do not so reason and that they would recoil from such a conclusion. But again we find an inconsistency. There is no restriction in the text, but they do restrict the text when it suits their purpose.

When repentance and faith are given as requirements for baptism, it should be evident that they are directed to those who can believe and not to infants who are incapable of such activity.

We therefore conclude that repentance and faith are not the conditions of either salvation or baptism in the case of infants.

3rd Objection: The bad record of baptized infants.

Answer: The sad record of many baptized in infancy but who never come to make their own confession of faith before the church is of deep concern and appears to be an argument against infant baptism.

This sad condition is always worse in the periods of apostasy and a decline in the spiritual life of the church. So it is today. But that very condition should goad us to be diligent in praying for a true revival in the church and especially for the covenant children.

Too many have rejected God's sign and seal of their interest in the covenant of grace. They thereby reject God's claim upon their lives. We cannot deny the sad record. But the perversion and the abuse are not proper arguments against the institution of infant baptism. The objection is equally applicable against "believer's baptism." Far too many who have been baptized on their own confession have proved unfaithful and have lived godless lives.

We should learn from this sad record that the covenant of grace always carries with it responsibilities and obligations. God's promises demand acceptance and response.

John Murray wrote: "Too often those who are the beneficiaries of this institution of grace rest upon the institution rather than upon the God whose administration it is (*Christian Baptism,* page 75).

We should also remember that the objection of the bad record could also have been made against the practice of infant circumcision in the Old Testament period.

4th Objection: We can't draw an argument from circumcision because of the great difference between circumcision and baptism.

Answer: This objection concedes that if an analogy can be established between circumcision and baptism then the case for infant baptism has been established.

We believe that there is an essential identity of meaning existing between circumcision and baptism. Throughout this study we have consistently maintained the unity and the continuity of the covenant of grace in both the Old and the New Testament. We have further maintained that in the Old Testament circumcision was the sign and the seal of the covenant, in accordance with Genesis 17, and that baptism is the sign and seal of the covenant in the New Testament, in accordance with Matthew 28:19. There is therefore an identity of meaning between these two sacraments. See chapter 14 for a discussion of Matthew 28:18-20.

Colossians 2:11-12

To further establish the identity of meaning of circumcision to baptism it is fitting that we briefly refer to Colossians 2:11-12.

It is apparent from these verses that at least a part of the Colossian heresy was caused by the influence of Judaizing teachers who maintained that the new Gentile Christians must submit to the rite of circumcision, together with other Mosaic laws and ceremonies. Against this heresy Paul maintains the superiority and the all-sufficiency of Christ.

William Hendriksen translates verse 11: "In whom also you were circumcised with a circumcision made without hands by the putting off of the body of the flesh in the circumcision of Christ, [verse 12] having been buried with Him in your baptism in which you were also raised with Him through faith in the operative power of God who raised Him from the dead."

a. To those Christians in Colosse Paul writes, "you were circumcised." You don't need to be circumcised because you have already been circumcised. Every New Testament Christian, Jew or Gentile has been circumcised. Philippians 3:3: "For it is we who are the circumcision, we who worship by the Spirit of God, who glory in Christ Jesus, and who put no confidence in the flesh."

b. "a circumcision made without hands." Our circumcision is not made by the hands of man. This is the circumcision performed by God's Almighty Hand. Here is the real, the true circumcision, not of the flesh but of the heart. Romans 2:28-29: "For he is not a Jew who is one outwardly; neither is circumcision that which is outward in the flesh; but he is a Jew who is one inwardly; and circumcision is that which is of the heart, by the Spirit, not by the letter; and his praise is not from men, but from God" (NASB).

c. The reference is to the Holy Spirit and His divine work of regeneration. See Titus 3:5. It is clear from Romans 2:29 that the work of the Holy Spirit in regeneration is equal to the inward circumcision. It is the spiritual cleansing of the body.

d. "the circumcision of Christ." There can be no doubt that what Paul is writing about is Christian circumcision. In verse 12 he shows us how this circumcision is of Christ.

Verse 12: "having been buried with Him in your baptism in which you were also raised with him."

a. Here is the parallel passage to Romans 6:4 which we have previously studied in detail. Paul is teaching the same thing in this passage. What is the Christian's relationship to Christ?

The Christian is joined to Christ in the fullness of His redemptive activity. When He died we died; when He was buried we were buried; when He arose we arose. The baptism referred to is the cleansing and the regenerating work of the Holy Spirit because we were joined to Christ. As circumcision referred to in verse 11 is the true inward circumcision, so here too the baptism referred to is the true inward baptism; the regenerating work of the Holy Spirit.

b. Paul is not ascribing here any magical efficacy to the rite of water baptism. Water is not even mentioned. Water baptism does not consummate our union with Christ but it is the sign and seal of that true and inward baptism consummated by the Holy Spirit. One purpose of the passage is to warn against resting simply upon the external rite of circumcision without the inward cleansing of the heart. That same warning is equally appropriate to the rite of water baptism.

c. The new life issues forth in faith. It is a faith which originates in the operative power of God. He demonstrated that power when He raised Christ from the dead. We therefore believe that the same divine power is working in us and that He will provide our every need for both time and eternity.

d. The clear implication of this passage is that in the New Testament baptism has taken the place of the Old Testament circumcision but that the identity of meaning is there for both sacraments. Paul takes for granted the identity of meaning.

David Kingdon, writing in *Children of Abraham,* refers to Colossians 2:11-12 on pages 28-29. It appears to me that he comes to the same conclusion as we have in this study. He writes on page 28: "Now it can hardly be denied that baptism in the New Testament has much the same meaning and import."

Page 29: "In the light of such expressions, 'Putting off the flesh,' 'putting on Christ,' it is plain that baptism is close in meaning to the symbolic significance of circumcision."

Also on page 29 he quotes Paul Jewett: "If this be so, the only conclusion we can reach is that the two signs as outward rites symbolize the same inner reality in Paul's thinking."

Yet on page 28 he wrote objecting to our position: "It is this identity of meaning to which I object, but not the analogy itself."

He tries to maintain his position by stating that circumcision had a national reference "as a mark of national separation to God." In this sense circumcision would be a sign of citizenship rather than church membership.

Answer to Kingdon's Argument

1. Israel was so constituted that it was both a nation and a church but these two formed but one theocracy. Israel was ruled by God. To belong to the nation was to belong to the church and vice versa.

2. Romans 4:11: "And he received the sign of circumcision, a seal of the righteousness of the faith which he had, being uncircumcised." From this passage we learn that circumcision had special reference to the church, as distinguished from the nation.

3. It seems to me that Kingdon misses the kingdom aspect of the New Testament church, and the kingship of Christ in this present age.

Colossians 1:13: "Who hath delivered us from the power of darkness and hath translated us into the kingdom of His dear Son.''

See also: I Timothy 1:17: "Now unto the King eternal, . . ."

Psalm 2:6: "Yet have I set My King upon My holy hill of Zion."

Kingdon's position also misses the import of Ephesians 2:11-22. See verse 19 to the effect that Gentiles are no more foreigners, we're no longer outside the commonwealth, but we are fellow citizens with the saints. See chapter 13 for a more detailed study of this passage.

Questions for Discussion

1. What New Testament passages strongly infer that children received the rite of baptism?

2. Does not the New Testament require repentance and faith before baptism? To whom are such passages as Acts 2:38, Acts 16:31 and Mark 16:16 directed?

3. What biblical warrant do we have for baptizing children without repentance and faith?

4. Can we justly base an argument against infant baptism on the observation that so many never really come to a saving faith in Christ?

5. Can we demonstrate an identity of meaning between circumcision and baptism? What is the importance of that identity to infant baptism?

6. Prove from the New Testament that every Christian has been circumcised. Discuss the meaning of circumcision in these passages. Do these passages prove the identity of meaning between circumcision and baptism?

7. What is a theocracy? Are Christians part of a theocracy? Who is the king?

26

WHAT PROFIT INFANT BAPTISM

Romans 3:1-4

Introduction

1. We are still dealing with objections to infant baptism. The objection under consideration might be variously stated:

Of what value is infant baptism? What good is accomplished by baptizing a little child who is unconscious of what is taking place?

2. Even some who believe in infant baptism have sometimes been constrained to ask: What is the value in infant baptism?

3. Let us first state that the mere performance of a ceremony brings no good whatsoever other than having a sentimental value. A superstitious attachment to infant baptism is of no value to the infant baptized. Baptism is a means of grace but it is not a means of conferring grace. Infant baptism only has meaning and value when it is performed as a sacrament within the context of the covenant of grace.

Romans 3:1-4

a. In this passage Paul, once for all, answers the old objection: "What profit is there in infant baptism?" But some may object and state that Paul is speaking about circumcision and not baptism. That's quite true but we have concluded that the sacrament of baptism replaced circumcision. Did we not discover that Paul teaches the identity of meaning for both these sacraments in Colossians 2:11-12?

b. In the consideration of this objection we must never forget that the same objections made against infant baptism could be made against infant circumcision. "What profit was there in infant circumcision?" It was precisely the anticipation of that question that prompted Paul to write as he did in Romans, chapter 3.

c. What caused Paul to anticipate this objection? In chapter 2:26-27 he had written to the Jews: "If therefore the uncircumcision keep the ordinances of the law, shall not his uncircumcision be reckoned for circumcision? And shall not the uncircumcision which is by nature, if it fulfill the law, judge thee, who with the letter and circumcision art a transgressor of the law?" On the basis of Paul's argument it might appear reasonable to conclude that there had been no good reason to submit to circumcision and that there had been no benefits gained. Paul anticipates that reasoning and gives his response in chapter 3.

Verse 1:

What advantage then hath the Jew? or what is the profit of circumcision?

a. In this verse Paul formulates the objection. He anticipates their conclusions and gives expression to them in these two questions. Are there no privileges in being born a Jew; that special nation chosen to reveal God's glory to the world? Was there no gain to be born within the pale of God's covenant people and from having received the sign and seal of that covenant?

Verse 2:

Much every way: first of all, that they were entrusted with the oracles of God.

a. Paul gives a clear answer; the Jew has a great advantage and much profit over the Gentiles; much in every respect. Circumcision was by divine institution and Paul allows no depreciatory reflection to be cast upon it.

b. He introduces the Jews' advantage with the statement "First of all." This would appear to introduce a series of items but at this point he only states one advantage. This probably influenced the King James translators to translate as "chiefly." Paul could have listed several other advantages even as he did in chapter 9, verse 4 when again he is expressing concern "for my brethren, my kinsman according to the flesh."

c. "They were entrusted with the oracles of God."

"Oracles" refers to communications, the revelations. NIV translates: "the very words of God." In Acts 7:38 it is said that Moses at Mt. Sinai "received living words to pass on to us" (NIV).

What does this expression "oracles of God" refer to? He is undoubtedly referring to the Old Testament in its entirety. It is the Scripture as the written Word of God. II Timothy 3:16 states that all Scripture is God breathed. It is the Scripture that constitutes "the very words of God."

It was the very words of God that were "entrusted" to the Jews. It is the written Word of God that constituted God's speech. It is those very words written in Scripture that were given as a trust to Israel. The divine words have a fixed and an abiding form. It was in that abiding Word that Jehovah established His covenant with the Jews and signified the sign and the seal of that covenant.

That was the advantage of the Jews. What a great privilege was theirs. No other nation in the world had for their possession "the very words of God."

In the Bible we hold God's Word in our hands.

Verse 3:

For what if some were without faith? shall their want of faith make of none effect the faithfulness of God?

Paul again anticipates questions and again he has given verbal expressions to those questions.

What he is dealing with is the problem of unbelief on the part of those who had received the sign of the covenant. As it was true in Israel so it is true today that many born within the pale of the church never come to faith in Jesus Christ. But the question is: "Though many have proved faithless, will their faithlessness destroy the faithfulness of God?" "Will He forget His promises?"

God's promises are contained in the written Word of God, and those born within the church have had the privilege of possessing the divine oracles. That privilege is carried on from one generation to another with greater and lesser degree. We should diligently seek to be faithful to that responsibility. This generation is desperately in need of that warning.

Will man's faithlessness cause God to be faithless to His covenant promises contained in His Word? It is that question which Paul answers in verse 4.

Verse 4:

God forbid: yea, let God be found true, but every man a liar; as it is written, That thou mightest be justified in thy words, and mightest prevail when thou comest into judgment.

Paul is horrified at the suggestion that the faithfulness of God might be called into question. God is faithful to His Word. The promises of God are not annulled even though rejected by sinful men. God will be faithful to His covenant promises and will redeem His people.

II Timothy 2:13: "If we are faithless, He remains faithful: For he cannot deny Himself" (NASB).

God is true and faithful to His Word even though every man should prove false and faithless to their promises.

b. Paul confirms this thought by an appeal to Psalm 51:4. As the first part of Psalm 51:4 shows, sin is directed against God. So it is that God's judgments pronounced against sin serve the purpose of vindicating God's words of judgment. His judgments show His justice. Man's sin and faithlessness cannot make void the faithfulness and the truth of God. It seems extremely difficult for us to learn the lesson that God's judgments also demonstrate His faithfulness.

Even if it were possible to bring the justice and faithfulness of God to trial, nevertheless God would not only be found just but His righteous character would be triumphantly displayed. God will be found to be true even though every man be a liar.

c. The unbelief of some is no objection against the covenant of God, nor against His faithfulness to His covenantal promises.

So with Paul, we must conclude that there is much profit in being born within the pale of the church and receiving the sign of God's covenant and having the oracles of God. His covenant promises are found in His church.

Deuteronomy 7:9: "Know therefore that the Lord thy God, he is God, the faithful God, which keepeth covenant and mercy with them that love Him and keep His commandments to a thousand generations."

Men's unbelief does not make void the faithfulness of God; nor does men's unbelief make void the advantage of being born within the pale of the church and thereby receiving the sign and seal of the covenant; rather it adds to the responsibility of being judged a covenant-breaker. God is faithful in grace and in judgment.

Concluding Remarks

a. God's Faithfulness

Jehovah is a covenant-making and a covenant-keeping God. The Lord has bound Himself to the covenant consummated with Abraham for all eternity. He has promised in the everlasting covenant "to be a God unto thee and to thy seed after thee."

The sign of God's faithfulness to His everlasting covenant in the Old Testament was circumcision. However, circumcision is not designated as the everlasting sign. So, the sign of God's faithfulness to His covenant is changed in the New Testament to baptism. We are so prone to forget that on God's part baptism is the sign and seal that He will be faithful to His Word. It's God's claim of ownership.

"Great is thy faithfulness," O God my Father,
There is no shadow of turning with thee;
Thou changest not, thy compassions, they fail not;
As thou hast been thou forever wilt be.

b. To Parents

History is the record of God's faithfulness to His covenant promises. Each successive generation has been the recipient of His grace. The Lord has demonstrated that our covenant children are the objects of His special care. The sacrament of infant baptism should be a comfort and an encouragement to parents. It is a sign that God has extended His promises to covenant children. It is a sign that children are the objects of His love. It speaks to us of God's eternal blessings bestowed upon our children and with the promise that those same blessings shall also be bestowed upon our children's children.

The sacrament and its vows bind us as parents to bring up our children in the nurture and admonition of the Lord. They should be brought up with a consciousness of their privileged covenantal relationship to the Lord. It is by this means that God's covenant grace and promises come to fruition. They should also understand that covenant privileges also bring covenant responsibility. We must teach them that the covenant demands faith and obedience.

By fulfilling our covenant obligations we can have the assurance that God's faithfulness to His covenant promises will be passed on to our children.

c. To Children

Were you, in God's providence, born as a covenant child and did you receive the sacrament of infant baptism? Then it is your obligation to remember that you bear the sign and seal of God's ownership. At the appointed time of your baptism your parents made solemn vows, and by faith they claimed God's gracious promises for you. By baptism you became a member of the church of Jesus Christ. Throughout the years the church has fed and nurtured you by its faithful teaching and preaching of the Word of God.

The question which is now before you has eternal consequences. Have you laid hold of those covenant promises by faith in Jesus Christ? Have you by faith claimed the promises of the covenant or have you rejected them? Will you continue to disown the privileges claimed for you by your parents and will you continue to disown the covenant obligations to love and serve Jehovah as your God? Are you following the footsteps of Esau, who despised his birthright and willingly sold it to his brother for a bowl of vegetable soup? Like Esau, the day may come when you may find no place for repentance, though you seek it carefully with tears.

It seems appropriate and fitting to close this study with the prayer written by Edwin Hall in 1840 as he came to the conclusion of his series of messages printed under the title "The Law of Baptism":

O, God of our fathers! our covenant God!
Save our children from such a doom as this!
Seal them thine own, by working in their souls
the reality of that which is signified by the
outward sign. Make them thine own by the
washing of regeneration and the renewing of
the Holy Ghost; and thy name shall have all
the praise for ever. Amen.

Questions for Discussion

1. Why do many who do not belong to the church request baptism for their children?
2. What is it that gives baptism meaning?
3. Is there any advantage of being born of godly parents?
4. What is the specific advantage given in Romans 3:1-4? Could Paul have listed other advantages?
5. How do we question God's faithfulness?
6. How does Paul respond to the questioning of God's faithfulness? How do we respond?

7. How does Paul handle the problem of unbelief on the part of covenant children? Can you relate your answer to the question: "What advantage then hath the Jew?"

8. What is the relationship of God's faithfulness to infant baptism?

9. What are the obligations of parents to their covenant children? What comfort can parents receive from the covenant?

10. What are the benefits received by covenant children? What are their obligations?